Praise for *Hades*

"*Hades* is a wonderfully lyrical book that will forever change the way you think about one of the most dreaded Greek gods, Hades. Drawing upon deeply personal experience and detailed research, Waggoner teaches the perfect blend of mythology, history, and practice. This book is loaded with storytelling, correspondences, rituals, and exercises that will enrich the practice of both beginners and adepts."

—**KATE FREULER**, author of *Of Blood and Bones*

"Waggoner has created a stunning patchwork quilt ... seamlessly incorporating the beauty of folklore with the knowledge of history while providing readers the tools they need to connect with something so much bigger than themselves."

—**AMANDA WOOMER**, author and creator of *The Feminine Macabre: A Woman's Journal of All Things Strange and Unusual*

"Waggoner expertly guides the reader through the lore, correspondences, and magical practices of the Unseen One. Her personal insight adds a profound depth to the book, especially the various trance journeys to the Underworld. Highly recommended."

—**ASTREA TAYLOR**, author of *Modern Witchcraft with the Greek Gods* and *Intuitive Witchcraft*

"A volume full of clear-eyed wisdom and practical exercises.... *Hades* is packed with information about herbs to be used for offerings and in magical work, rituals and meditative practices to begin or deepen a relationship with this god ... and a startling variety of hands-on exercises that bring it all together. Open it to discover fascinating tidbits drawn from history and mythology, or use it as a guide to a profoundly sacred path, but read this book."

—**TERENCE P WARD**, editor of *Host of Many: Hades and His Retinue*

T0285674

"*Hades* is simultaneously celebration, evocation, and exploration....Waggoner's journey toward Hades is frightening and exhilarating, and her personal anecdotes and exercises invite the reader to explore their own relationship with the much-maligned Lord of Tartaros and Elysium. This is a much-needed text in an age when so many, even in the Pagan/polytheist community, fear death and the Holy Powers who watch over us as one life ends and the next begins."

—**REBECCA BUCHANAN**, author of *Host of Many: Hades and His Retinue* and editor of *Eternal Haunted Summer*

"A comprehensive and insightful exploration of the Greek god Hades. Waggoner draws on a wide range of sources, including myth, folklore, and her own personal experiences, to paint a complex and nuanced portrait of this often-misunderstood deity....Waggoner's writing is clear and engaging, and she provides a wealth of information that is both scholarly and accessible. The book is a well-researched work that I believe will be a great source of inspiration for many Pagan practitioners."

—**DEAN JONES**, host of the *Calling the Quarters* podcast

HADES

About the Author

Jamie Waggoner (Alabama) is a Pagan priestess, philosopher, writer, and teacher. Jamie has studied esoteric and occult subjects since 1995. She holds a BA in philosophy, magna cum laude, from the University of Idaho and Kingian Nonviolence Level I Trainer Certification from the Selma Center for Nonviolence, Truth, and Reconciliation.

Jamie uses her skills and experience gained over twenty years of magical praxis to lead workshops, rituals, sacred circles, and study programs. Her work as a priestess is highlighted in the Red Tent documentary film *Things We Don't Talk About* (2012) and the *Goddess on Earth Oracle* (2021).

In addition to her independent projects, Jamie is a cofounder of and teacher for Way of the Weaver, an all-gender inclusive program of magical inquiry, social justice, and community building. She has been a devotee of Hades since 2016. Visit her online at jamiewaggoner.com.

HADES

MYTH, MAGIC & MODERN DEVOTION

JAMIE WAGGONER
Foreword by Morpheus Ravenna

Llewellyn Publications | Woodbury, Minnesota

FIRST EDITION
First Printing, 2024

Book design by R. Brasington
Cover design by Shannon McKuhen
Interior illustrations by Llewellyn Art Department

Llewellyn Publications is a registered trademark of Llewellyn Worldwide Ltd.

Library of Congress Cataloging-in-Publication Data
Names: Waggoner, Jamie, author.
Title: Hades : myth, magic and modern devotion / Jamie Waggoner.
Description: First edition. | Woodbury, Minnesota : Llewellyn Publications,
  [2024] | Includes bibliographical references. | Summary: "One of the
  most recognizable but misunderstood Greek gods, Hades plays a valuable
  role that has not garnered much adoration. Using myth, storytelling, and
  practical exercises, author Jamie Waggoner shows how Hades is more than
  the keeper of souls and the land of the dead"— Provided by publisher.
Identifiers: LCCN 2023048807 (print) | LCCN 2023048808 (ebook) | ISBN
  9780738775753 (paperback) | ISBN 9780738775814 (ebook)
Subjects: LCSH: Hades (Greek deity) | Gods, Greek. | Mythology, Greek. |
  Magic. | Hell.
Classification: LCC BL820.P58 W34 2024 (print) | LCC BL820.P58 (ebook) |
  DDC 292.2/113—dc23/eng/20231127
LC record available at https://lccn.loc.gov/2023048807
LC ebook record available at https://lccn.loc.gov/2023048808

Llewellyn Worldwide Ltd. does not participate in, endorse, or have any authority or responsibility concerning private business transactions between our authors and the public.

All mail addressed to the author is forwarded but the publisher cannot, unless specifically instructed by the author, give out an address or phone number.

Any internet references contained in this work are current at publication time, but the publisher cannot guarantee that a specific location will continue to be maintained. Please refer to the publisher's website for links to authors' websites and other sources.

Llewellyn Publications
A Division of Llewellyn Worldwide Ltd.
2143 Wooddale Drive
Woodbury, MN 55125-2989
www.llewellyn.com

Printed in the United States of America

Disclaimer

Studying, working magic, and engaging in ritual with Hades and the denizens of the Underworld can sometimes bring up challenging emotions and situations. If you should ever find yourself in serious mental or emotional distress after a magical working, ritual, or trance journey, please seek professional psychological help. The magical operations and invitations for practice in this book are not a replacement for professional medical attention, mental healthcare, or legal advice.

The information about flowers, trees, herbs, and other plants included in this book is based on historical record, folklore, and the author's own experience working with these plants in an esoteric capacity. Any magical, medicinal, or ritual use of these plants is at the sole discretion and responsibility of the reader. Readers are responsible for educating themselves on proper plant identification, safe harvesting and handling, recommended dosages, and contraindications, which is beyond the scope of this book. The author and publisher therefore take no responsibility, legal or otherwise, for any misuse of these plants resulting from poor judgment or misinformation on the part of the reader.

Contents

Exercises

FOREWORD

Sooner or later, we will each meet death. Like Kore in the meadow of flowers, death's chariot bears down on us and we cannot escape it. The inevitability of that meeting and the inexorable movement of our steps toward it is something all human beings share. The gods present when we face that encounter may differ for each of us within our various traditions, communities, and cultures, but the task of coming into relationship with this immensity is part of our shared humanity. Mortality is a shadow that walks beside us always, and if we can come into relationship with that shadow, it may make the joys in our lives shine all the brighter.

This immensity is best faced in the company of friends, and I couldn't imagine a better companion on the journey than Jamie Waggoner. I first met Jamie at a workshop on sorcery. I remember her presence being characterized by a calm, centered sense of curiosity and wonder. As we discussed potent, challenging topics related to trauma, justice, and baneful magics, she carried herself with both a rootedness and a lightness that spoke to me of someone who has dived deep into self-reflection and found the ground of their own being. A companion who is gentle and full of courage.

Bringing this same grace and warmth to her writing, in this book Jamie invites us on a shared journey into a luminous and shadowy realm, the realm of death, the dead, and of the dread beings who hold and oversee that domain in the Hellenic mythic worldview: Hades, Persephone, and their kin. It's like taking a walk into the Underworld arm in arm with a trusted friend. She offers a nourishing balance of knowledge distilled from historical scholarship on Hades in ancient Greek religion, alongside vibrantly contemporary interpretations of that lore for living practice. Her prose is lucid, vulnerable, and brave, making even the most distressing aspects of Hades' world feel approachable.

She tackles difficult topics such as the abduction of Persephone and the traumas it evokes and the encounter with one's own mortality with this same vulnerability and grace and a focus on justice and liberation.

As a dedicant of the Morrígan, the Irish goddess of war, death, and the Otherworld, I have some experience of walking with khthonic gods, their frightful retinues, and the violence their mythologies sometimes dwell on. I have sometimes sensed a feeling of concern from others that spending too much time with gods of death might somehow put a person at risk, like J. R. R. Tolkien's hobbit Frodo growing wan and spectral from the nearness of phantoms, as if intimacy with death and its spirits could suck the life out of you, or as if contemplating myths that encompass death and violence could weaken your sense of the value of life.

But my experience has been the opposite: spending my life in close company with a being many consider a "dark" goddess has clarified for me what is most important in life and strengthened my commitment to our shared humanity. There is a reason why the ancient myths dwell on such themes as death, tragedy, and violence and why ancient peoples venerated gods who operate in these realms. They are inexorable forces that visit our lives and that we must find a way to confront and to live with. These myths, and the ritual traditions connected with them, offer a sacred framework within which we can orient ourselves and find the threads of meaning, resilience, and beauty that will carry us through these harrowing encounters. Making friends with the gods and spirits who embody these terrifying immensities can show us the way toward a more empowering and healing way of relating to them. And it can give us the tools to work toward greater justice in our society's collective relationships with them as well.

Jamie's work in this book illuminates how closeness with Hades and the realm of death can help us reconnect with our own lived values in new and deeper ways. How contemplation of these myths can help us find the insight to repair ancestral harms, the compassion and moral courage to face and transform our own fears. How personal devotional ritual can be part of a liberatory practice that can heal and connect both the living and the dead. She offers a vision of a way of life that is unafraid to look at death and violence, deeply rooted in contemplation of the immensities of death, and nourished by life-affirming ritual that connects us to ourselves, to each other, and to the earth all around us.

This pathway she has made into the shadow realms leads the reader through all the elements needed to create a strong polytheist practice inspired by Hellenic customs and the lore of Hades: spiritual purification techniques, altar practice, offerings and invocations, protection and grounding, trance and spiritual journeying to the Underworld, oaths and devotional bonds, and more. Her rituals are simple and heartfelt, with an emphasis on bringing elements of ancient myth into everyday life with beauty and gravitas and connecting with traditional plants, stones, and other natural elements to invite a deepening of relationship with Hades and his kin. Each step builds on the last as the pathway opens into further mysteries of the Underworld.

The way is open, the path awaits, and you couldn't wish for a better guide into the shadow lands. May your journey be a blessed one.

Morpheus Ravenna
May 2023

INTRODUCTION

I had to give myself permission to love Hades. Polydegmon, Klymenos, Eubuleus, Plouton: an ancient Greek god who is not well understood, perhaps not entirely good, and who genuinely scares some people. His presence in mythology is assumed but rarely acknowledged. Hades is always described through the lens of someone else's experience—cast in a supporting role in many stories, but never starring in his own. It can be difficult to get to know him, yet as soon as I began working with Hades, I knew I had stumbled upon something meaningful: a god who was different, serious about his duties, protective of his realm and family, multifaceted, dedicated, and ultimately worth pursuing.

The descent to the Underworld was arduous and harrowing, but like the heroes of legend, I somehow returned to tell my tale. Today I am a proud priestess of Hades, and this book, dear reader, is a guide. It is a love song to death, darkness, shadows, and determination. I wrote it in case you, too, are drawn to the depths of the Underworld.

My Descent to the Underworld

In 2016 I was asked to serve on the ritual facilitation team for a week-long Pagan and witchcraft-centric camp. The theme of camp was "Persephone's Descent." Each member of our ritual facilitation team decided to take on one of the roles in the myth. We agreed to study and engage deeply with our roles while doing our planning and preparatory work, so that we would be prepared to hold the energy of our individual god within the container of the camp. Because of my age and feminine presentation, I expected that the group would ask me to take on Persephone, but this was not the case. I waited until last to choose my role, and no one had claimed Hades. I had not worked with Hades in a magical sense prior to this; taking on his role felt a bit risky to me, but I

1

was also intrigued, so I cast my lot. I was tickled about the gender-bending role play and potential reclamation work we as a team could bring to the story.

During the next six months, I tried to learn all that I could about Hades' mythology, purview, energy, and personality. I was immediately frustrated that I could only find a scant handful of approachable resources that analyzed his mythology with any depth, and even less material on how to build a relationship or magical rapport with him. So I pressed forward as best I knew how. My method of getting to know him involved many hours of trance journey in the Underworld, experimenting with subtle plant and mineral energies to discover his correspondences, collecting digital works of art and literature, listening to a wide variety of mythology-based podcasts, and asking all my other gods and guides for protocols and advice. After preparing to the best of my ability, I surrendered myself to the not-knowing and packed my bags for camp.

My experience at camp that year was awe inspiring, construct shattering, gratifying, and terrifying—in the best of ways. In addition to the challenge of holding the energy of Hades' role within the theme of camp, once on-site I was also asked to aspect him in three rituals. *Aspecting* is a magical technique in which a priest/ess/x invites the metaphysical energy of a deity into their physical body, oftentimes giving the deity control over their movements and voice, so that the god can interact directly with participants inside a ritual container. Deep in this possessive trance state, I experienced firsthand the fathomless well of solace that Hades—the god and the Underworld—has to offer. I felt his gravitas, the pull of his magnetism. I witnessed his sacred interactions with participants and, in doing so, was honored to overhear the tender, grounded counsel he shared. Feeling his feelings as if they were my own, I also understood, in my very bones, the guardianship and responsibility Hades feels for the dead. I also felt the enduring love he has for Persephone, and the crushing, devastating loneliness he experiences when she leaves the Underworld each spring. This energetic merger was, and is, incomparable to anything else I have experienced in my spiritual practice.

After camp, I was incredibly grateful for my profound experiences, but I was also ready to put my relationship with Hades to rest for a while. I needed some time to digest everything I had learned over the past months. Hades' energy was temptingly compelling and charismatic, but I was not sure how—or if—he would fit into my life and magical praxis after that summer. I designed a solo ritual for the specific purpose of releasing our bond: I placed the magi-cally charged items that I had used in conjunction with Hades into a jar, which I then deposited at the base of a cypress tree in a local cemetery. I broke the bifurcated branch I had been using as Hades' bident over the jar, in symbolic action of severing my ties to him, and purposefully walked away without a backward glance.

I would soon realize that Hades was not ready to let me go. Stubborn and persistent, he came to me in dreams. He showed up in my trance journeys. With the patience of mountains that mark time on a geological scale, he kept courting me. And when I continued to ignore him, Persephone even began entreating me on his behalf. The following year, in May 2017, I made my first trip to Italy. A curious phrase had risen out of my dreamscape while planning our itinerary: *Pythia khthonia*. Through etymology research and Google magic, I learned about the Antro della Sibilla (the Cave of the Sibyl) in Cuma, Italy—also described as an entrance to the Underworld in Virgil's *Aeneid*. This was obviously another dream communication from Hades, so I decided to put him to a test. My partner and I would make a petition for his aid—one with a very big ask—at the Antro della Sibilla, and if granted, I would reconsider picking up my relationship with him.

My amazing partner figured out the two trains, one bus, and a hike that were required to get us from Rome to the archaeological site in Cuma. We went to the cave; we explored the surrounding landscape, laid offerings, and made our petition—making sure to stomp the ground three times to call the attention of the Underworld. Indubitably, we received confirmation that our petition was granted before the end of that year. The opportunity we had asked Hades to provide arrived with ease and timeliness. Still slightly hesitant, I made a final decision: if the jar I left in the cemetery almost two years ago was still resting at the base of that cypress tree, I would take it as a definitive sign, and give this Hades thing a go.

Of course, I found the jar right where I had left it.

My Approach to Study and Praxis

I'm a Pagan polytheist. In case you're not familiar with that terminology, it sim-ply means my spiritual beliefs are not necessarily an organized religion, such as Christianity; rather, they include facets of animism, folklore, mythology, and

ecstatic practices (such as ritual and trance journey) in addition to deity veneration. I am what is known as a *hard polytheist*, which means I believe that there
are countless distinct, real, existing gods, all with their own independent agen-
cies and agendas. In other words, I don't just believe in one god, I believe in all
of them. And I worship and interact with a small, select contingent.

This book was written through a lens of applied, post-modern Paganism.
It is meant not to be read as academic mythological theory. I am not a trained
Classical scholar, nor am I a Hellenic reconstructionist Pagan. The devotional
hymns, imaginative retellings of stories from Greek mythology, discussion and
analysis, trance journeys, and invitations to practice included in these pages
emerged from more than twenty years of my personal, eclectic theurgic and
magical praxis.

There is an amazing amount of ancient Greek and Roman texts and text
fragments available to us, many of which cover the same stories and characters;
sometimes these accounts are equivalent, and other times they are markedly different from one another. In this book I present the versions of myth and folklore
that have become near and dear to my praxis over the years, and I include references to primary source materials when available. Primary sources are those
considered closest to the origin of the subject matter: in this case, extant pieces
of historical records, poetry, prose, philosophy, art, and theater from the Mediterranean region circa 2900 BCE to 400 CE. In instances where I share my personal gnosis about Hades, I have endeavored to clearly state it as such, so as not
to confuse my observations with material found in primary sources.

It should also be noted that *ancient Greece* is a very vague term. You'll see
me using it as shorthand throughout the pages of this book, often accompanied by a primary source reference and its approximate date. Since these references span several centuries (roughly 1600 BCE to 1000 CE), a quick timeline
will help you remain oriented. As delineated by author Johan August Alm, the
history of Greece before the Common Era is usually divided into the following
time periods:

- 6000–2900 BCE: Neolithic Period
- 2900–2000 BCE: Early Bronze Age
- 2000–1400 BCE: Minoan Age (on the island of Crete)
- 1600–1100 BCE: Mycenaean Age (on the Greek mainland)

- 1100–750 BCE: The Dark Ages
- 750–500 BCE: Archaic Period
- 500–336 BCE: Classical Period
- 336–146 BCE: Hellenistic Period[1]

The events of the Trojan War took place in the Mycenaean Age (1600–1100 BCE). The mythos of Zeus and the Olympians defeating the Titan generation of gods emerged during the Mycenaean Age; these stories speak to major cultural and ethnic changes that were going on at the time—including the gradual shift to patriarchy.[2] In the following Dark Ages (1100–750 BCE), Hesiod composed his *Theogony*, and Homer wrote down the *Iliad* and the *Odyssey*. Their works were likely based on earlier oral traditions. Influential pre-Socratic philosophers such as Pythagoras and Empedocles emerged in the sixth century BCE. Later, Socrates and Plato were active during the Classical Period (500–336 BCE). After the Hellenistic Period (336–146 BCE), Greece was conquered by the Romans and would eventually be folded into the Byzantine (Eastern Roman) Empire. Byzantium persisted until the fall of Constantinople in 1453 CE.

The names of gods, places, and concepts—all subject to a wide variety of spellings, translations, and pronunciations—can be one of the biggest hurdles encountered in studying Greco-Roman mythology. The pronunciation of the Greek language has changed over millennia. The Classical period of the ancient Greek language is considered to be during the fifth century BCE. After this period, Koine ("Common Greek") was spread throughout the regions Greek-speaking peoples conquered and colonized until about the fourth century CE.[3] Byzantine Greek and Modern Greek followed afterward. Similar to Classical scholars such as Sarah Iles Johnston, for this book I have chosen to use English transliterations that come closer to the Classical Greek spellings of these words. Where relevant, I have included their Latinate transliterations in the glossary. For an excellent guide on how to pronounce Classical Greek words,

---

1. Johan August Alm, *Tartaros: On the Orphic and Pythagorean Underworld and the Pythagorean Pentagram* (San Pablo, CA: Three Hands Press, 2013), 2.

2. Alm, *Tartaros*, 4.

3. Luke Ranieri, "How to Pronounce χαῖρε in Greek: Classical Greek, Attic Greek, Koine Greek, Modern Greek," polýMATHY, August 19, 2019, YouTube video, 7:46, https://www.youtube.com/watch?v=yCv5dK1DOgw.

as well as interesting facts on how the language has changed over the years, I recommend checking out Luke Ranieri's polýMATHY video series on YouTube.

How to Use This Book

Each chapter of this book begins with a creative retelling of a myth or fragment of folklore associated with Hades. These retellings are written in Hades' voice, from his perspective, resulting from the many hours I've spent talking with him in trance journey. They are intended to give you insight into Hades' thoughts and personality and to assist you in making an emotional connection with an enigmatic god that, at first, might seem stoic, formal, and distant. I then move into analysis and discussion of Hades' mythos as it is described in primary sources, how these themes are still relevant today, and what the takeaways are for modern devotees.

Information on Hades' symbols, attributes, and corresponding flora and fauna is included in the midsection of each chapter. Greek mythology is full of plants and animals, and these beings are important parts of the full story—they have the power to enrich our comprehension and understanding of complex, multifaceted mythological figures like the gods. All the plants I have included either grew wild or were cultivated in the ancient Mediterranean, with the possible exception of *Datura stramonium*. Ancient peoples would have been familiar with these plants, even if their historical use of them differs from our usage today. Discussion of correspondences is followed by information on how to find Hades in the modern landscape: sacred temples, natural features, and archaeological sites that exist today.

In the final section of each chapter are invitations to practice. As the chapters progress, the skills and exercises in the invitations to practice build upon the previous ones, giving you a direct path to build a devotional relationship with Hades. I believe in anchoring magical and spiritual exploration with a strong foundation, so I've included some how-to basics such as circle casting, warding, evocation, and grounding, as well as an introduction to trance journey. Some of these operations will be familiar to readers who have already spent time developing their own magical praxis. However, it is my hope that in applying these techniques in the context of working with Hades and the Underworld, you will perhaps discover something new or come to see them in a different light. The invitations to practice section also includes a concise summary of when to call upon the specific aspect of Hades or the Underworld denizens discussed in that chapter, with an accompanying original devotional hymn written by me.

Studying, working magic, and engaging in ritual with Hades and the denizens of the Underworld can sometimes bring up challenging emotions and situations. You may find yourself confronting intensely emotional topics, such as death and dying, personal or collective traumas, or the shadowy or hidden aspects of your own personality. If you should ever find yourself in serious mental or emotional distress after a magical working, ritual, or trance journey, please seek professional psychological help.

Finally, if the content in these pages resonates with your own desires and yearnings, please use it in your personal magical and spiritual practice with my blessing. I invite you to get in touch with me and share what you have discovered. However, if you find your path or beliefs diverge from this material, please know that you have my utmost gratitude and respect for your time and attention. I wish you well as you seek your heart's calling elsewhere.

Welcome friends, and khaire Hades!

CHAPTER 1
THE UNSEEN ONE

Hades speaks:

What is it like to be suspended in the belly of time? It is being able to hear but unable to speak. It is being able to sense but unable to see. It is being enveloped by constant darkness, while left with a distant, lingering memory of the light.

My father is the devourer of ages. Some say he is the personification of time itself, but that's not quite right ... He is the forward thrust of an unwelcome past, forever threatening to swallow the present, recklessly and selfishly destroying the potential of the future. I have only one memory of Rhea, my Titaness mother. It is a stolen vignette of a moment, close-up and out of focus. I remember the sheen of sweat on her brow, the soft glow of her cheek by firelight. And then ... darkness.

At length, I found my sisters in the dark. Hestia, Demeter, and Hera had been swallowed before me. Their childish hands reached out, fumbling to grasp my shoulders, to feel the outline of my face, to find the edges of my being. My siblings. Eventually Poseidon joined us, too, and together we taught him the ways of our dark imprisonment (such as they were). This is how we grew up: five scared, lonely children. Holding hands in the dark.

And then, one day, our father swallowed a stone instead of his sixth child, Zeus. Clever Rhea hid the baby—and clever Zeus grew to adulthood. He disguised himself as a cupbearer and fed Kronos an emetic potion. With a great contraction and heaving force, our father suddenly spat out the rest of us. Blinded, breathless, and confused, we were immediately swept away to recover at the threshold of Tartaros.

Tartaros is a deep abyss. It is as far beneath Hades as the Underworld is beneath the earth. It is a mysterious place where the cosmos and its multitude of forms were born, yet no light can pass its boundaries. It draws all, consumes all. Nothing escapes Tartaros without the twin efforts of cunning and outside assistance.

Our father was strong, and in order to win our freedom from him, my siblings and I needed help from the Titans. Imprisoned within Tartaros were the Cyclopes, three one-eyed Titan brothers who were skillful blacksmiths and armorers, and the Hekatonkheires, three hundred-handed Titan brothers who were fierce warriors. So we freed these prisoners, and in their gratitude they agreed to ally with us against Kronos.

The Cyclopes forged our weapons for battle. Zeus was gifted the thunderbolt, and my brother Poseidon the trident. My weapon, however, was different. The gift the Cyclopes crafted for me was not meant to burn flesh or draw blood. My weapon was not meant to wound, but to conceal: the Helm of Invisibility. I placed the newly wrought helm on my head. My body instantly dissolved into mist and shadows, until I was undetectable. Unseen. Armed and eager, together we marched against Kronos.

The battle waged for ten years. Thunder rolled as Kronos and the Titans who allied with him fought to preserve their dominance. Day after day the Cyclopes swung their mighty battle axes; hour after hour the Hekatonkheires were a relentless blur of bristled arms and lethal hands. Finally the moment came when Zeus and Poseidon cornered Kronos on the battlefield. As he raged against their entrapment, I slipped on the Helm of Invisibility. I crept closer, and closer still. Soundless. Unseen. Screaming his anger at my brothers, our father took no notice as I quickly clamped manacles around his ankles. He barely understood what was happening when swiftly I closed the second set around his wrists. And it was then that I removed the Helm to look him in the eye—his silent shock was louder than his rage had ever been: the once-mighty Kronos, devourer of his own children, now defeated.

Tartaros was, and still is, the perfect prison for the unjust. When the battle was over and Kronos secured in the abyss, Zeus proposed that he, Poseidon, and I draw lots to divide the world among ourselves. As she had been given dominion over crops, grains, and agriculture, our sister Demeter gathered straws of varying lengths in her hand for the lottery. We each chose a straw. Zeus drew the longest straw and for his lot was given the realm of the Skies. Poseidon drew the middle straw and for his lot was given the realm of the Seas. Demeter's face grew sympathetic as I drew the last straw, the short straw ... and for my lot was given the Void.

Aides, Aidoneus, and Hades: The Unseen One

The origins and exploits of the gods of Greek mythology are recorded in numerous manuscripts, as well as several scattered fragments of text, from the ancient world. However, there are two primary sources that remain extremely influential (and relevant to our topic): the works of the poets Hesiod and Homer, both circa 800 to 700 BCE. Hesiod's *Theogony*, thought to be composed sometime around 730 to 700 BCE, is an epic poem describing the genealogy of the gods and ancient Greek cosmology. Homer, whether a singular author or a compilation of several poets using the same moniker, is best known for the epic poems the *Iliad* and the *Odyssey*—two extensive volumes bursting with stories of war, adventure, heroes, and interactions between humans and the gods. To this day, the *Iliad* and the *Odyssey* are considered foundational to the evolution of Western literature; in fact, if you grew up in the United States, they were most likely assigned reading at some point during your high school or college days. Related to these two epics are the *Homeric Hymns*, likely composed a bit later around 600 to 500 BCE, which consist of thirty-three anonymous poems celebrating the Greek gods. The hymns are deemed *Homeric* because they share the same poetic meter and dialect as the *Iliad* and the *Odyssey*.

Because of these extant primary sources, we know that the god we now call Hades was recognized throughout antiquity as Aides, or sometimes by the longer poetic form Aidoneus, both names that trace their roots back to the proto-Indo-European word **n-uid-*, meaning "unseen."[4] This mysterious, primordial name implies that whatever lies beyond death is invisible to the living, and so it must also follow that the ruler of death's domain is likewise unseen. In other words, Kronos didn't see Hades coming, and neither will we. These older names evolved into their more familiar form, Hades, by the fourth or fifth century BCE.[5]

---

4. Avi Kapach, "Hades," Mythopedia, last modified 7, 2022, https://mythopedia.com/topics/hades.

5. James Diggle et al., eds., *The Cambridge Greek Lexicon*, vol. 1 (Cambridge: Cambridge University Press, 2021), 19.

In Hesiod's *Theogony*, Hades is the fourth child of the Titans Kronos and Rhea, in birth order after sisters Hestia, Demeter, and Hera. Kronos was the king of the Titan generation of gods and was the god of time, particularly time viewed as a destructive, all-consuming force. After it was prophesied that he would be overthrown by one of his own children, Kronos swallowed each of his offspring as they were born. Hades was the first of three brothers born to Kronos and Rhea, and the first male child to be swallowed by his father—eventually followed by Poseidon and a stone disguised as Zeus. Kronos is tricked into regurgitating his children, and after waging ten years of war against their father, the younger generation finally overpowers the Titans, locking Kronos away in Tartaros. Duties and dominions are divided amongst the siblings and their sympathizers. Hades becomes responsible for the third realm: the Void (as Homer refers to it), or as we have come to know it, the Underworld.

We can only speculate about how Hades felt in the aftermath of the Titanomachy—the name Classical scholars gave to the overthrow of the Titan generation of gods by the Olympians and their sympathizers—because the poets and historians of the ancient world did not tell us. From primary source texts, we know that his siblings waved goodbye, claimed Mount Olympus for themselves, and blithely began having children and consolidating their power. So-called after their chosen dwelling place, the Olympian gods of Greek mythology would grow to include not only Hestia, Hera, Demeter, Zeus, and Poseidon, but also Aphrodite, Hephaestus, Ares, Athena, Apollo, Artemis, Hermes, and sometimes Dionysus (depending on the source text). Hades, although their contemporary, is noticeably absent from this roll call. Why?

When Hades drew the lot of the Void, he had no choice but to part with the newly formed cohort of Olympians to build his home in the misty, ancient, and obscured realm of the dead. He is rarely recorded visiting Mount Olympus, instead preferring to interact with other gods and humans within the borders of his khthonic realm. The term *khthonic* comes from the Greek word *khthónios*, meaning "in the earth, under the ground, or subterranean," and it refers to something being of or related to the Underworld.[6] We could assume the reason for his missing presence is that Hades' tasks as ruler of the Underworld keep him quite busy; however, I also think that his perspective may have

---

6. Diggle et al., eds., *The Cambridge Greek Lexicon*, vol. 2, 1501.

shifted over the years, as the concerns of the dead are quite different than those of the living. It's not hard to imagine Hades feeling more and more like an outsider among his livelier Olympian family, especially over millennia. Writing on Hades' origins and history, author Jesse Harasta observes, "Of all of his siblings, Hades is unique. He is the only one of the gods to not be considered an 'Olympian,' and he is the only one not to live on Mount Olympus. This simple fact defines the nature of Hades more than any other and transforms the way that he was understood, worshiped and discussed amongst the Greeks."[7]

Although we can find a plethora of descriptive passages about his realm, there are very few stories about the deeds of Hades himself. He does not take part in the conflicts of mortals, such as the Trojan War, nor is he the patron of any heroes. While the other Olympian gods and goddesses fill page after page of epic verse with their escapades, Hades is frequently absent, or cast in the role of a tertiary character subordinate to the main action. In the grand tradition of Greek theater, Hades enters mythology stage left—a theatrical term that refers to the left side of a stage from the point of view of a performer facing the audience. In some forms of ancient Greek theater, it was customary for tertiary characters (sometimes called the tritagonist) to enter from stage left. Hades often fills the shoes of the notorious outcast, unlikely benefactor, or implacable adversary necessary to move the protagonist's story forward. Does this mean Hades was not important to the ancient Greeks? The answer is quite decisively and unequivocally no. And yet, it is complex: Hades was extremely important—his primary responsibility as ruler of the Underworld was, and is, to keep the balance between the world of the living and the realm of the dead. The Unseen One plays a very valuable role in the pantheon of Greek gods but not one that historically garnered adoration.

Hades' Realm and Responsibilities

The word *Hades* continued to evolve, eventually becoming the name of a god as well as the name of the Underworld over which he presides. For purposes of clarity, in this book I will always refer to the god as *Hades* and to his realm as the *Underworld*. The Underworld of Greek mythology is the land of the dead, the place all mortals are destined to go once they cross the threshold from life to

---

7. Jesse Harasta, *Hades: The History, Origins and Evolution of the Greek God* (self-pub., CreateSpace, 2013), loc. 225, Kindle.

death. There are many non-mortal denizens of the Underworld, too, and most of these beings report to Hades. The Underworld provides a clearly delineated home for mortal souls who are in between lifetimes; in doing so, it is a key factor in preventing our world from descending into chaos. In the Underworld, mortal souls appear as *shades*—the ephemeral or ghostly semblance of their last physical form.

Hades is fair-minded. He treats everyone equally after death, whether you are a king or a commoner, and it would be accurate to say he's a stickler for rules. He is most definitely the executive administrator—or Host, if you will—of the Underworld, much more so than a judge or punisher of the dead. Hades usually delegates the responsibilities of judgment and sentencing to a trusted trio of Underworld judges named Aiakos, Rhadamanthus, and Minos, or sometimes to his wife, the Dread Queen Persephone. And as for punishment? Well, that's the sphere of the Erinyes. Otherwise known as the Furies, the Erinyes are a terrifying trio of serpent-haired, winged goddesses of vengeance. They brandish whips and torches of yew and are particularly concerned with crimes of homicide, perjury, incest, sexual assault, and offenses against the gods.

Many people mistakenly assume Hades is the god of death, or the supernatural being who comes to claim you at the end of life—but no, that's the winged daimon Thanatos, who works in his employ. Likewise, Hades has no control over the length of a lifetime, or the chosen hour of death for any given individual; that responsibility belongs to another Underworld trio, the Moirai, otherwise known as the Fates. The Moirai consist of three sisters: Clotho, Lachesis, and Atropos. Clotho, with a distaff in her hand, presides over the moment we are born. Lachesis, working the spindle, turns out the hours and days of our lives. And Atropos, the eldest sister of the trio, ends the thread of our mortal life with a sharp pair of scissors.

In addition to the Underworld itself, Hades' domain also includes all the riches beneath the surface of the earth: rocks, gems, metals, minerals, and fertile soil. It is because of these precious resources, in addition to the abundance of shades that inhabit his realm, that Hades is often referred to as the Wealthy One among the gods. *Plouton* is the epithet given to him in this role.[8] An *epithet* is an adjective or short description that expresses the character of a person or

---

8. Diggle et al., eds., *The Cambridge Greek Lexicon*, vol. 2, 1146.

thing—essentially, an illustrative nickname or surname. Ancient Greeks commonly used epithets to honor the gods in poetry, literature, art, and statuary. It was by the epithet *Plouton* that Hades was most commonly referred to in the ancient world; this euphemism called up images of abundance and prosperity, rather than separation and death.

Hades Worship in the Ancient World

You'll recall that Hades was gifted the Helm of Invisibility during the Titanomachy, which may be another reason why he is known as the Unseen One. But it is also important to recognize that he was quite literally unseen among the living—purposefully pushed out of sight, and out of mind, unlike the other members of his Olympian family. Death has always been an uninvited guest knocking at the door of humanity; its presence was perhaps even more intimidating in a world before modern advances in science and medicine.

In their day-to-day lives, the ancient Greeks preferred not to dwell on death and the afterlife, for fear of drawing it closer to home and hearth. In her book *The Path of Shadows*, writer and esoteric philosopher Gwendolyn Taunton observes, "Hades occupies a role which fills mortals with dread, for as the King of the Underworld, his task is as necessary as it is unpleasant. As such, it is obvious that mortals would revile Hades for separating them from their loved ones and bringing grief to humanity, for death is an inescapable consequence of mortality."[9] To avoid speaking of Hades or looking upon his image was a simple act of apotropaic magic: a way to protect oneself and one's family, deflecting premature harm. Taunton continues, "The fact that the face of Hades is forever unseen is depicted in iconography. Hades is sometimes shown with his brothers—Zeus and Poseidon—with his head turned back to front, implying that despite his power, he is forever unknown to mortals."[10]

Offerings to Hades in the ancient world were not common; however, people occasionally found themselves in sticky situations. In the *Odyssey*, the witch Circe gives Odysseus explicit instructions on how to beseech Hades, Persephone, and the dead with offerings. She tells him to dig a hole in the ground one cubit wide and one cubit long. A *cubit* is an ancient unit of measurement, approximately

---

9. Gwendolyn Taunton, *The Path of Shadows: Chthonic Gods, Oneiromancy & Necromancy in Ancient Greece* (Colac, Victoria, Australia: Manticore Press, 2018), 10.

10. Taunton, *The Path of Shadows,* 10–11.

18 to 20 inches (45 to 50 centimeters), or the length of a human forearm from the elbow to the tip of the middle finger. Odysseus is to pour libations into the hole—milk mixed with honey, then wine, and then water. After libations, barley is to be sprinkled on the ground. Ritual sacrifice of animals is also prescribed, including one ram and one black ewe. Odysseus and his men are to turn away as they make these sacrifices.[11]

If it became necessary to seek favor from the Unseen One, the task of making khthonic offerings was almost always handled by trained priests—professional ritualists who were hired specifically for the occasion. An individual or family who desired to make an offering to Hades would purchase a black animal, the first choice being a sheep and the second choice being a goat. They would then commission a pit to be dug directly in the earth. The pit served as the *bothros*, a dedicated altar to receive the sacrifice.[12] The hired priest would approach the bothros at night, slitting the throat of the sacrificial animal, and letting its blood drain into the pit while looking away.

The individuals paying for the offering were not usually present during this ritual, but if they were, they stood solemnly with their backs to the earthen pit. Accidentally looking upon the face of the Unseen One, or any of his Underworld retinue, was to be avoided at all costs. Any ritual libations would be poured out entirely into the bothros, rather than shared between Hades and participants. Prayers or hymns to Hades, if included, would be sung solemnly with hands lowered toward the ground. And then, finally, the priest and any others who were still present would stomp on the earth or beat upon it with their hands to call the attention of the Underworld to the sacrifice.

Although occasional offerings were made out of necessity, ancient temples and cult sites dedicated to Hades were even more rare. Most notable among these were the Nekromanteion of Ephyra in northern Greece, the Hades temple at Elis in the Greek Peloponnese, and the Ploutonium at Hierapolis in Asia Minor in modern-day Turkey. All these sites served a very particular function: they were oracles of the dead—temples where the living could petition and speak to the dead during necromantic rites. Necromancy, in the sense of con-

11. Homer, *The Odyssey*, trans. Emily R. Wilson (New York; London: W. W. Norton & Company, 2018), 10.517–35.

12. Sarah Kate Istra Winter, *Kharis: Hellenic Polytheism Explored*, 2nd ed. (self-pub., CreateSpace, 2019), 132.

sulting with the dead for the purposes of divination, was quite popular in the ancient world. Gwendolyn Taunton explains: "Despite its sinister reputation, necromancy was a very widespread practice throughout the ancient world. It was not associated with evil or horror in most circumstances, but instead was a socially acceptable form of magic in which one obtained a prophecy from the dead."[13] Hades, of course, was the patron god of necromantic rites. His temples were staffed by reclusive priests who conducted the seance-like oracles, and sometimes also by other professionals of similar trades, such as *manteis* (diviners who were not officially licensed by the city-state) and *psuchagôgoi* ("soul-drawers"—specialists who evoked uneasy ghosts in order to coax them into being at rest). Brave people seeking advice or prophecies from the dead often traveled great distances to visit these liminal places; they were considered focal points of spiritual power, providing direct access to the Underworld.

Exploring the Lore

You may be wondering: If so few stories about Hades exist, how do I approach building a relationship with him? How do I learn to recognize his energy or his presence? What should I do if I'm drawn to working magic with Hades, or other denizens of the Underworld, but don't know where to start? What are the ground rules? Are there any hidden dangers to be aware of? These are all valid questions.

In order to see the Unseen One, we must learn to look between the lines. Context is our ally in this pursuit.

Context Clues: Finding Hidden Gems in Stories

One of my favorite ways to discover the wisdom encoded in myth and story is to mindfully, deeply explore any fragments of context that survived within the narrative. Details like a description of a character's attributes or garments (such as Hades' Helm of Invisibility), or specific places, plants, and animals, add layers of nuance and meaning to mythological tales. These elements of the story are oftentimes more familiar to our human experience. For example, we know what it's like to walk outside to smell the unique fragrance of a certain plant, or to enjoy running our fingers through the fur of a beloved pet. Some

---

13. Taunton, *The Path of Shadows*, 142.

of us may even know what it is like to wear a military-style helmet on our head. In studying and magically exploring these details, we unearth valuable clues about the nature of beings (such as gods like Hades) who are vastly different from us.

In his book *Ancient Magic: A Practitioner's Guide to the Supernatural in Greece and Rome*, author and Classical scholar Philip Matyszak advises, "To study ancient magic, start by forgetting about the 'supernatural.' In the ancient world, there was no such thing. This is not because nothing was magical in that world, but because everything was. The ancient world was *numinous*, which means 'infused with divine power.' Nature was packed with magic."[14] The terrain of myth and story is saturated with meaning because everything in the world was *meaningful* to the poets, playwrights, and storytellers who gave us these narratives. When it comes to re-enchanting our modern world, myth and story contain encoded instructions hiding in plain sight. Animals could be gods in disguise. The color someone wore could magically protect them. Certain plants are mentioned by name to call upon their *spiritus viridis*, or green spirit. Here are some investigative questions to ask as you approach mythology and folklore:

- What characters, in addition to the protagonist, are present in the narrative?
- What are their roles and functions?
- How is the appearance, demeanor, or energy of different characters described?
- Do any of the characters have a signature item of clothing, a distinctive physical attribute, or a specific place that they inhabit?
- Do the characters instigate, harm, heal, support, grow, and/or change? If so, how?
- Are there any sequences of actions or events in the narrative that seem ritualistic?
- Are there any specific times, days, or seasons mentioned?
- Are there any specific plants, animals, and/or minerals mentioned?

---

14. Philip Matyszak, *Ancient Magic: A Practitioner's Guide to the Supernatural in Greece and Rome* (New York: Thames & Hudson, 2019), 7.

Throughout the chapters of this book, I'll tease out contextual clues from mythology that give us insight into Hades' enigmatic nature—specifically, any symbols, plants, and animals (ordinary or extra-ordinary) mentioned in association with him. Many of these clues come from the epic poetry of Hesiod and Homer, as previously discussed, but there are a few other, more obscure sources that also warrant exploration. Our studies begin with a context clue from the myth of the Titanomachy: Hades' Helm of Invisibility.

Symbols of Hades: The Helm of Invisibility

In Hesiod's *Theogony*, the Cyclopes gift Zeus with his infamous lightning bolt, Poseidon with a trident, and Hades with the Helm of Invisibility. The Cyclopes are a trio of brothers named Brontes (Bright), Steropes (Thunder), and Arges (Lightning). Their names reflect their skill in creating weaponry, including terrifying thunderbolts. They are said to be massive in size and strength, and each share the key feature of having a singular eye in the middle of the forehead. The Cyclopes are sons of the primordial deities Ouranos (the Sky) and Gaia (the Earth). They were imprisoned by their father in Tartaros, and later released by Zeus and his siblings to aid in their battle against the Titans.

The Helm of Invisibility is just that—it renders the wearer invisible. This object is also sometimes called the Cap of Invisibility or the Helm or Cap of Darkness, depending on the translation. Hades put the helm to good use in the war against his father, Kronos, but other figures in Greek mythology have borrowed the helm, too. Athena utilized it to influence the Trojan War, Hermes wore it in battle against the giant Hippolytus, and Perseus donned it to escape the immortal gorgons Sthenno and Euryale after he decapitated their sister, Medusa. The Helm of Invisibility, however, always returns to reside in the Underworld with its original owner, Hades.

It is interesting to note that it was Hades who was gifted the Helm of Invisibility even before drawing the short straw—before becoming ruler of the Underworld. Did the Cyclopes have some kind of prescience about his future role as the Unseen One? Perhaps their trademark large singular eye, placed directly over the location of the pineal gland in the middle of their foreheads, lent the Cyclopes brothers extra-ordinary insight when forging armaments for the gods. The pineal gland, located deep in the center of the brain, helps the body interpret the presence or absence of light in the environment in order to regulate circadian rhythms and melatonin secretion. Many spiritual traditions believe this "third eye" serves as a connection between the physical and spiritual worlds. So was it intuition? Clever foreshadowing? Maybe both.

English philosopher, occultist, and statesman Francis Bacon (1561–1626) referenced the Helm of Invisibility in his short essay entitled *Of Delays*: "For the helmet of Pluto [Hades], which maketh the politic man go invisible, is secrecy in the counsel, and celerity in the execution."[15] In other words, underneath the Helm of Invisibility, actions can be undertaken swiftly and secretly. Bacon's essay goes on to advocate that secrecy is sometimes advisable in public affairs, in order to preserve an individual's or group's options—once you speak or act publicly, it is on the record.[16] Perhaps occasional loaning of the Helm of Invisibility empowers not only those who are wearing it to act toward their desired ends, but also Hades himself, networking behind the scenes to influence events and outcomes? Hades would certainly have the necessary strategic perspective to move chess pieces across the board into checkmate.

Of course, on the other side of this metaphorical coin is the concern that hidden moves are suspect because they lack transparency. Maybe the real lesson lies in developing the discernment to know when invisibility is advisable and when transparency is the order of the day. Who better to aid us in this quest than the guardian of the Helm of Invisibility himself?

In His Dark Garden: Bay Laurel and Hellebore

In studying the myth of the Titanomachy, as well as the origins of Hades' name and his worship in the ancient world, some common themes arise: victory, invisibility, prophecy, and divination. Bay laurel and hellebore are two plant allies that can help us better understand and align with these characteristics of the Unseen One, as well as aid us in communicating with beloved dead or the Underworld.

BAY LAUREL

Species: *Laurus nobilis*
Other Common Names: Laurel tree, bay, sweet bay, Grecian laurel

---

15. Francis Bacon, "Of Delays," in *Essays* (New York: John B. Alden, 1885), 84.

16. Bacon, "Of Delays," 84.

Toxicity: Nontoxic to humans (but toxic to cats, dogs, and other animals). Ingesting bay leaf is contraindicated for pregnant people and those with diabetes.

Keywords: Victory, success, oracles, divination, messages

Bay laurel is one of the oldest trees in cultivation. This evergreen shrub is commonly planted as a hedge or other structural feature, and its fragrant leaves are used to flavor a variety of savory foods. There is a popular origin story of the laurel tree recorded in Greek mythology. It speaks of the nymph Daphne, who asks Gaia to turn her into a tree so that she may avoid the unwanted advances of the god Apollo. Gaia grants her request, turning Daphne into the laurel tree. Apollo is the Olympian god of the sun, light, healing, poetry, and prophecy, and as he mourned the loss of his unrequited love, the laurel tree henceforth became sacred to him.

Why include this tree in the garden of Hades? What can it tell us about him? I assure you, the Unseen One has a prized bay laurel or two among his gardens. A wreath of fragrant bay laurel leaves was the quintessential sign of victory in ancient Greece and Rome—Hades, along with his siblings and their sympathizers, were ultimately victorious over the Titans. Additionally, because of its association with Apollo's divinatory arts, bay laurel was a fixture in the practices of ancient seers, such as the Pythia and the Sibyl. Artists of antiquity captured images of these prophetesses holding branches of laurel in one hand, while leaning over earthen vapors and peering into their scrying bowls. Extant sources do not explicitly tell us if priests of the Nekromanteion used bay laurel in their divinatory rites, but it seems logical that they, too, would have known how to ally with the spiritus viridis of this particular plant.

Bay laurel is an appropriate choice for works of magic or divination involving communication with the dead, not only because its leaves are slow-burning and fragrant, but also because their smooth texture and size are perfect for writing short petitions, messages, or sigils. Such messages can be inscribed before a single leaf is burnt on a small charcoal or before releasing a few leaves into a fire. The smoke of the burning leaves will carry your message to the Underworld. It's a good idea to keep your messages succinct, perhaps limiting yourself to one to three leaves at a time, to more easily determine if your messages are being received.

Hellebore

Species: *Helleborus orientalis, Helleborus niger*
Other Common Names: Black hellebore, Christmas rose, Lenten rose, melampodium
Toxicity: Highly toxic (never ingest, and use caution when handling)
Keywords: Astral projection, invisibility, madness

Hellebore is one of my favorite plants. A member of the buttercup family, it is an evergreen perennial with leathery leaves and winter-blooming flowers. *Helleborus niger* features white blooms, while *Helleborus orientalis* cultivars may have white, pink, green, mauve, or smoky purple blooms. In *The Philosophy of Natural Magic*, Henry Cornelius Agrippa includes hellebore in his list of Saturnine plants: "Amongst plants and trees, the daffodil, dragon's-wort, rue, cummin, hellebore, the tree from whence benzoin comes, mandrake, opium, and those things which are never sown, and never bear fruit, and those which bring forth berries of a dark color and black fruit, as the black fig-tree, the pine-tree, the cypress-tree … [are] deadly, and dedicated to Pluto."[17]

Hellebore is extremely toxic but was commonly used by ancient peoples as a treatment for madness. An example of this folk usage is documented in the Greek narrative tale "Cure of the Proetides." In this anecdote, the god Dionysus struck the daughters of King Proetus of Argos and Tiryns with madness as punishment for scorning his worship. His daughters, collectively known as the Proetides, were named Iphianassa, Iphinoe, and Lysippe. A local seer named Melampos, upon hearing the pleas for assistance from King Proetus, searched for the Proetides and found them wandering in the nearby mountains, naked and mooing like cows. Melampos cured their madness with hellebore.[18]

Centuries later, European witches were infamous for their alleged use of flying ointment. They rubbed a salve of herbs and rendered fat over themselves and then took off "flying." Hellebore featured prominently in these concoctions, alongside belladonna and other toxic plants. Flying ointment was a dan-

17. Henry Cornelius Agrippa, *The Philosophy of Natural Magic*, trans. L. W. de Laurence (Chicago: de Laurence, Scott & Co., 1913; electronic reproduction by John Bruno Hare, Internet Sacred Texts Archive, 2008), 102–3.

18. Pliny the Elder, *The Natural History*, trans. John Bostock and H. T. Riley (London: Taylor and Francis, 1855), 25.21.

gerous high—both hellebore and belladonna can disrupt heartbeats and cause hallucinations. Hellebore's other magical use during this time period was as an invisibility powder.[19] Witches were said to grind the flowers into a fine powder, sprinkle it onto the earth, and then walk on the powder to make themselves invisible.

Hellebore can be a useful ally when we wish to be undetected. Due to its toxicity, hellebore should never be ingested, and extreme caution used when handling the plant. In order to ally with hellebore for invisibility or trance journey, I suggest growing your own plant (keeping it well out of reach of any children or pets) and simply sitting in its presence. Alternatively, you can draw or meditate on an image of hellebore. To venerate Hades as the Unseen One, place the plant or its image on your altar. Once you've spent some time getting to know hellebore, you can begin asking its spiritus viridis how to incorporate more of its insight into your magical and ritual practices.

Khthonic Bestiary: The Black Ram

Sacrifice was the most important ritual action in ancient Greece. Most sacrifices involved animals; the main species chosen for these rites were pigs, sheep, goats, and cattle.[20] Symbolism was sometimes incorporated into the choice of animal—as specifically mentioned in Homer's *Odyssey*, black sheep were preferred sacrifices for Hades. One possible reason for this choice is that the sheep's ebony coat honors Hades' hair and beard, believed to be as dark and curly as black sheep's wool. One of Hades' epithets, *Euchaites*, means "The Beautiful Haired One."[21] Another possible reason is that the color black is reminiscent of fertile soil and of Erebos, the primordial god of darkness who encircles the Underworld. Black rams made for particularly potent offerings—rams figure prominently as metaphors of strength and courage throughout Greek mythology. Apotropaic rams' heads, in the form of beads carved from amber, have even been found in ancient graves. These beads are interpreted by some

19. Occvlta, "Hellebore," *Materia Venefica* 18 (February 2023): 22, https://www.occvlta.org/.

20. Simon Hornblower, Antony Spawforth, and Esther Eidinow, *The Oxford Companion to Classical Civilization*, 2nd ed. (New York: Oxford University Press, 2014), 690.

21. Hornblower et al., *The Oxford Companion to Classical Civilization*, 353.

to function as both "ornament and amulet," lending the wearer protection and fortitude in the afterlife.[22]

Animal sacrifice is still a sacred act celebrated by many people around the world, although it is less common in spiritual practices descended from Western European traditions. Unless you are a farmer or hunter who knows how to lawfully and humanely slaughter an animal, it's best to explore other alternatives. A perfectly suitable alternative practice is to "sacrifice" a savory cake or biscuit in lieu of an animal. You can shape the dough into the form you seek to represent and use food coloring or decorative icings to add color to your offering. Chapter 6 contains a recipe for maza, a type of ancient barley cake, which works well for this purpose.

Finding Hades in the Landscape: Nekromanteion of Ephyra

The Nekromanteion of Ephyra was a famous temple of necromancy devoted to Hades and Persephone. According to ancient sources, the Nekromanteion was located on the banks of the Akheron river in Epirus, near the city of Ephyra. In 1958, the archaeologist Sotirios Dakaris discovered ancient ruins on a hilltop near the confluence of the Akheron, Phlegethon, and Kokytos rivers in the vicinity. The ruins are seventy-two feet square, with eleven-foot-thick walls, and subterranean chambers. Dakaris excavated the site from 1958 to 1964 and 1976 to 1977 and identified it as the ancient Nekromanteion based on its geographical location and similarities to descriptions in Herodotus and Homer.[23] However, its topographical location on the top of a hill does not exactly align with the account in primary sources, and the ruins themselves date no earlier than the late fourth century BCE (the works of Hesiod and Homer are both circa 800–700 BCE). Although the archaeological site is still officially identified as the Nekromanteion, later scholars have proposed that the ruins may have been a fortified agricultural tower, with underground storage areas for water or grain.

---

22. Faya Causey, "Rams' Heads," *Ancient Carved Ambers in the J. Paul Getty Museum* (Los Angeles: The J. Paul Getty Museum, 2012), https://www.getty.edu/publications/ambers/objects/groups/8/.

23. Annetta Black, "Necromanteion of Ephyra," Atlas Obscura, March 27, 2010, https://www.atlasobscura.com/places/necromanteion-of-ephyra.

The modern archaeological site is called the Nekromanteion of Akheron. It is open to visitors and is located in the region of Thesprotia, approximately four and a half hours northwest of Athens by car (242 mi/390 km). The surrounding area is beautiful, regardless of whether or not the current archaeological site is actually the ancient Nekromanteion. There are areas set aside along the Akheron river for picnicking and camping. The river itself is cool and shallow in the summertime. In the month of August you can walk its waters all the way to the spring at its source.[24]

Invitations to Practice

Invoke Hades the Unseen One for necromantic divination, communicating with ancestors and the dead, aligning with cycles of death and rebirth, and assistance with situations requiring invisibility or transparency. Symbols and correspondences that resonate with the energy of Hades in this aspect are the Helm of Invisibility, bay laurel, hellebore, and black sheep (especially rams).

Hymn to the Unseen One

The following hymn can be spoken or sung (to a melody of your choice) to connect with Hades at any time. It offers honor and praise to the Unseen One and asks for his divine protection.

Hear me, Unseen One, you who are
Eternally cloaked in mist and shadows—
Invisible to the eye, yet not
Invisible to the heart.
I offer honor and praise to thee, called Aidoneus,
I pray you will watch over me with kindly spirit
And stealthy might, I ask you to please protect me
As I walk above, until I descend below
To rest in your fields once more.

---

24. Christos Vasilopoulos, "4 Gates of Hades Locations Not to Miss in Greece," Mindful Experiences Greece, April 13, 2023, https://mindfulexperiencesgreece.com/gates-hades-underworld-greece/.

Creating an Altar to Hades

If you'd like to begin exploring a relationship with Hades, a good first step is to create an altar dedicated to him. An altar is a conduit to invite the presence of the Unseen One into your life, via a particular physical space, and serves as a designated place for offerings and acts of devotion. When starting a new relationship with any god, I find it helpful to focus my altar on them specifically, rather than including multiple beings from their realm or other gods from entirely different pantheons. For me, this helps provide a more distinct sense of their particular energy. Once I can clearly discern their particular energetic signature or personality, I may choose to begin adding more elements. For example, when I built my first Hades altar, I did not include Persephone because I wanted to get a sense for Hades as himself, not as part of a couple. After some time passed, I began to add touches of Persephone, as well as other denizens of the Underworld, such as Kharon and Nyx, to expand the altar.

First you must choose a location for your altar. These are some helpful questions to consider:

- Will the altar be inside or outside?
- Do you want your altar to be a large area that influences a whole room or a small and compact shrine?
- Does your living situation necessitate a private altar so that no one else will take notice unless invited by you (such as in a closet or cabinet)?
- Do you need to situate it out of the reach of curious pets or children?
- Do you want the altar where you will see it every day, occasionally, or only rarely?
- Can you comfortably spend time at your altar? Do you need to have a chair, meditation cushion, warm blanket, light source, or other accommodations?

There are no right or wrong answers to these questions. It is important that you choose an altar space that works for your lifestyle and magical practices. If your altar is not in the right spot, you may find yourself disinclined to interact with it or maintain it. At that point, it just becomes decoration. Engagement with and maintenance of your altar helps keep its energy fresh and focused.

Correspondences and Altar Tending

Correspondences, in the magical sense, are things that share close similarity, connection, or equivalence. Corresponding items are included on altars to honor and attract the gods. They are included in rituals and other magical operations to attract specific energies or entities desired for the working. Similar to employing an increasingly more powerful magnet, layering correspondences (such as including sacred symbols, plants, and animals on an altar or considering the time of day, phase of the moon, and location, etc., in your ritual planning) enhances your ritual, spellcasting, or other magical operation by making it "louder" and clearer to the universe. Discarnate beings, such as the gods, are drawn by correspondence.

The idea of correspondences (as I apply them to magic and ritual) stems from two main philosophical theories:

The Platonic Microcosm and Macrocosm: The Platonic concept of the microcosm and macrocosm is captured in the Hermetic axiom "as above, so below." For example, the blaze of a roaring bonfire is present in the light of a small, single candle. Likewise, the blaze of a bonfire can be equated to the blaze of passion in the heart or the heat of action in the solar plexus.

Sympathetic Magic: Sympathetic magic is the idea that a magical practitioner can influence something by using an object that resembles it or an object that is somehow in relationship to it. This concept shows up in folk magic practices around the world and throughout history.

Altars are a creative exercise and there are many, many ways to put them together. You don't need to invest a lot of money buying corresponding objects (unless you want to). Simply walk out into the world with the intention of calling items for your Hades altar to you—you'll be surprised what you find on the sidewalk, at the thrift store, in the grocery aisle, or in Grandma's attic. Here are a few suggestions for an altar dedicated specifically for Hades:

- Portrait or sketch of Hades—yours or that of an artist you admire
- Artwork depicting a place you associate with Hades or his Underworld realm
- Statues to represent Hades (and perhaps also Persephone)

- Reproductions of Classical art from ancient Greece or Rome
- A metal representation of Hades' bident or a bifurcated (forked) branch of wood
- Responsibly sourced stones, minerals, crystals, and/or a small dish of soil to represent the riches of the earth
- Coins to represent wealth
- Hades' sacred plants (there are many mentioned throughout this book)
- Images or physical items related to Hades' sacred animals, such as black sheep (a bit of black wool), the owl (a feather), or his three-headed dog Kerberos (a dog toy or treat)
- Periodic food and drink offerings: red wine, bitter chocolate, and olive or truffle oil

In my home, our Hades altar is located in the entryway, just opposite the front door. We painted the wall a deep purple, similar to the color of black figs. On the wall hangs a beautiful portrait of Hades and a letterpress print of a poppy field near Cuma, Italy, a place where we explored the Antro della Sibilla (Cave of the Sibyl) and made offerings to him. A shelf is placed just below, with a mix of iconic items to represent the Unseen One: dark stones such as smoky quartz, black tourmaline, and pyrite; coins for wealth; and a forged iron bident. Recently we've added a pair of reproduction Etruscan bronze statues of a man and woman to represent Hades and Persephone as a couple. This is a very central spot in our home, so I frequently pass by the altar during the day. Each time, I nod my head to Hades in recognition or sometimes touch two fingers to my lips and then to his portrait.

There are many ways to tend and interact with altars. Common altar-side activities include lighting candles, leaving offerings of food or incense, maintaining fresh flowers or plants, drawing a tarot or oracle card each day, singing hymns or chants, praying, journaling, letter writing, drawing, doing ritual, engaging in trance journey, or simply sitting in mindful contemplation. You don't have to do all these things. To start, choose one or two activities that appeal to you and that you can commit to doing on a regular basis. Consistency is the key. You can always add more engagement later.

Your Body as a Living Altar

Your body can be a living altar. If you'd like to physically embody more of Hades' energy, choose colors, scents, jewelry, and other accessories that remind you of your connection with him. You don't need to empty your closet or get a total makeover—just try working something small into your ritual of getting dressed each day. For example, I make a blend of earthy essential and carrier oils that I keep in a small glass roller bottle. Each morning after I step out of the shower, I use the roller bottle to draw the astrological sign of Pluto on my right forearm. While drawing this sigil, I ask Hades to watch over and protect me throughout my day. You could use a purchased essential oil or perfume roller in the same way.

Astrological Symbol for Pluto

Over time, I have curated a collection of rings, bracelets, necklaces, and earrings that I wear to remind me of my connection to Hades; I rotate through different pieces, but I'm usually wearing at least one of them every day. Sometimes I also tuck a small Hades-aligned touchstone into my purse or pocket. When I want to feel even more immersed in his energy, I plan my outfit to include colors, textures, and stylistic elements that are evocative of the Underworld.

Here are a few correspondences to help you embody Hades' energy:

Colors: Black, gray, dark blue, deep purple

Scents: Cypress, vetiver, oakmoss, patchouli, clove, spearmint, fig

Textures: Fabrics that have a luxurious feel (e.g., velvet, brocade, soft wool, ethical fur)

Stylistic Elements: The *meandros* ("Greek key" pattern), snakes, skulls

Bling: Whatever this means for you—rings, necklaces, earrings, etc.—in gold or silver

Stones: Black or brown tourmaline, smoky quartz, amethyst, pyrite, obsidian, onyx

If your job restricts your ability to wear specific clothes or jewelry (such as having to wear a uniform or working a manufacturing job that prohibits jewelry for safety reasons), you can tuck a talisman in your pocket or wallet. In my wallet, I carry a miniature portrait of Hades with a devotional hymn printed on the reverse. I've also added a beautiful antique key to my everyday key ring, right next to my house and car keys. The Key to the Realm is another one of Hades' sacred symbols, but anyone looking at my key ring just thinks it's a cool old key.

Purification and Consecration Techniques

Purification and consecration are basic magical techniques. Purifying a space, person, or object cleans and neutralizes its energy. Consecrating a space, object, or activity is a way of dedicating it to a specific purpose. You want to both purify and consecrate the location you choose for your altar, as well as the altar itself and the objects it holds.

The purification technique called *khernips* (literally meaning "hand washing") comes from ancient Greece.[25] To perform this purification, you will need a small bowl of water, a small sprig of rosemary or a few bay leaves, and a fire source. Spring water is recommended, but filtered tap water is fine, too—you may want to include a pinch of salt if you are using tap water. Carefully light the sprig or leaf on fire, and once it is smoldering, plunge it directly into the bowl of water. The water is now purified and can be used for hand washing or can be sprinkled on objects, offerings, and spaces. The rosemary sprig makes a handy tool for sprinkling khernips on yourself and your altar. To properly dispose of used khernips, pour the water outside in your garden, at the base of a tree, or even into a planter. It is not respectful to dump spiritually charged water down the drain.

To consecrate your altar, write or pick out a song, prayer, or hymn of dedication. After purifying your space, building your altar, and then purifying the altar and yourself with additional khernips, you are ready to stand at the altar and consecrate it by reading your dedication out loud. Be very clear in your mind and words that you are dedicating this altar space to Hades, not dedicating yourself to him—that's a matter I'll discuss later in chapter 10. If you have

---

25. Patrick Dunn, *The Orphic Hymns: A New Translation for the Occult Practitioner* (Woodbury, MN: Llewellyn Publications, 2018), 20.

specific intentions for exploring a relationship with Hades, you can state these out loud, too. And it's perfectly fine to leave a copy of your dedication on or near the altar so that you can refer back to it or periodically renew it aloud.

Khaire is a Classical Greek expression of salutations and honor, meaning "Rejoice!"[26] You may want to finish consecrating your Hades altar with a warm and heartfelt salutation: "Khaire Hades!"

---

26. Ranieri, "How to Pronounce χαῖρε in Greek."

CHAPTER 2
HOST OF MANY

𒀭𒀭𒀭𒀭𒀭𒀭𒀭𒀭𒀭𒀭𒀭𒀭𒀭𒀭𒀭𒀭𒀭𒀭

Hades speaks:

How small the straw looked lying in my palm: the third lot, the Underworld.

I stood stunned while my brothers congratulated each other on their destinies. They slapped each other on the back, relieved, laughing in celebration. My face remained stoic as the sunlight began to fade. A sinking feeling invaded my gut, and one by one, I watched my siblings depart for their new realms and responsibilities. I closed my eyes tight against the inevitable. At length, I was left standing alone—or so I thought—until I felt soft fingers slip into my own. Hekate, the goddess who allied with us against the Titans, squeezed my free hand: "Hades. Let us go home."

I followed Hekate beyond the great river of Oceanus, past the setting sun … and then down, far below the earth, to a liminal realm hidden from the living. Behind its shroud of mist, the Underworld was not at all the empty void I had feared it to be—there were mighty rivers to explore, landscapes to chart, fields to cultivate. And I was not alone: other deathless ones such as Nyx, Erebos, Kharon, Thanatos, Kerberos, the Moirai, and Menoites live here. They welcomed me as their leader. Eventually I built a home for myself, the Halls of Hades, and planted an orchard of pomegranate trees. It was not long before the shades of mortals began arriving on my shores.

These days, I watch from my balcony as shades drift aimlessly across the Asphodel Fields. This balcony is where I retreat when I need a few moments to myself, my favorite spot in the halls for quiet contemplation. Mortal shades appear gray, amorphous, ephemeral. Sometimes melancholy. But the shades floating in the Asphodel Fields never fail to renew my spirit, because of one simple reason: within their shadowy frames I can still see the faint, yet ever-present, glow of their souls. Delicate, golden, and precious. They rest here in my fields for a time, until they are ready to be born again and re-enter the great cycle. I watch over and care for them. And I am uplifted by their infinite potential.

Hades Polydegmon: The Host of Many

The epithet *Polydegmon* (Host of Many) refers to Hades' eternal hospitality, extended to the mortal dead, as well as to various other inhabitants of the Underworld. Greek mythology tells us that hospitality was the sacred right of guests and the sacred duty of hosts. Inns and hostels in the ancient world were few and far between; travelers often depended on the hospitality of strangers for shelter and food along the way. The gods sometimes disguised themselves as mortals, making it impossible to know whether a weary traveler was human or a very powerful divine being. It was common courtesy to treat all guests like gods, just in case. Hades, in his role as Polydegmon, fulfills a sacred duty—on a divine scale!—by hosting the shades of mortals traveling between lifetimes.

It is difficult to speak of Hades the god without also evoking the Underworld he rules; the two are so intertwined that they even share the same name. As with most ancient myths, descriptions and accounts of the Underworld sometimes vary from source to source, but there are many commonalities. Let's take a closer look at some of the major features of the Underworld.

Underworld Rivers and Pools

The rivers of the Underworld are bodies of water, and they are also gods or *daimons*, a term from Greek mythology used to describe a category of lesser deities or spirits, who were oftentimes humanoid personifications of abstract concepts.

In *Underland: A Deep Time Journey*, author Robert Macfarlane chronicles his explorations beneath the surface of the earth. Macfarlane theorizes that the reason Greek and Roman mythology flows with so many Underworld rivers is geological—the landscape that these myths grew from is largely karstic in nature. Karst is a type of topography formed by dissolution of soluble rocks and minerals like limestone, gypsum, and dolomite. "Below the surface—if karst can be said to have a surface—aquifers fill and empty over centuries, there are labyrinths through which water circulates over millennia, there are caverns big as stadia, and there are buried rivers with cataracts, rapids and slow pools," writes Macfarlane.[27] He describes this natural terrain as seemingly magical: karst hydrology can feature springs seeming to rise from rock, disappearing and reappearing rivers, lakes with no visible source, sinkholes, and natural shafts. The rivers and pools of the Underworld reflect this topography.

River Styx (Shuddering, Unbreakable Oaths and Vows)

Infamously renowned, the Styx is the principal river of the Underworld. It is a branch of the Oceanus river, and it encircles the border of the Underworld seven times, separating the realm of the dead from the land of the living. According to *Encyclopaedia Britannica*, the ancient Greek word *styx* literally means "shuddering" in reference to mortal loathing or hatred of death.[28] Shades of the dead are ferried across the river by Kharon, who collects an *obol* (coin) from each soul for their fare.

The Olympian Zeus is recorded using a golden jug of water from the Styx to settle disputes among the gods. In Homer's *Iliad*, Styx is called "the fearful oath-river" because if a god swore falsely by the water, they would be deprived of ambrosia for a year, in addition to being banished from the company of the other gods for nine years.[29] Ambrosia is the food or drink of the gods, with the power to gift immortality to anyone who consumes it. For this reason, ancient vows were often sworn (metaphorically) on the Styx, to ensure that they were binding.

River Akheron (Woe, Misery)

The Akheron is the River of Woe or the River of Misery, and in some source texts it is the principal river of the Underworld instead of the river Styx. In those tales, the ferryman Kharon transports departed souls across the Akheron from the upper to the lower world.

In the ordinary world, there are actually many rivers named Akheron. Most notable among these is the river Akheron in Thesprotia (northern Greece).

---

27. Robert Macfarlane, *Underland: A Deep Time Journey* (W. W. Norton & Company, 2019), loc. 178, Kindle.

28. *Encyclopaedia Britannica Online*, s.v. "Styx," accessed March 3, 2023, https://www.britannica.com/topic/Styx-Greek-religion.

29. Homer, *The Iliad of Homer*, trans. Richmond Lattimore (1951; repr., Chicago: University of Chicago Press, 1961), 2.755.

It flows through deep gorges, occasionally disappearing underground, before emerging to meet the Ionian Sea. You may remember from chapter 1 that the Nekromanteion of Ephyra was located alongside the river Akheron.

River Kokytos (Wailing, Lamentation)

If a dead person is not given proper burial rites, including the obol for their fare, Kharon cannot ferry them to the Underworld. These shades are doomed to wander the banks of the Kokytos, forever restless, unable to settle into a peaceful afterlife. The ice-cold Kokytos is called the River of Wailing or River of Lamentation because its waters are filled with their cries of despair. Its shores are scoured by frigid winds, and spots along the river often freeze over.

River Lethe (Oblivion, Forgetting)

Lethe is the River of Oblivion or the River of Forgetting. It is named after its tutelary goddess, Lethe, the goddess of forgetfulness. Lethe is the daughter of Eris, the goddess of strife and discord. Upon entering the Underworld, shades of the dead drink the waters of Lethe to forget about their former lives. Eventually their souls will be born again, but they will remember nothing of their previous incarnation.

River Phlegethon (Fire)

Phlegethon is called the River of Fire because it travels directly to the depths of the Underworld, passing through lands filled with the flames of funeral pyres, eventually leading to the abyss of Tartaros. In Plato's *Phaedo*, Socrates describes the River Phlegethon—sometimes also referred to as the Pyriphlegethon—as erupting with boiling jets of lava and streams of fire before disappearing into the abyss.[30]

Pool of Mnemosyne (Memory)

Mnemosyne is the goddess of memory, and she keeps an Underworld pool located near the Halls of Hades. Inscriptions on gold leaves found in the tomb of a dead woman in Thessaly, dated to 400 BCE, caution the newly dead to keep their memories by avoiding drinking from the Lethe and to drink instead from

---

30. Plato, *Phaedo*, in *The Dialogues of Plato*, vol. 1, trans. Benjamin Jowett (New York: Scribner, Armstrong, and Co., 1874), 442–43.

the babbling stream that flows from the Pool of Mnemosyne. The woman has an obol resting on her lips, a coin inscribed with the image of a gorgon. Classical scholars speculate that the ability to drink from the Pool of Mnemosyne, and remember past lives, may have been a boon granted to initiates of mystery cults—such as the cult of Demeter and Persephone at Eleusis.

Where Mortal Shades Dwell

When shades cross the River Styx, they are greeted by Kerberos, a monstrous canine with three heads and a serpent's tale, who guards the gates to the realm of the dead. Kerberos' duties include ensuring only those who have gained proper entrance pass through the gates, and that none leave. The judges Aiakos, Rhadamanthus, and Minos meet with the newly arrived deceased and usually assign them to dwell within one of four main regions of the Underworld, based on their actions in life.

Asphodel Fields

Most shades are assigned to drift through the Asphodel Fields (also sometimes called the Asphodel Meadows). This is the home for mortals who were neither particularly good nor particularly bad. The Asphodel Fields serve as a sort of way station, like an airport lounge where their souls rest between lifetimes instead of flights. These shades drink from the waters of Lethe, and thus they have no memory of past lives when their soul is born into a new body.

Elysian Fields

The Elysian Fields, or Elysium, are the home for mortals who lived virtuous lives, or perhaps were initiated into various mystery cults. These fields are sunny and pleasant, abundant with food, drink, and conversation. Sometimes the shades drink from the Pool of Mnemosyne, rather than the River Lethe, and may recall lessons learned in previous lives. If a shade is assigned to the Elysian Fields for three consecutive lifetimes, they can choose to escape the cycle of life and death by retiring to the Isles of the Blessed.

Isles of the Blessed

The Isles of the Blessed are the home of heroes, the thrice-blessed virtuous, and other mighty dead. These shades are the valedictorians, so to speak, of the Underworld: overachievers and first in their class. Upon being welcomed to the Isles of the Blessed, they leave the cycle of life and death behind, hanging out with the deathless ones (a.k.a. gods), and indulging in the ultimate eternal staycation.

Tartaros

The abyss of Tartaros predates Hades the god and was originally quite distinct from the Underworld. Archaic poets and playwrights describe Tartaros, Nyx, and Erebos existing even before Ouranos—the primordial sky god, father of the Titan Kronos, and ruler who imprisoned the Cyclopes and the Hekatonkheires in Tartaros. Nyx is the goddess of night; Erebos is her consort, the god of darkness. Both Nyx and Erebos chose to dwell in or near the Underworld after the Titanomachy. Earliest Tartaros was conceptualized as an infinite chasm, a yawning mouth, in whose depths the cosmos was born.[31] In the center of this Tartaros burned a mysterious fire, the *axis mundi* around which the whole universe revolved. Over the centuries, Tartaros lost some of its earlier philosophical connotations and became an impenetrable dungeon of imprisonment for the fallen Titans and the worst of mortal offenders. For most who end up there, Tartaros is an eternal sentence with no escape.

The Halls of Hades

The Halls of Hades are the home of the god himself, and his wife Persephone, when she is at residence in the Underworld. It is in these halls that we find their audience room and the dual thrones symbolic of their sovereignty. In Homer's *Odyssey*, the witch Circe sends Odysseus to the Halls of Hades to speak with the then-dead seer Tiresias, now in the service of the Dread Queen Persephone. It is also in this audience room that Hades and Persephone receive Orpheus, the mortal bard who plays such a moving song for the king and queen of the dead that it melts Hades' stoic heart into bending the rules for a pair of young lovers. Outside the Halls of Hades lies an orchard tended by Askalaphos, son of the daimons Styx and Akheron.

---

31. Alm, *Tartaros*, xi.

Exploring the Lore

For the ancient Greeks, Hades was often portrayed as passive rather than evil; his role was to host the deceased in his domain and to help maintain a relative balance between the living and the dead. However, a common modern misconception is equating the Underworld with Christian notions of hell and Hades with the figure of the Devil.

Hold tight for a bit of disambiguation: when it comes to the Christian Bible, some meanings have been lost in translation over the centuries. In the Hebrew scriptures of the Old Testament, the word used to describe the realm of the dead is *Sheol*. This word refers to a dark, still place where some departed souls reside. In the Greek scriptures of the New Testament, the word *Sheol* was translated as *Hades*, despite the concepts of Sheol and the Greek Underworld being somewhat inequivalent. Over time, this mistranslation led to Hades (the realm) mistakenly becoming synonymous with the Christian concept of hell.[32] However, outside of personal beliefs or religious doctrine—purely etymologically speaking—neither of these Hebrew or Greek terms originally referred to a fiery inferno of eternal punishment.

Another one of the main sources we have to thank for this confusion is the medieval Italian poet and philosopher Dante Alighieri (ca. 1265–d. 1321), who sprinkled characters and landscapes from Greek mythology into his three-part *Divine Comedy* with artistic abandon. In *The Inferno*, the first book of the *Divine Comedy*, Dante describes his journey through hell, guided by the ancient Roman poet Virgil. "Perhaps the most important Christian chronicler of the Underworld, Dante, was well aware of the Pagan worldview when he wrote *Divine Comedy*, placing many Pagan figures, images and terms in the various levels of Hell. Dante's work has had such a formative role in the Western literary imagination that it could be said that he formalized the fusion of Pagan and Christian beliefs," writes Jesse Harasta, in *Hades: The History, Origins and Evolution of the Greek God*.[33]

---

32. *Encyclopaedia Britannica Online*, s.v. "hell," by Carol Zaleski, last modified May 18, 2023, https://www.britannica.com/topic/hell.

33. Harasta, *Hades*, loc. 466, Kindle.

To be clear, we're talking about two totally different sets of mythology: the Christian mythos and the ancient Greek. Hades as we speak of him in these pages is not the Devil, nor is his realm equivalent with hell.

Symbols of Hades: The Key to the Realm

Pausanias, Greek traveler and geographer circa 110 to 180 CE, was one of the original travel bloggers. He was born in Asia Minor under the Roman empire but remained deeply connected to his Greek roots. He spent the majority of his life traveling through mainland Greece, recording his observations and encounters at various temples, venerated spaces, monuments, and notable geological formations. His simple and straightforward style of writing left us with a multitude of matter-of-fact details about life in ancient Greece.

In *Description of Greece*, Pausanias wrote about a particular scene he saw depicted on a table in the temple of Hera at Olympia: "On one side are Asclepius and Health, one of his daughters; Ares too and Contest by his side; on the other are Pluto [Hades], Dionysus, Persephone and nymphs, one of them carrying a ball. As to the key (Pluto holds a key) they say that what is called Hades [the Underworld] has been locked up by Pluto, and that nobody will return back again therefrom."[34]

The khthonic goddess Hekate is associated with keys in Greek mythology. But many do not realize that Hades, too, is often depicted with a key or a ring of keys to show that he alone holds the power to unlock the gates of the Underworld. It's part of his eternal balancing act, keeping the shades of the dead where they belong. To this day, keys remain symbolic of many things: hidden mysteries, responsibility, freedom (or lack thereof), security, privacy, and attainment.

In His Dark Garden: Mint and White Poplar

Unlike most of the Olympian gods, Hades seems to be a faithful partner and companion to his wife Persephone. Only two instances of Hades engaging in romantic entanglements outside of marriage are recorded in primary sources—these are Hades' relationships with the nymphs Minthe and Leuke, both of whom became plants sacred to him.

---

34. Pausanias, "Description of Greece," in *Complete Works of Pausanias*, trans. W. H. S. Jones (Hastings, East Sussex, UK: Delphi Classics, 2014), 5.20.3.

MINT

Species: *Mentha spicata*
Other Common Names: Garden mint, green mint, spearmint, spire mint
Toxicity: Nontoxic to humans (but toxic to cats, dogs, and other animals)
Keywords: Clarity, desire, passion, sexuality

The mint plant belongs to the family Lamiaceae, which includes such aromatic and culinary herbs as basil, hyssop, rosemary, sage, marjoram, thyme, oregano, and lavender, among many others. The plants in this family are widely cultivated and distributed. In ancient Greece, mint and rosemary were often used in funerary and cremation rites, most likely to help cover the smells of death and decay. Conversely, in a nod to mythology, it was also used an aphrodisiac.[35] Good hosts would rub the leaves on their banquet tables as a symbol of hospitality. Mint provides a satisfyingly sharp top note in typically earthy khthonic incense blends.

It is unclear from mythology if Hades' relationships with the nymphs Minthe and Leuke occurred before or after he was married. However, in the case of Minthe, it was Persephone (or sometimes Demeter, depending on the source text) who trampled the nymph under her feet after hearing Minthe boast that Hades would put aside his wife and return to her bed. Upon Minthe's death, the mint plant sprung from the earth. After studying this particular bit of myth, I concluded that it seems offensive to use mint when Persephone is present in the Underworld, and I do not wish to offend the Dread Queen. (Although it may be an interesting experiment, and in alignment with the myth, to strew mint leaves on the ground to be walked upon as an offering.) It is for this reason that I only use mint in my Hades practice at those times of the year Persephone is above ground, fulfilling her duties in the land of the living. In North America, this equates to the span of days between the vernal (spring) equinox and the autumnal (fall) equinox.

WHITE POPLAR TREE

Species: *Populus alba*
Other Common Names: Silver poplar, silver leaf poplar

---

35. S. Theresa Dietz, *The Complete Language of Flowers: A Definitive and Illustrated History* (New York: Wellfleet Press, 2020), 142.

Toxicity: No reported toxicity

Keywords: Affection, remembrance, wealth

White poplar is a large, fast-growing deciduous tree. This tree is central to the story of Leuke, a nymph whom Hades loved. Leuke lived with Hades in the Underworld, and when the span of her life was over, Hades transformed her body into a white poplar tree in the Elysian Fields. The white poplar thus became a symbol of a blessed afterlife and beloved remembrance of those who had passed on. There may also be a connection between Leuke and the white poplar trees purported to grace the banks of the river Akheron in Thesprotia, where the ancient Nekromanteion was located.

White poplar trees love moist riverbank soil and can be easily spotted by their smooth, whitish bark with diamond-shaped markings. Their rounded leaves are dark green on top and covered with downy white hairs on the underside. The trees flourish in central and southern Europe. In another bit of folklore, it is said that laying white poplar leaves or buds on the body aids in astral projection and that carrying a white poplar leaf in your pocket will attract wealth.[36]

Khthonic Bestiary: Hades' Herd of Sable-Black Cattle

A daimon named Menoites keeps watch over Hades' herd of immortal, sable-black cattle. Cattle are social animals who become very stressed when they are isolated. Hades' cattle are said to freely wander the Asphodel Fields, perhaps providing comfort and companionship to the shades who dwell there.

Menoites' name roughly translates to "doomed might." When the hero Herakles traveled to the Underworld to complete his twelfth labor, he slew one of Hades' cattle. Menoites, enraged by this sacrilegious act, challenged him to a wrestling match. Herakles broke one of Menoites' bones before Persephone stepped in to stop the fight.

Finding Hades in the Landscape: Mt. Minthi

Named after the nymph, Mt. Minthi is located in southern Elis in the western Peloponnese in Greece. Its highest elevation is 4,413 feet, or approximately

---

36. Dietz, *The Complete Language of Flowers*, 172.

1,345 meters. The mountain is situated between the towns of Zacharo in the west and Andritsaina in the east.

There is a small village on the mountain slope, also named Minthi, which can be reached by car. Just past the village square is an unmarked trailhead leading to a primitive hiking path that summits the mountain. The trail begins at an altitude of 2,887 feet (880 meters). For experienced hikers, sweeping views of the surrounding countryside await at Mt. Minthi's summit.[37]

Invitations to Practice

Invoke Hades Polydegmon for assistance with matters of hospitality, rituals featuring the Underworld and its denizens, unlocking hidden mysteries, and seeking an existential sense of belonging. Symbols and correspondences that resonate with the energy of Hades in this aspect are the Key to the Realm, white poplar, mint, and his herd of Underworld cattle.

Hymn to Hades Polydegmon

The following hymn can be spoken or sung to connect with Hades Polydegmon. It is particularly helpful to recite this hymn before receiving guests in your home, such as for a party or extended visit. You can also use this hymn as a personal prayer for Hades to help you learn how to cultivate more rest and pleasure in your own life through self-care.

Hades, Host of Many, with your vast halls
And fields of the dead, your sable-black cattle
Grazing an orchard of pomegranate trees.
Hades, teach me to be a good host
To welcome each guest with your sacred hospitality
Host of Many, teach me how to cultivate
Solace, easement, rest, and pleasure—
For myself and others, Polydegmon, teach me
How to receive them home.

---

37. Athanasios Kouris, "Trail Minthi Mountain," Athanasios Kouris Productions, March 27, 2019, https:// athankproductions.com/en/trail-mountain-minthi/.

Creating a Hades Ritual Calendar

Ancient Greek religion was very syncretic, meaning that new ideas and belief systems were frequently integrated into the old, with very little issue. Their proximity to trade routes and the Mediterranean Sea exposed the ancient Greeks to ideas from Egypt, Syria, and Anatolia—just to name a few. They often incorporated gods they encountered along their travels, such as Hekate, into their pantheon. When the Romans conquered Greece, they absorbed Greek religion (along with other aspects of Greek culture, such as literary and architectural styles) into their own. The Greek gods were synthesized into the pantheon of Roman deities. The Heraklion Archaeological Museum (Crete, Greece) contains a pair of ancient Roman statues of Persephone (as Isis) and Pluto (as Serapis), circa second century CE.[38] These statues are a prime example of Greco-Egyptian syncretism.

The eventual decline of Greco-Roman polytheism may have been due in part to this syncretic nature; Greco-Roman philosophical schools began to incorporate elements of Judaism, Early Christianity, and Mithraism as the Roman empire expanded. Eventually these newer mystery religions became more popular than older pagan beliefs.

There were no ancient festivals explicitly dedicated to Hades; if he was honored, it was typically as part of seasonal fertility rites and in conjunction with Persephone. But considering the syncretic nature of ancient Greek religion, I believe that we can confidently create new, meaningful festivals and observances to enrich our modern Hades practice. Keep in mind that this is not a blank check to co-opt or appropriate someone else's cultural traditions, such as reading a few articles about *Día de los Muertos* (the Day of the Dead, from Mexican tradition), and then adding it to your Hades ritual calendar. Instead, it's an opportunity to take what you are learning about Hades' ancient worship, sacred attributes, and correspondences and apply that knowledge to select days and times, perhaps in innovative ways. To create a Hades ritual calendar, start by considering the following suggestions.

---

38. Unknown artist, *Statue Group of Isis-Persephone and Serapis-Hades*, 180 CE, marble, Heraklion Archeological Museum, Crete, Greece, https://www.heraklionmuseum.gr/en/exhibit/isis-persephone-and -sarapis-hades/.

Vernal (Spring) Equinox

Day and night are of equal length during the equinoxes. In the Northern Hemisphere, the vernal equinox signals the season of growth. For Hades devotees, this might be a time of quiet solidarity, since our Host of Many is entering the season of missing his queen. But we could also use this time to cultivate plants and trees sacred to Hades, which can be harvested for later use in offerings and rituals.

Autumnal (Fall) Equinox

Heralding Persephone's annual descent to the Underworld, the autumnal equinox occurs in the middle of harvest season. Fall is a good time to take stock of progress made during the past months and to hold feasts celebrating the return of the Dread Queen. It's also an appropriate season to venerate ancestors and care for places of the dead, such as cemeteries and other burial sites.

Winter Solstice

The longest night of the year occurs at the winter solstice. In the Northern Hemisphere, plants and animals have decreased their activities, and the whole world seems to have a quality of stillness. Deep in the belly of winter, Hades devotees can meditate on the mysteries of death and renewal.

Monthly on the Waning Dark Moon

The moon wanes almost to darkness on the last day of its monthly cycle. Its aspect is reminiscent of the original Tartaros, the void of creation. The night of the waning dark moon is a beautiful time to commune with the Underworld, hold sacred conversation with Hades, and engage in divination or trance journey.

Daily at Twilight

Twilight is the magic hour, occurring twice daily at sunrise and sunset, when the sky is neither completely dark nor fully lit. Natural light is much lower in contrast at twilight, lending a sense of liminality to the transition between day and night. In some accounts, the Underworld is described as being just past the setting sun, so it follows that sunset twilight would be a powerful time to make daily prayers or devotions to Hades.

Anniversary of Dedicating Your Altar to Hades
Celebrate the anniversary of building and consecrating your Hades altar by cleaning and dusting it, removing any offerings or objects no longer needed, performing khernips, and re-reading your altar dedication.

Can you think of other days and times? Are there any unique dates that have specific meaning for you, and your growing relationship with Hades? Add them to your calendar. You can observe these dates and times with the scale of activity that works for your lifestyle. Some fantastic rituals only take five minutes; others can last a day or more. Take the time to list, collage, or draw your emerging ritual calendar. Place this physical reminder of your intentions on your Hades altar.

Don't worry if you can't celebrate seasonal shifts such as the equinoxes, or if you are not in the Northern Hemisphere. In the Southern Hemisphere, your Hades observances will simply be aligned opposite of those listed earlier, to correspond with the prevailing energy of the season you are in. It can be a lot to wrap your brain around at first, but remember that the gods exist outside the confines of linear time. Hades does not care that the belly of winter occurs in June in Australia—your devotion to his mysteries is what truly matters.

Making Offerings to Khthonic Gods

When making periodic offerings of gratitude, devotion, and supplication to Hades, you can use olive or truffle oil; I find truffle oil makes a particularly potent offering, with its deep earthy smell and decadent nature. Red wine is an excellent poured offering as well, or if you prefer a nonalcoholic option, use mint tea, dark grape juice, or milk mixed with honey. And of course, you could always use ethically acquired sheep or goat blood—bonus points if it comes from a black animal—but unless you are friends with a local farmer or butcher, blood may be a bit harder substance to procure these days.

You may wonder, why not use pomegranate juice? Pomegranates are closely associated with Persephone, so I tend to utilize other options when making offerings specifically to Hades. However, if you are making an offering to both Hades and his wife, pomegranate juice is an appropriate symbolic offering to celebrate their partnership.

The substance you choose for your offering will be poured on the ground. When making your selection, be mindful of the guardian spirits of the place that you have chosen to perform the offering, as well as any etiquette regarding the type of offerings that are considered respectful by the Indigenous peoples of the land. (For example, some Indigenous peoples do not consider it respectful to pour alcoholic beverages onto the earth.) They have been stewarding the land for a very long time, and their counsel should be respected. I make offerings to Hades at a designated spot in my own backyard. If you live in a city block or apartment, you can seek out a quiet spot in a nearby park or natural area to make your offerings.

To perform the offering, begin by purifying yourself and the offering with khernips. Next, recite a hymn or speak words of gratitude to consecrate your offering to Hades. Pour out the whole substance of your offering directly on the ground, and do not reserve any for yourself. It is up to your discretion whether or not you choose to turn your back during or immediately after pouring your offerings; I choose not to turn away, despite the ancient custom. Complete your offering by stomping on the ground three times to contact the Underworld. If you prefer to kneel while making your offerings, you can lean forward and (gently) touch your forehead to the ground three times instead of stomping your foot.

Timing your offerings to an exact date (such as an equinox) might be difficult if you need to travel to perform them. If this is the case for you, try to procure the substance of the offering (bottle of oil, wine, etc.) beforehand and place it on your Hades altar as a symbol of your intent. You can recite a hymn or speak your words of gratitude at your altar on the exact date and then travel afterward to perform the offering when your schedule permits.

Planning Seasonal Feast Days

The myth of Hades and Persephone, featured in chapter 3, functions in part to explain the turning of the seasons each year—the earth is cold and barren when Persephone lives in the Underworld, and springtime returns once she emerges into the light. In our household, we mark these transitions with feast days on the vernal and autumnal equinoxes.

For each of these feast days, we set our dinner table for guests—using special plates, fancy drinking glasses, cloth napkins, and decorations such as fresh herbs or flowers. We always dish out the first and best portion of food for Hades and his Underworld retinue (and Persephone as well, if it is the autumn feast). We light candles and play soft music as we mindfully share our meal together. Once we have completed our dinner, we take the plates of food and drink that were reserved for the deathless ones outside to our backyard. Hearkening back to the tradition of the bothros, we dig a shallow hole in which to deposit their food. We also pour in any wine or other drinks and any other small offerings we choose to make. We cover the food with a thin layer of dirt and symbolically stomp three times to contact the Underworld. It feels appropriate to perform these rites at night, lit only by moonlight.

Planning the food menu for feast days is fun and rewarding. We incorporate what we know of plants, animals, and foods sacred to Hades and improvise with some modern additions of our own. Here are two example menus from equinox feasts we've celebrated in the past, with a sampling of our recipes included.

Autumnal (Fall) Equinox Feast

Our autumnal equinox feast is one of celebration as we welcome back the Dread Queen Persephone, returned beneath the surface to claim her Underworld crown. We include more festive foods and beverages. Here's an example menu:

Aperitif: Pomegranate fizz cocktail

Appetizer: Crusty artisan bread dipped in herbed olive or truffle oil

Main Course: Lamb chops, fragrant pistachio rice, fresh figs, grapes, and pomegranate

Wine Pairing: Light- or medium-bodied red varietals such as Pinot Noir, Grenache, or Sangiovese

Dessert: Goat cheese drizzled in honey, rosemary crackers, Lebanese- or Turkish-style coffee

POMEGRANATE FIZZ APERITIF
- Fresh pomegranate seeds
- 1 cup chilled prosecco

- 1 tablespoon pomegranate liqueur (such as Pama)
- Fresh thyme sprigs

Place 6 pomegranate seeds in the bottom of a white wine glass. Pour chilled prosecco into the glass. Add pomegranate liqueur and swirl gently to mix. Pluck a fresh sprig of thyme, rubbing it along the rim of the wine glass to release its fragrance. Tuck the sprig into the drink for a bit of festive decoration.

For a nonalcoholic version of this cocktail, substitute seltzer water for the prosecco and pomegranate juice for the liqueur. Follow all other directions as stated. Enjoy!

FRAGRANT PISTACHIO RICE
- ⅔ cup shelled pistachios
- 2 tablespoons olive oil
- 1 small yellow onion, finely diced (about 1 cup)
- ½ teaspoon kosher salt; more to taste
- ½ tablespoon coriander seeds lightly smashed, or ground coriander
- 1 tablespoon ground cumin
- 1 bay leaf
- 3-inch cinnamon stick (or a generous ½ tablespoon ground cinnamon)
- 2 cups basmati rice
- 2¾ cups low-salt chicken broth
- 1 cup dried black currants or raisins

Position a rack in the center of your oven and preheat it to 325 degrees Fahrenheit (160°C). Spread the pistachios on a baking sheet. Toast the pistachios in the oven until golden and fragrant, approximately 7 to 10 minutes. Transfer the baking sheet to a wire rack to cool. Once cooled, roughly chop the nuts and set aside.

Heat the olive oil in a medium saucepan over medium-high heat. Add the diced onion and salt, sauté for 4 to 5 minutes, and then add the coriander, cumin, bay leaf, and cinnamon to the saucepan, mixing to coat the onion. Continue to cook for another 1 to 3 minutes, stirring occasionally, until the onion is softened and turning brown. Add the rice and continue stirring until the rice is well-coated with oil and slightly translucent, about 3 minutes.

Next add the chicken broth. Bring the mixture to a boil and then reduce the heat to low, cover, and let simmer until the liquid is absorbed and the rice is tender, about 15 minutes. Discard the bay leaf and, if necessary, cinnamon stick. Fluff the rice with a fork and mix in the dried currants. Season to taste with salt. When ready to serve, sprinkle the rice with the chopped pistachios.

Vernal (Spring) Equinox Feast

Our vernal equinox feast is more subdued, since Hades must once again say goodbye to his beloved Persephone to ensure the survival of the living. We include more comfort foods and beverages. An example menu:

Aperitif: Vermouth and tonic water spritzer (Roots Divino is a great non-alcoholic vermouth option, made in the Greek style, and comes in both white and red versions)
Appetizer: Selection of cheeses with fig jam
Main Course: Lamb koftas with harissa yogurt sauce, saffron yellow rice, and side green salad with balsamic vinaigrette
Wine Pairing: Medium to full-bodied red varietals such as Cabernet Sauvignon, Montepulciano, or Malbec
Dessert: Squares of fine bitter chocolate, mint tea

LAMB KOFTAS
- 2 tablespoons minced cilantro
- 2 tablespoons grated fresh yellow onion
- 2 tablespoons Greek-style yogurt (Use the full-fat yogurt—this is a comfort food feast.)
- 1 teaspoon ground cumin
- 1 teaspoon ground coriander
- 1 teaspoon turmeric
- 1 to 2 cloves finely minced garlic, about 2 teaspoons
- ½ teaspoon salt
- ½ teaspoon black pepper
- 1 pound ground lamb (You may substitute a 1:1 mixture of ground beef and lamb, if lamb alone tends to be too rich for your palate.)

Combine all ingredients, mixing gently but well. Shape the mixture into approximately 3-inch (8 cm) oblong patties, resembling small sausages. Next, heat a large nonstick skillet over medium high heat, coating lightly with cooking spray or extra-virgin olive oil. Add the koftas to your pan without crowding them, working in batches if necessary. Cook each batch for approximately 10 minutes, turning the koftas occasionally, until the patties brown on all sides. Allow the koftas to rest for 4 to 5 minutes before serving.

HARISSA YOGURT SAUCE
- ½ cup plain Greek-style yogurt
- ¼ cup chopped roasted red pepper
- 1 teaspoon cumin
- 1 teaspoon coriander
- 1–2 cloves garlic, finely minced (about 2 teaspoons)
- ½ teaspoon harissa powder or crushed red pepper
- ¼ teaspoon salt

Combine all ingredients and mix well. Place the sauce in the refrigerator to chill until the meal is served. When ready, plate the yogurt sauce to accompany koftas. If desired, this sauce can be prepared ahead of time and chilled overnight.

CHAPTER 3
NOTORIOUS

Hades speaks:

Would she have said yes? It is a question that will never be answered. Because I was too impetuous, too enraptured, too terrified ... and I did not wait.

I see her for the first time, near the cypress grove on the slopes of Mount Aetna. Kore is picking flowers in the meadow, following a wandering trail of narcissus in bloom. Does she know she walks among my sacred trees? The grace of her footsteps, the sunlight falling on her hair. The secret smile on her lips as she trails her fingertips through the blossoms. Cypress trees swaying languidly in the breeze. My heart is shot through with eros, and I realize with perfect clarity: I ache for her and her alone.

I dread going to Olympus. After so many years in the Underworld, the blindingly bright halls of my brother's home pain my eyes. The quarrels and squabbles of the gods above seem superficial when I compare them to the weight of my duties. I am gravitas; it is my nature. Yet on this day I travel there with all haste, out of respect for tradition, because (whether I like it or not) Zeus is her father. I bow my head and ask my youngest brother for his permission to marry Kore. Humbling myself before Zeus does not matter to me; I would bow a thousand times, and always at least once more after that, for my love. With a sly grin, Zeus says yes.

I waste no time. Gathering my chariot and team of horses, I ride for the cypress grove. Kore is startled by my sudden appearance, but not so startled that she runs. I cannot decipher the expression on her face. I barely know her, yet somehow, I know everything about her: crushed petals and soft skin, a sharp contrast to her eyes that burn with ancient fire. "Come with me to the

Underworld and be my queen." My heart stills in my chest as she parts her lips to speak ... and then I seize her.

My arms capture her waist. I pull her into the chariot and hold her to my side. The wind whips through the grove, bending the trees, sounding an alarm. Kore screams. My horses buck and snort as I slap their reigns, urging them to run. The earth cracks open at my command.

Together, we dive.

Would she have said yes? I was too scared to wait for her answer. After all, who would want to live in my kingdom ... considered the short straw, an eternity among shades, a realm without sun? Who would want to be surrounded by darkness and death when they could live in warmth and light? Who could find a scrap of tenderness buried deep in the heart of a khthonic king?

Her shock fades as days pass. So different from the world she knew above, Kore explores my realm with wonder. Shades gather to glide beside her as she crosses the Asphodel Fields. The Fates proudly show her their thread, loom, and scissors; the Furies promise her their undying loyalty. She does not fear walking the banks of the Rivers of Forgetting, Wailing, or Fire, nor does she flinch from peering into the depths of Tartaros. Monstrous Kerberos, guardian of the gates, snores peacefully at her feet. It seems all of Hades is rendered spellbound by her presence.

Ultimately, she cannot stay. I learn that the world above dies with her mother's grief. My younger brother implores me to return her to Demeter, lest the humans perish too soon from cold and hunger. "There must be respite," he argues. "No," I counter, "there must be balance." I walk the Halls of Hades, and I think. My pensive footsteps echo down corridors of obsidian, amethyst, and adamant. Occasionally I pass by the great audience room; I see her sitting tentatively on the throne my artisans have crafted. Unaware of my presence, she tests the armrests, rubbing her palms along darkly gleaming carved crystal. That secret, tentative smile. Kore leans her head against the padded backrest, closes her eyes. A gentle sigh.

She cannot stay ... but I cannot let her go.

"I have found a way," I whisper to her one morning, as I reveal a ripe pomegranate from the grounds just outside my halls. I split its flesh with a paring knife. Sweet red juice drips down my arm as I offer half of the fruit up to her, my queen upon her throne. "Those who eat the fruit of the Underworld *are bound to this place. We can rule together, for half of each year, our days measured by the equinoxes. Your return above will herald the growing season, your return below will be the swing of the scythe. The poets will tell our story over and over, for millennia, unable to decide if it is a love song or a tragedy. We will be notorious."*

I hold my breath. Once again my heart stills in my chest. But this time, I wait.

She does not look away.

Persephone lifts the pomegranate to her lips as she replies, "Then let us be notorious."

Klymenos: Hades the Notorious

The epithet *Klymenos* means "renowned"—but it's not a completely positive implication. Hades is notorious, not celebrated. The most well-known myth connected with Hades is the story of how he obtained his beloved wife, Persephone. A notoriously dramatic kidnapping, and a notoriously tempting pomegranate, are at the heart of this tale.

Persephone's kidnapping is the inciting event in the *Homeric Hymn to Demeter* (ca. 600–500 BCE). The hymn serves as an allegory for the changing of the seasons, recounting the story of Demeter's search for her lost daughter, Persephone, also known as Kore, whose name is translated as "maiden" or "daughter." Kore is a minor goddess of springtime. Hades spots Kore walking a meadow in full bloom, falls instantly in love, and carries her away to the Underworld. Demeter searches frantically for her missing daughter. As she sinks deeper into grief and despair, the harvest is ignored, and the world above begins to wither and die. Eventually Demeter is reunited with Kore, but there is a caveat: Kore has eaten some pomegranate seeds while in the Underworld, binding her to Hades' realm.

A compromise is reached when Kore agrees to marry Hades and spend the number of months equivalent to the seeds she has eaten with him in the Underworld. The exact number of seeds varies from one text to the next; sometimes she eats as few as three, sometimes as many as nine. Each year when Persephone returns to the land of the living, the world celebrates by bursting into spring. When she descends to the Underworld, the upper world grieves with Demeter, growing cold and barren.

A Different Vision of the Sacred Feminine

Persephone is a goddess who defies attempts at categorization: she is both a youthful girl with flowers in her hair and the sovereign queen of the Underworld. Each year's harvest depends on Persephone's descent to the Underworld, following roots and seeds underground, to emerge once again in the spring. Persephone embodies the interweaving of life in death and death in life; if Demeter can be said to represent growth and life, and Hades to represent decay and death, then Persephone is the link between the two.[39]

Meadows, especially meadows in flower, are places betwixt and between. Flowers are a physical representation of the transition from immaturity to sexuality and fertility. Hades unexpectedly shows up in the meadow where Kore is picking flowers. Kore is a young goddess, naive and as yet unaware of her own potential—and Hades is a stranger to her, someone beyond her scope of experience, quite possibly even dangerous. But he also represents the prospect of who she can become in the fullness of her own power, if she is willing to leave her mother's side: she will become a sovereign queen.

Her full and accurate title is the Dread Queen Persephone. When she marries Hades, she becomes his equal in power. Dynamic feminine beings like Persephone are too threatening for the gilded, misogynistic court of Mt. Olympus, but they thrive in the Underworld. Mythology tells us that Hades often defers to his queen in tricky matters of judgment; their thrones sit side by side in the audience room of the Halls of Hades. The Erinyes (Furies), relentless avengers of injustice, fly at her command. The seasons turn by her clock. Persephone's descent to Hades—both the god and the Underworld realm he represents—may provide a type of gateway to self-actualization, but the Dread Queen is a guardian of Underworld mysteries through her own merit.

In addition to her role as Underworld queen, Persephone was worshiped alongside her mother Demeter in the Eleusinian Mysteries. Initiates of the Mysteries were promised a blessed afterlife through their participation in the ceremonies of this agriculture-based religious cult. In the Orphic *Hymn to Persephone* she is called *Praxidike*, an epithet meaning "exactor of justice."[40]

---

39. Neel Burton, *The Meaning of Myth: With 12 Greek Myths Retold and Interpreted by a Psychiatrist* (Acheron Press, 2021), 142, Kindle.

40. Dunn, *The Orphic Hymns*, 29.7.

Persephone was also frequently invoked on ancient *katadesmoi*: curse tablets, referred to as *defixiones* in Latin, made from thin sheets of lead that were inscribed, rolled up, and then pierced with nails or needles.[41] The purpose of katadesmoi (singular, *katadesmos*) were to petition the gods, the dead, or the spirits of a place to compel someone to do something or to enact some form of retribution. These tablets were usually buried underground, placed in graves or tombs, or thrown into bodies of water.

Persephone was, and still is, a beloved agricultural goddess, an honored wife, and a khthonic Dread Queen both respected and feared. She presents us with a uniquely compelling vision of the sacred feminine, one that remains inspirational in its broad range of influence and expression.

Exploring the Lore

I want to take a few moments to acknowledge that the subject matter of this particular myth can be difficult. To be honest, when I initially dedicated myself to Hades, I was afraid that I would not be able to reconcile my deep feelings of devotion with the infamous account of his kidnapping, and potential assault, of Persephone. From time to time, I still feel the urge to lean wholeheartedly into feminist retellings of this myth, in which Persephone has the agency to descend with Hades of her own volition. But I also realize the value in pausing to recognize the very real trauma of sexual assault in our modern culture. Consent is still violated. Bodily autonomy is still disrespected. And there is absolutely no excuse for these crimes.

"Compared to other forms of story, a myth tends to be more morally ambiguous and open to interpretation: it is not a simple narrative of good versus evil, and fate, as we shall see, plays a more important part than fortune," posits psychologist Neel Burton, in *The Meaning of Myth*. He goes on to add: "Monsters aside, few characters in Greek myth are entirely good or evil, least of all the gods."[42] As a priestess of Hades, I recognize that some people may never be able to see this myth in any sort of positive light, especially if they have experienced trauma. I encourage anyone who is considering working with Hades to realize that negative responses to this subject matter are completely valid, and that the

41. HellenicGods.org, "Persephone: The Epithets," accessed May 2, 2023, https://www.hellenicgods.org/persephone-the-epithets.

42. Burton, *The Meaning of Myth*, loc. 6, Kindle.

thoughts, feelings, and opinions of individuals whose reception of this myth differs from our own should be respected—never attacked, dismissed, or belittled.

Aurora Sun is a devotee of the Dread Queen Persephone. In an interview for this book, she graciously shared some of the insights she has gleaned from Persephone regarding the primary sources for this myth, as well as its modern retellings: "The lens of patriarchy is present in older versions of the myth, and some newer pop culture versions glamorize their relationship, ignoring any harm. Both of those things are problematic, and I get the sense that Persephone doesn't appreciate either version. There's far more complexity to this myth."[43] As Hades devotees, we have an opportunity to hold space for sacred conversations around these complexities, as well as to educate ourselves and others about consent in the spirit of reparations.

Navigating Transgressive Themes in Mythology

If we choose never to engage with myths that have transgressive or disturbing themes, we might miss the deep lessons they convey. Should you spend all your time contemplating these acts? No, most definitely not. However, it's not a liberatory or justice-oriented practice to simply avoid discussing past harms and uncomfortable situations. We cannot learn from them if we bypass them. We have a responsibility to research the period of history in which primary source materials were recorded. For example, Persephone's abduction by Hades followed all the proper laws of marriage during this time period, because Hades got permission from her father first. This is decidedly not how we would conduct matters today, but it was consistent with the cultural context.[44]

The ancient Greeks were colonists. They were patriarchal. They enslaved people and treated women like property. These values, however despicable they may be, are still very much reflected in their mythology and art; one has only to look at the mythical antics of Zeus or his son Apollo to observe how pervasive transgressive misdeeds and violent behaviors were in ancient Greek society. In later Roman retellings of this story, such as Ovid's *Metamorphoses*, the mythic waters become even more murky as the story of Hades and Persephone starts being referred to as "The Rape of Proserpina." *Proserpina* is the

---

43. Aurora Sun, Persephone Devotee, interview with the author, January 4, 2023.

44. Overly Sarcastic Productions, "Miscellaneous Myths: Hades and Persephone," February 12, 2021, YouTube video, 20:28. https://www.youtube.com/watch?v=Ac5ksZTvZN8.

Roman name for Persephone. The dramatic word choice of *rape* in this title is derived from the Latin word *rapere*, meaning "to steal, seize, or carry away."[45] In Classical Latin, during the time of Ovid (ca. 100 BCE–100 CE), the word *rapere* was very rarely used to indicate an act of sexual violence. By the medieval period, however, the word had taken on a more salacious connotation. This later connotation still influences our perception, and reception, of the myth.

Navigating transgressive and violent themes in mythology can be uncomfortable and sometimes even painful. Go gently into the myth. Remember to read primary sources with an open and critical mind. Do your research and have a trusty red pen at the ready to mark over anything that does not stand the test of time or your personal code of ethics. If you are struggling, here are some questions to ask yourself:

- What did these acts of violence mean in context of the culture of the time?
- How did this story help humans process and understand the violence that was part of their everyday lives?
- What are the possibilities that the violence is a colonizer, patriarchal, or monotheistic overlay added to an earlier version of the myth, meant to force an agenda on the audience?
- What does the violence teach us as a metaphor?
- What steps can we take to repair these harms?

I believe myths are just like us: they are enlivened, ensouled beings—manifestations that are meant to evolve and change over time. This animist perspective is especially true of oral stories and histories. Two human beings come together and create a child; that child is its own unique being, yet it is also a mixture of their DNA and the DNA of generations before. Stories evolve and change in much the same way: each telling is a new, unique creation between storyteller and listener—a moment in time that can never be duplicated. But at its core, the DNA of the original story remains. We are a vital part of every story's evolution. Mythologist Sharon Blackie speaks eloquently about the importance of myth: "Myth is many things, but above all, myth is meaning. If we

---

45. Online Etymology Dictionary, s.v. "rape," by Douglas Harper, last modified July 27, 2022, https://www.etymonline.com/word/rape.

fall out of myth, we fall out of meaning."[46] When we rediscover, reimagine, rewrite, and retell problematic stories, transformation begins. Meaning shifts and harm is repaired. There is the potential for acts of violence to be replaced by agency and compassion.

The opening passages of each chapter in this book are my own creative retellings of Greek mythology. These narratives are the product of many hours of trance journey and conversation with Hades, in which I've asked him to recount the myths in his own words, from his perspective. I find it fascinating that in his retelling of Persephone's kidnapping, she never says yes or no—even in the end. She seems agreeable to Hades' pomegranate proposal, but we're still left wondering what her answer truly was. It is a question that will never have a clear answer, a question that continues to spark ethical debate and lead to potent conversations, even now—thousands of years since it was first told. Perhaps this myth's controversial nature is part of its brilliance.

Symbols of Hades: Golden Chariot and Black Horses

In Greek mythology, horses were associated with power, speed, and the primal force of lust. Many primary sources mention Hades having a chariot pulled by four black horses. In the *Homeric Hymn to Demeter*, his chariot is described as "golden," and the horses as "immortal" and swift.[47] Persephone is carried away to the Underworld in Hades' chariot and later returned to Demeter by way of this same vehicle—driven by Hermes on her return. The horses pulling the chariot are able to traverse seas, rivers, glens, mountains, and even the air with equal ease.

Claudius Claudianus, more commonly known simply as Claudian, was a Latin poet of late antiquity. His most important nonpolitical work was the unfinished mythological epic *De raptu Proserpinae*, of which three books were completed before his death around 404 CE. This poem is worth mentioning because it introduces names for the four black horses who pull Hades' golden chariot: "The dread fury Allecto yokes to the chariot-pole the two fierce pairs of steeds that graze Cocytus' banks and roam the dark meads of Erebus, and, drinking the rotting pools of sluggish Lethe, let dark oblivion drip from their

46. Sharon Blackie, "The Mythic Imagination," online course, 2016, https://sharonblackie.net/.

47. Evelyn-White, Hugh G., trans., *The Homeric Hymns*, in *Hesiod, the Homeric Hymns, and Homerica* (London: William Heinemann, 1914), 289–91.

slumbrous lips—Orphnaeus, savage and fleet, Aethon, swifter than an arrow, great Nycteus, proud glory of Hell's steeds, and Alastor, branded with the mark of Dis [Hades]."[48]

Classicist Eleftherios Tserkezis holds a BA in Classics and an MA in Byzantine history from the Aristotle University of Thessaloniki. He breaks down the etymology behind Claudian's names for the horses: "The name *Orphnaeus* comes from, or is etymologically connected to, the Greek word *orphnē*, which means 'darkness,' 'night.' *Aethon* (Greek *aithōn*) means 'blazing,' 'burning.' *Nycteus* is connected to the Greek *nuks* and the Latin *nox*; both mean 'night.' *Alastor* was the name and/or epithet of various individuals, including Zeus himself; it means 'destroyer' or 'avenger.'"[49]

So it seems Hades drives a golden chariot, pulled by a team of four black, immortal, and supernaturally fast horses named Darkness, Blaze, Night, and Avenger. Notorious, indeed.

In His Dark Garden: Narcissus and Pomegranate

The *Homeric Hymn to Demeter* opens with an idyllic scene that quickly takes a more sinister turn: Kore "was playing with the deep-bosomed daughters of Oceanus and gathering flowers over a soft meadow, roses and crocuses and beautiful violets, irises also and hyacinths and the narcissus, which Earth [Gaia] made to grow at the will of Zeus and to please the Host of Many, to be a snare for the bloom-like girl— a marvelous, radiant flower."[50]

From fragrant meadows full of flowers to the mist-shrouded regions of the Underworld, narcissus and pomegranate both play central roles in the story of Hades and Persephone.

NARCISSUS

Species: *Narcissus hispanicus, Narcissus tazetta*
Other Common Names: Asphodel, daffodil

---

48. Claudian, *Claudian, Volume II: On Stilicho's Consulship 2–3. Panegyric on the Sixth Consulship of Honorius. The Gothic War. Shorter Poems. Rape of Proserpina*, trans. M. Platnauer, Loeb Classical Library 136 (Cambridge, MA: Harvard University Press, 1922), 1.284–5.

49. Eleftherios Tserkezis, "What Are the Names of Hades' Stallions in Greek Mythology?," Quora, May 9, 2017, https://qr.ae/py76RB.

50. Evelyn-White, trans., "The Homeric Hymns," 289–91.

Toxicity: Highly toxic (never ingest, and use caution when handling)

Keywords: Hope, new beginnings, rebirth, regard, singular love, vanity

Narcissus rises gracefully from bulbs buried in the ground, with slender green leaves and six-petaled flowers, featuring a prominent trumpet-shaped corona (crown) in the center. Its appearance is often a precursor of spring, and its bright yellow petals are reminiscent of the color of Hades' golden chariot. This sunny flower is considered baneful, however, due to the toxic alkaloids in its bulbs and leaves.

Asphodel is a vague name or descriptor that ancient poets often applied to the narcissus flower. As noted in *Encyclopaedia Britannica,* "The asphodel of the poets is often a narcissus. That of the ancients is either of two genera, *Asphodeline* or *Asphodelus,* containing numerous species in the Mediterranean region. In Greek mythology, the asphodel flowers were associated with the underworld, death, and mourning."[51] Narcissus is also known as daffodil, an English name derived from the Greek word *asphodelos.* If you say the two words aloud (asphodel and daffodil), their similarity is readily apparent.

Is this clever wordplay an instance of foreshadowing? If so, on the day Hades appears to kidnap her, Kore is in the midst of quite literally plucking her destiny from the earth—she later becomes queen of the Underworld, including the Asphodel Fields. To honor the Dread Queen Persephone, consider growing narcissus around your home, or try combining a few narcissus blooms with other flowers to make an offering bouquet.

POMEGRANATE TREE

Species: *Punica granatum*

Other Common Names: Apple of Granada, grenadier, melagrana, pound garnet

Toxicity: No reported toxicity. Pomegranate extract may lower blood pressure, however, so ingestion is contraindicated for those who take medication to control their blood pressure.

Keywords: Abundance, bonds, divine feminine, fertility, love, marriage, sensuality

---

51. *Encyclopaedia Britannica Online,* s.v. "asphodel," accessed August 12, 2021, https://www.britannica.com/plant/asphodel-plant.

Pomegranate is a fruit-bearing deciduous shrub or small tree, producing reddish-orange flowers that, once fertilized, turn into a deep red fruit containing a multitude of seeds buried inside a tough rind. The pomegranate tree has been cultivated for millennia and was commonly found growing in ancient orchards alongside apple, pear, fig, and olive trees. For the ancient Greeks, the pomegranate fruit was sacred to Hera and was one of her attributes as goddess of marriage. The profusion of blood-red seeds inside the fruit was representative of fertile ovaries.

It's no coincidence that Hades offers Kore a pomegranate while she is in the Underworld—the pomegranate symbolizes a marriage proposal. By eating a few of the seeds, Kore accepts. For obvious reasons, pomegranate was one of the foods prohibited in the mystery initiations of Demeter and Persephone at Eleusis.[52] Pomegranate is a wonderful inclusion in any feast celebrating the return of Persephone to the Underworld. The fruit, seeds, and juice are available in most grocery stores.

Khthonic Bestiary: The Screech Owl

Back in chapter 2 we met Askalaphos, the son of Styx and Akheron, who tends the fruit orchards outside the Halls of Hades. Askalaphos plays a role in this myth, too: according to the account in Ovid's *Metamorphoses,* the orchardist saw Kore eating pomegranate seeds in the Underworld and was called upon to bear witness before the gods.

Persephone was not pleased by Askalaphos' account. In her anger, she turned Askalaphos into an owl: "The Queen of Erebus [Persephone] grieved, and changed the informer into an accursed bird, and turned his head, sprinkled with the waters of Phlegethon, into a beak, and feathers, and great eyes. He, thus robbed of his own shape, is clothed with tawny wings, his head becomes larger, his long nails bend inwards, and with difficulty can he move the wings that spring through his sluggish arms. He becomes an obscene bird, the foreboder of approaching woe, a screech owl, a direful omen to mortals."[53]

---

52. Aaron J. Atsma, "Flora 2: Plants of Greek Myth," Theoi Project, accessed January 22, 2023, https://www.theoi.com/Flora2.html.

53. Ovid, *The Metamorphoses of Ovid*, vol. 1., trans. Henry T. Riley (London: George Bell & Sons, 1893; Project Gutenberg, 2007), 5.538–57.

Sunset twilight is sometimes called "owl light." Owls are a bird apart—they stand on the threshold, reminding us of the ever-present realities of nighttime, darkness, and death. Hunting at night, owls seek prey mostly by flying low over open ground, watching, and listening; they have excellent vision in low light levels and hearing so precise that they can strike prey in total darkness. Their silent flight recalls the invisible nature of the Unseen One. Perhaps the account in Ovid's *Metamorphoses* also explains why some examples of ancient Hades iconography feature him holding a staff topped with a screech owl instead of his usual symbol of office, the bident.

Finding Hades in the Landscape: Lake Pergusa

The ancient precinct of Enna was renowned throughout Sicily and Italy as a center of cult worship dedicated to the goddesses Demeter and Persephone. Demeter's sacred grove in Enna was known as the *Umbilicus Siciliae*—the Navel of Sicily. In Ovid's *Metamorphoses*, Lake Pergusa (in Italian, Lago di Pergusa) is the site where Hades appears in a flowery meadow to kidnap Demeter's daughter to the Underworld.

Approximately three miles (5 km) from the hilltop town of Enna, Lake Pergusa is now encircled by the Autodromo di Pergusa, a famous racetrack. Nearby is the archaeological site of Cozzo Matrice. This site is composed of a prehistoric fortified village constructed around 8000 BCE, in addition to the remains of a sacred citadel, necropolis, and temple dedicated to Demeter that date back more than 2,000 years.

Invitations to Practice

Invoke Hades Klymenos for courage when taking bold action, for assistance navigating difficult family situations, for seeing multiple perspectives or sides of a story, and when swift forward movement or momentum is needed in your endeavors. Symbols and correspondences that resonate with the energy of Hades in this aspect are his golden chariot and team of black horses, narcissus, pomegranates, and the screech owl.

Hymn to Hades Klymenos

The following hymn can be spoken or sung to connect with Hades Klymenos. You may want to memorize this succinct hymn so that you can recite it on short notice. Utilize these words on the fly to ask Hades for a quick injection of courage, discernment, and skillful action.

Notorious Klymenos, come with all haste!
With your immortal horses, golden chariot, and fearsome gaze—
Grant me courage and decisiveness,
Grant me discernment and skill,
Make brave my heart and measured my actions!

Trance Journey: Going to the Origin

As the written word gained predominance in Western Europe, it was gatekept and propagandized for centuries by the hierarchy of the Christian church. Written words had power and permanence, and in equating the Bible with ultimate spiritual authority, the church convinced society to believe written words held more value than inner wisdom. This notion persists to the present day, and here's where I encourage you to subvert the paradigm: I want you to go directly to the origin, to the gods, fearlessly and often. Seek the truth, and the paradox, of their stories for yourself. Let the gods tell you their stories in their own words. In the end, it matters little what my (or anyone else's) interpretation of these stories is; what is important for your personal practice is their meaning to you. That's where the real magic is.

How do we do this? We engage in trance journey.

In trance journey, we enter a meditative state with a specific intention in mind, such as meeting Hades in a cypress grove for a conversation. As our body sinks into the trance state, our consciousness journeys into the liminal space of the Otherworld—a place where we can interact with gods, beings, and spirits (such as the spiritus viridis of plants) who don't usually have embodied forms. Trance journey gives the magical practitioner access to a wide variety of experiences that are not readily available in the everyday world.

There are many approaches to trance journey; you can find a plethora of books and online courses that focus specifically on this subject. In our collaborative magical studies program, Way of the Weaver, Murphy Robinson and I teach students how to build a personal trance journey practice over the course of nine months. The following introduction to trance journey is based on our approach and is intended to give you an overview of the basics.

Entering the Trance State

Choose a location where you will not be disturbed. Cast a circle or set wards of protection around your physical body to divert any hindrances and help you remain focused while you journey. You may want to lie down, cover yourself in a light blanket, or limit outside light sources in your immediate space. Place your journal, writing implement, and a glass of water near at hand for when you finish your journey.

When you are ready, close your eyes. Begin paying attention to your breath. As you breathe, and if you are able to do so comfortably, gently roll your eyes (while still closed) upward and slightly in, as if looking toward the center of your forehead. This subtle pressure will help stimulate your third eye. Breathe in, breathe out, slowing and lengthening each breath. In and out, try to make your inhale the same length as your exhale. In and out, pausing slightly at the top of the inhale. In and out, pausing slightly at the bottom of the exhale. In, pause. Out, pause. Narrow your focus to this pause, the liminal space between breathing in and breathing out. It is this liminal space that will lead you to the liminal place: through the third eye into the imagination, the wild mind, the mythic landscape of the Otherworld. The place where we are all the characters in all the stories ever told, the place where we can talk to gods, plants, and animals, the place that is everywhere and nowhere, betwixt and between.

Your Otherworldly Headquarters

A nice place to land in the Otherworld is at some sort of headquarters (HQ) you create for yourself. This can be any structure you like, but it should be something or somewhere that gives you a sense of security. I've practiced trance journey for over twenty years, and I've had a few different HQs during that time: a wood cabin, a sacred wishing well, the roots of a giant hollow tree. Once you enter the Otherworld, you can stop here to get your bearings and pick up any accoutrements you might need for the journey (for example, a sprig of rosemary to offer to Hades).

Traversing Extra-ordinary Realms

Once you've geared up at HQ, it's time to pursue your intention for being in the Otherworld. To keep using our example, you're here to meet Hades in a cypress grove for conversation. Many people find it helpful to call for a guide when setting out on their travels. Guides are beings that help you navigate the terrain of the Otherworld. They can take a variety of forms, such as animals, ancestors, or figures from mythology and folklore. You may meet different guides in different trances, or you may have a guide that shows up frequently. Building a strong relationship with your guides is a good idea; they are your allies in these extra-ordinary realms.

When a new guide shows up, introduce yourself and state your intention. Spend a few moments in their presence, chatting with them or simply getting a feel for their energy. If you feel this guide has good intent to help you on your journey, respectfully ask for their assistance. As you leave HQ, take note of your surroundings and the path you traverse to get to the cypress grove (or wherever you might be going). This will be very important later—you always want to return to your HQ exactly the same way. Once you reach your destination, you may find Hades waiting for you, or you may need to call out for him. Similar to meeting your guide, introduce yourself and state your intention. Be open to conversations and interactions that may occur, even if they seem strange or anachronistic to you—you are in the realm of myth and metaphor, and it takes practice to learn the highly symbolic language of this place.

There are some general precautions about the Otherworld that come from myth, folklore, and fairy tales: don't eat or drink anything in the Otherworld, don't fall asleep there, treat everyone you meet with respect, and don't make any agreements you cannot keep.[54] You still have agency and consent in the Otherworld, as well as the power to negotiate or reject anything that you are not comfortable with. Similarly, you are responsible for your own actions—in the Otherworld and when you return.

Once you are finished talking, be sure to offer your gratitude. Courteously take your leave, and travel back to your HQ by the same route. Thank your guide and prepare to return to your physical body.

Exiting the Trance State

To exit the trance state, bring your attention back to your breath. Breathing in and out, inhale and exhale, begin to let the breath return to its normal pace. This is the pace that supports your waking body, your own breath leading you

---

54. Murphy Robinson, "Trance: A Working Guide," October 2019, 2–3.

back to the physical plane, to the here and now. Start to make small movements to wake your body: wiggle your fingers and toes, move your head gently side to side. Circle the hands around the wrists, circle the feet around the ankles. Yawn and stretch your arms far over your head. You are safe, you are awake, you are home. Welcome back.

You may want to capture your experiences in your journal while they are fresh in your memory. Some people experience trance journey visually, as if they are in a movie. Others may get intuitive impressions, feel sensations in their body, hear songs or phrases, or recognize smells. All of these are valid experiences and great sources of information. When you are finished journaling, release your circle or wards.

From Theory to Praxis

Ready to journey to the Otherworld? I suggest engaging in a few initial trance journeys in which you simply go to your HQ, spend time equipping it with supplies, and get a feel for the experience of sending your consciousness outward from your physical body into this liminal space.

Once you feel comfortable with this, try the example we used above: journey with the intent to meet Hades in a cypress grove (not in the Underworld just yet—there'll be an opportunity for that later) and have a conversation. You can talk to him about your altar, show him your ritual calendar, or ask him questions about his myths. The best way to get to know him is by spending time with him.

CHAPTER 4

GOOD COUNSEL

Hades speaks:

Sitting side by side on our thrones, I held Persephone's hand as we watched him enter the room. A skinny youth, pretending to be grown, with dirty shins and the dust of the road on his sandals. He looked tired but determined. He pleaded. And then, he bargained.

"Let me sing and play my lyre for you," said Orpheus. "And if your hearts are moved by my song, then let my beloved return with me to the land of the living."

I frowned. The rules, as they say, are the rules. How will I remain a just king if I bend the rules for one mortal but not another? But my Dread Queen leaned close and whispered in my ear, "Let the boy play." Her eyes were lit with curiosity. I value her judgment and so nodded my assent.

"Well then, Orpheus," I offered, "play."

His fingers trembled as he prepared the lyre. He cleared his throat, twice. At first, only a few screeching, off-key notes emerged. Orpheus tapped his foot, cleared his throat again. And then ... transcendence.

I did not realize until that moment that music had the power to echo through all the chambers of my heart, vibrate in my immortal bones, sing in my khthonic blood. I was pierced by the longing of his song. The acute pain of parting, the long and lonely grief of separation, these emotions were brought up from the depths of my own deathless being to crest like a tidal wave crashing into the room. I squeezed Persephone's fingers, and she caressed the back of my hand with her thumb. His music, her tenderness. I remained transfixed as wave after wave the grief came, until at last, the song ended. I blinked. A single, pitch-black tear made its way down my cheek; Persephone caught it on her fingertip, tucking it away for safekeeping.

"Bring the shade of Eurydice," she instructed, "for Orpheus has done the impossible."

I advised Orpheus not to look back. To hold his beloved's hand, returning the way that he came, back to the land of the living. To look only toward the future. "If you look back," I cautioned him, "all that you desire—all that you've worked for and won—will disappear. Just hold her hand, keep moving, and don't turn around until both of you are once again warmed by the rays of the sun."

Oh, Orpheus.

Eurydice's shade soon returned to the Underworld. We embraced her with sorrow.

The bard had not heeded my advice.

Eubuleus: Hades the Good Counselor

In the Orphic *Hymn to Plouton* the epithet Eubuleus is used in connection with Hades.[55] *Eubuleus* means "good counsel" or "consoler." Its use in the hymn suggests that Hades gives good advice and that his fair-minded, dependable stoicism is a consolation to the shades of the dead that find themselves inhabiting his Underworld realm. Composed sometime in the first four centuries of the Common Era, this collection of eighty-seven devotional poems is attributed to Orpheus, superstar bard of the ancient world.

Orpheus, Eurydice, and Mystery Cults

Orpheus was a musician and poet from Thrace. His father was the god Apollo, who gave him a lyre and taught him how to play it. Orpheus' playing was said to be so enchanting that even the plants, animals, and rocks could be caught dancing in its thrall. The young musician fell in love with a sweet, beautiful wood nymph named Eurydice and they soon married. But their marriage was doomed from its beginning: shortly after the wedding, Eurydice was enjoying a walk when a rogue satyr tried to accost her. In her rush to escape the unwanted attention, she stepped on a venomous snake and was bitten. She died instantly.

---

55. Dunn, *The Orphic Hymns*, 18.16.

Orpheus was so bereft with grief that he traveled from Thrace to the tip of the Greek peninsula, where there was a known entrance to the Underworld. With lyre in hand, he played his way through the Underworld, past the shades of the dead and all manner of obstacles, all the way to the Halls of Hades. When Orpheus was granted an audience before Hades and Persephone, he sang his most beautiful poem in an attempt to sway them into permitting Eurydice to return with him to the land of the living. The king and queen were so moved by his music that they broke their own rule of prohibiting the dead to leave their realm and sent for Eurydice's shade. Stoic Hades shed one sooty, pitch-black tear.

Orpheus grasped his lover's hand, and as the couple left to return to the world above, Hades gave them one final stipulation: at no time during their journey was Orpheus to look back to see if Eurydice was following him. Off they went, following shadowy pathways back through the gates of the Underworld, across the river Styx, leading to lands once again lit by rays of sunshine. In his utter glee, Orpheus slipped up—he looked back to smile at lovely Eurydice, and just like that, she began to fade back to the Underworld. He wept as she whispered one final word to him before she disappeared: "Farewell."

So why didn't Orpheus take more care to follow Hades' advice? Psychologist Neel Burton proposes that sometimes we are our own worst enemies: "Often, it is not Hades that we doubt, but ourself. Because we deem ourself unworthy of good things, and in particular of happiness, we sabotage ourself just before attaining the very thing that we were striving for. ... If something is too good for us, we find a way of passing over it."[56] Despite his failure to heed Hades' warning and bring Eurydice home, Orpheus was celebrated as someone who had special knowledge of life after death. He had traveled deep into the Underworld, arguably further than any hero of mythology, to stand before Hades and Persephone in their throne room. His return from the Underworld sparked interest in the possibility that death could be transcended, and thus he became a central figure of his namesake Orphic mystery cult.

At cursory glance, it can be easy to compartmentalize ancient Greek religion—or even Greek mythology for that matter—into a common, clearly understood set of stories and practices. In truth, however, religious beliefs and

---

56. Burton, *The Meaning of Myth*, loc. 136, Kindle.

practices in ancient Greece varied widely. Public festivals and sacrificial rites were usually organized at the community or civic level, with some overlap in form and function from one community to another, but with plenty of local traditions and substitutions.[57] Mystery cults were part of this religious melee. Different from public celebrations, the rituals of mystery cults were celebrated privately among initiates. These rites were reported to be ecstatically trans-formative for participants, but little is known about them because they were purposefully shrouded in secrecy—their inexplicable nature was part of their attraction.

The Orphic mystery cult focused on death and what follows after. Orphic initiates viewed the myth of Orpheus and Eurydice as an allegory for the rescue of the soul from the cycle of death and rebirth. So-called Orphic tablets, thin sheets of gold inscribed with instructions on how to navigate the Underworld and cautions against drinking from the forgetful waters of the river Lethe, have been found in graves across a wide area spanning Sicily, southern Italy, northern Greece, the Peloponnese, and Crete.[58] The theology of the Orphics also diverged from the mainstream and focused on a thrice-incarnated Dionysus as the savior of humanity. In Orphism, Dionysus is the son of Zeus and either Persephone or Demeter, depending on the version of the myth. Within Orphism itself there were quite a few variations of myths and stories, but orthopraxy—that is to say, shared rites, rituals, and sacrifices—seemed to be more important to initiates than belief.[59]

In his work *Hermes: Guide of Souls*, philosopher and Jungian psychologist Karl Kerenyi observes, "It belonged to the essence of the Greek mysteries that through their initiations one came into friendly relation with Hades. (From this it follows that for one who is initiated, death is not 'the worst gift'.)"[60] As it turns out, it was not only the initiates of ecstatic mystery cults who thought Hades wise and worth building a relationship with—Socrates, the influential thinker and self-proclaimed Gadfly of Athens, was also a big fan of Hades.

---

57. Dunn, *The Orphic Hymns*, 13.

58. J. Paul Getty Museum, "Underworld: Imagining the Afterlife," accessed November 10, 2022, https://www.getty.edu/art/exhibitions/ancient_underworld/inner.html.

59. Dunn, *The Orphic Hymns*, 19.

60. Karl Kerenyi, *Hermes: Guide of Souls* (Thompson, CT: Spring Publications, 2015), loc. 56, Kindle.

Why Socrates Loved Hades

Socrates was a philosopher, teacher, and orator who lived in the city-state of Athens around 470 to 399 BCE. Socrates himself authored no texts during his lifetime, but his philosophy and teaching methods were preserved in a series of dialogues written by one of his students: Plato. In his work entitled "Cratylus," Plato records the conversation between Socrates and two friends, Cratylus and Hermogenes, in which they ask the famous thinker to tell them about the nature of names. Are names merely arbitrary, or do they imply something intrinsic about that which they signify?

I love this snippet of dialogue between Socrates and Hermogenes; they are discussing the name Hades and what it reveals about the god who carries it. Its casual, conversational tone is very relatable for the modern reader or listener. Even reading the text of the dialogue in translation, we really get a sense of the rhythm and genius of the Socratic method of teaching critical thinking skills through inquiry and discourse. The following is from Plato's "Cratylus":

Socrates: As for Pluto, he was so named as the giver of wealth (πλοῦτος), because wealth comes up from below out of the earth. And Hades—I fancy most people think that this is a name of the Invisible (ἀειδής), so they are afraid and call him Pluto.

Hermogenes: And what do you think yourself, Socrates?

Socrates: I think people have many false notions about the power of this god, and are unduly afraid of him. They are afraid because when we are once dead we remain in his realm forever, and they are also terrified because the soul goes to him without the covering of the body. But I think all these facts, and the office and the name of the god, point in the same direction.

Hermogenes: How so?

Socrates: I will tell you my own view. Please answer this question: Which is the stronger bond upon any living being to keep him in any one place, desire, or compulsion?

Hermogenes: Desire, Socrates, is much stronger.

Socrates: Then do you not believe there would be many fugitives from Hades, if he did not bind with the strongest bond those who go to him there?

Hermogenes: Of course there would.

Socrates: Apparently, then, if he binds them with the strongest bond, he binds them by some kind of desire, not by compulsion.

Hermogenes: Yes, that is plain.

Socrates: There are many desires, are there not?

Hermogenes: Yes.

Socrates: Then he binds with the desire which is the strongest of all, if he is to restrain them with the strongest bond.

Hermogenes: Yes.

Socrates: And is there any desire stronger than the thought of being made a better man by association with some one?

Hermogenes: No, by Zeus, Socrates, there certainly is not.

Socrates: Then, Hermogenes, we must believe that this is the reason why no one has been willing to come away from that other world, not even the Sirens, but they and all others have been overcome by his enchantments, so beautiful, as it appears, are the words which Hades has the power to speak; and from this point of view this god is a perfect sophist and a great benefactor of those in his realm, he who also bestows such great blessings upon us who are on earth; such abundance surrounds him there below, and for this reason he is called Pluto. Then, too, he refuses to consort with men while they have bodies, but only accepts their society when the soul is pure of all the evils and desires of the body. Do you not think this shows him to be a philosopher and to understand perfectly that under these conditions he could restrain them by binding them with the desire of virtue, but that so long as they are infected with the unrest and madness of the body, not even his father Cronus could hold them to himself, though he bound them with his famous chains?

Hermogenes: There seems to be something in that, Socrates.

Socrates: And the name "Hades" is not in the least derived from the invisible (ἀειδές), but far more probably from knowing (εἰδέναι) all noble things, and for that reason he was called Hades by the lawgiver.[61]

I want to delve into several fascinating ideas put forth in this dialogue. First of all, Socrates suggests that mortal shades stay in Hades' realm out of desire, not compulsion, in order to be close to its ruler. Second, Socrates suggests that even the Sirens, infamous for their alluring songs that have the power to lead sailors to death and doom, are "overcome by his enchantments, so beautiful, as it appears, are the words which Hades has the power to speak."[62] Socrates counts Hades' skill as an orator and sophist—that is to say, a wise and well-spoken teacher skilled in his area of expertise—as an expression of his beneficence and generosity. And finally, he calls Hades a philosopher who can "restrain them by binding them with the desire of virtue."[63] Socrates pays the highest compliment to Hades: that he is a morally virtuous god. Hades Eubuleus knows "all noble things."[64] Hades is charismatic because he is a wise counselor.

Exploring the Lore

In chapter 2, we learned about the Elysian Fields: the Underworld home for shades who lived virtuous lives. The Greek word for virtue, in this context, is *arete*. Arete is a concept of excellence, a notion of complete fulfillment of potential or function. A kitchen knife has a function: to cut fruit, vegetables, cheese, and so on. There are certain virtues that will help a kitchen knife achieve its arete—complete fulfillment of its function—sharpness, cleanliness, and size, for example. Likewise, virtues help a human achieve arete, too.

61. Plato, "Cratylus," in *Plato in Twelve Volumes*, vol. 12, trans. Harold N. Fowler (Cambridge, MA: Harvard University Press, 1921), 403–4.

62. Plato, "Cratylus," 403.

63. Plato, "Cratylus," 404.

64. Plato, "Cratylus," 404.

In Socrates' time, the virtuous human was wise, courageous, temperate, and just. Each of these four virtues would help a person perform well in some area(s) of their life, and as a whole, they would work together to increase one's overall happiness.[65] These four cardinal virtues later made their way into Christianity, via Aristotle, where they are often referred to as prudence, temperance, fortitude, and justice. In "Cratylus," Socrates sets up Hades as the embodiment of these virtues but also awards him the skills to convey what he knows to others. Hades' words are enchanting and compelling. His generous counsel helps the shades of his realm on their quest for arete, for personal excellence.

You may have noticed that both Socrates and the Orphics emphasized the importance of separating the soul from the physical, material body. For Socrates, humans had to escape the cares and concerns of the body to be free to achieve their highest purpose—the arete of their soul. For the Orphics, the initiate's ultimate goal was to explore the mysteries of death and rebirth, in order to escape the cycle of reincarnation. Unlike Socrates, I don't believe that Hades only teaches or helps mortal souls achieve fulfillment once they are separated from the body—my own experiences with him are living proof (pun intended). And if we look at history, this line of thinking has led us down dangerous, oppressive paths. Author and activist Sonya Renee Taylor observes, "When we speak of the ills of the world—violence, poverty, injustice—we are not speaking conceptually; we are talking about things that happen to bodies."[66] She continues, "Racism, sexism, ableism, homo- and transphobia, ageism, fatphobia are algorithms created by humans' struggle to make peace with the body...how we value and honor our own bodies impacts how we value and honor the bodies of others."[67] It seems an antiquated, if not entirely antithetical, notion that a khthonic deity like Hades—the quintessential god of dark fertile soil, decaying bones, and composting flesh—would divorce the spiritual from the physical. Embodiment is one of the portals through which his wisdoms flow. Death and life are intimately connected; we cannot fully experience one without the other. So, too, are the body and the soul.

---

65. Plato, *The Republic*, trans. Benjamin Jowett (Oxford, UK: Clarendon Press, 1888; Project Gutenberg, 2017), bk. 4.

66. Sonya Renee Taylor, *The Body Is Not an Apology: The Power of Radical Self-Love*, 2nd ed. (Oakland, CA: Berrett-Koehler Publishers, 2021), loc. 4, Kindle.

67. Taylor, *The Body Is Not an Apology*, loc. 5, Kindle.

Symbols of Hades: The Single Pitch-Black Tear

In *Metamorphoses*, Ovid captures the moment when Orpheus held all who were present in the Halls of Hades in thrall with his song: "The story is, that then, for the first time, the cheeks of the Eumenides [Furies], overcome by his music, were wet with tears; nor could the royal consort [Persephone], nor he who rules the infernal regions [Hades], endure to deny him his request; and they called for Eurydice."[68] In my retelling of this myth, written from Hades' perspective, he describes himself shedding a single tear. The shedding of a single tear by a character in a book, film, or television series is a common trope: it signifies a moment wherein the character is deeply and exceptionally moved—so much so, that they momentarily drop their stoic countenance to shed a tear. What was it about Orpheus' song that moved him so? I believe it is because Hades truly loves Persephone and deeply misses his wife when she is above ground. Hades recognized his own story in the young lovers' plight of separation.

As mentioned in the previous chapter, my retellings of these myths are the product of many hours of trance journey and conversation with Hades. In my trance journey to retrieve this story, the tear I saw fall from Hades' eye was intensely black. The color black alludes to something mysterious, obscured, or not well understood. It also speaks to a sense of great sorrow, grief, and loss. Black is a powerful color that stands out, eclipsing anything surrounding it. One might assume that the color black is simply symbolic of the Underworld, but that is not necessarily true—various areas of the Underworld are described differently throughout myth, and the color black is usually reserved for descriptions of the abyss of Tartaros. To me, Hades' black tear suggests that his grief is intense, but also compacted over time, like coal. Through grief, his heart is moved to mercy and compassion.

In His Dark Garden:
Mediterranean Cypress and Dittany of Crete

Mediterranean cypress and dittany of Crete are excellent allies for working magic with Hades and the denizens of the Underworld. If I had to pick just one herb for my Hades praxis, it would definitely be Mediterranean cypress, for its

---

68. Ovid, *The Metamorphoses of Ovid*, vol. 2, trans. Henry T. Riley (London: George Bell & Sons, 1893; Project Gutenberg, 2008), 10.1.343.

lengthy historical association with death rites and cemeteries. Dittany of Crete, with its rare evocative properties, helps me connect deeply with the gods of Greek mythology.

Mediterranean Cypress Tree

Species: *Cupressus sempervirens*

Other Common Names: Italian cypress, Persian cypress, pencil pine, Tuscan cypress

Toxicity: No reported toxicity, but not recommended for ingestion. Cypress essential oil can be used aromatically and topically when properly diluted, but it is contraindicated for pregnant people.

Keywords: Death, mourning, necromancy, sorrow

The Mediterranean cypress is an evergreen, pencil-shaped tree with needle-like leaves and small cones. To this day, it is still the most commonly planted tree in cemeteries throughout Europe and the Muslim world. In pop culture, you may have seen images of the Mediterranean cypress gracing travel posters for Italy—the tree is closely associated with this region.

In ancient Greece, cypress boughs were placed over thresholds and within households to signify a state of mourning. The aromatic sap of the tree represented "tears" of sorrow. A garland or wreath of cypress was considered a suitable decoration to venerate a statue of Hades. Additionally, cypress trees were often planted near graves or in groves where necromantic rites were performed, thus consecrating them to Hades. Preparations for these rituals oftentimes included building a pyre made from cypress branches. A Greek funeral lamentation tells us that mourners placed oil lamps in the branches of cemetery cypress trees, perhaps to guide shades of the dead on their way to the Underworld: "On your branches I will hang lamps, / so that your friends can pass by and fill them with oil, / so that your mother can come and fill them with tears, / and so that your brothers and sisters can come and fill them to overflowing."[69]

Burn cypress tips for assistance in divination, especially necromantic divination. You can place a few boughs of cypress on your altar to venerate Hades, or weave them into a wreath for a ritual centerpiece. The fumes of burning

---

69. Loring M. Danforth, *The Death Rituals of Rural Greece* (Princeton, NJ: Princeton University Press, 1982), 98.

cypress also have a purifying effect, providing an added benefit to its resonance with Hades and the Underworld.

DITTANY OF CRETE

Species: *Origanum dictamnus*

Other Common Names: Erontas, hop marjoram

Toxicity: No reported toxicity. Ingesting dittany of Crete is contraindicated for pregnant people.

Keywords: Astral projection, love, spirit evocation and manifestation

Dittany of Crete is an indigenous Mediterranean herb of the mint family, similar to oregano and marjoram. This small shrub is easily recognizable by the soft, velvety hairs on its stems and leaves, and it features small pink blooms in the summer. In the wild, dittany of Crete only grows on the steep mountainsides and gorges of its namesake, the Greek island of Crete. Wild-grown dittany of Crete is classified as rare and is protected from extinction by European laws against over-harvesting. Nearby villages now cultivate dittany of Crete for commercial export. It is used in a variety of products, such as herbal tea, flavoring for vermouth, natural beauty remedies, and incense. In the ancient world, dittany of Crete was used to flavor wine, used to decorate temples and gardens, gifted as a love token, and prescribed as a medicinal cure-all. Collection of dittany of Crete was a very dangerous occupation—the men who risked their lives climbing the sheer rock faces where the plant grows were called *erondades* (love seekers). Use of dittany of Crete in love potions and spells persisted into the early modern period, especially in the folk magic of Italy.[70]

In Western ceremonial magic, Aleister Crowley popularized the use of dittany of Crete to summon spirits. The dried leaves are burned in copious amounts, and spirits are said to manifest in the ensuing smoke. However, since dittany of Crete is a rare and protected herb, you may want to be a bit more conservative with quantities than Crowley. I find that burning a small pinch of dried dittany of Crete helps create a beneficial environment for trance journey. I add it to animating potions or elixirs used to anoint scrying vessels, such as bowls or mirrors. Dittany of Crete is also a key component of incense blends that I make

70. Michelle Gruben, "Rare Occult Herbs: Dittany of Crete," Grove and Grotto, April 12, 2017, https://www.groveandgrotto.com/blogs/articles/rare-occult-herbs-dittany-of-crete.

for any ritual working that involves the Greek gods, and especially for my rituals with Hades—it assists in evocation of the god(s) into the ritual circle.

Khthonic Bestiary: Bats

In the *Odyssey*, Odysseus likens the spirits of Penelope's dead suitors to bats: "He [Hermes] led the spirits and they followed, squeaking like bats in secret crannies of a cave, who cling together, and when one becomes detached and falls down from the rock, the rest flutter and squeak—just so the spirits squeaked, and hurried after Hermes, lord of healing."[71] In Greco-Roman art, there are many examples of birds, butterflies, and sometimes bats metaphorically representing the soul departed from the physical body. The Greek word for bat is *nykteris*, which is related to "night," while in Latin, it is *vespertilio*, derived from "twilight."[72]

According to Bat Conservation International, bats have been on Earth for more than 50 million years. They are widely dispersed across six continents and are the second largest order of mammals, with more than 1,400 species.[73] With their membranous wings, bats are the only mammal capable of true flight. They are critical members of the worldwide ecosystem, providing pest control, nighttime pollination, and seed dispersion for an extensive variety of plants.

As nocturnal animals, of whom many species inhabit dark and vast cave systems, bats easily resonate with the murky and ineffable nature of the Underworld and its denizens. Contrary to popular belief, bats are not blind—they are equipped with exceptionally sensitive eyes, packed with photoreceptor cells that allow them to see in low light conditions that appear impenetrable to humans. These ancient animals can teach us much about skillfully navigating what may seem mysterious, inscrutable, or uncertain; in trance journey work, the bat in spirit form can serve as an excellent guide on your Otherworldly travels, as well as a teacher in magical arts such as scrying.

Finding Hades in the Landscape: Cape Tainaron

Cape Tainaron, also known as Cape Matapan, is situated at the end of the Mani Peninsula at the southernmost point of mainland Greece. It is surmised that

---

71. Homer, *The Odyssey*, trans. Emily R. Wilson, 24.5–10.

72. Chiara O. Tommasi Moreschini, "Bats in Greco-Roman Antiquity," *Bats* 29, no. 2 (July 20, 2011): 6–8.

73. Bat Conservation International, "Bats 101," accessed April 24, 2023, https://www.batcon.org/about -bats/bats-101/.

Orpheus entered the Underworld seeking Eurydice through the Cape Tainaron caves and also that the hero Herakles entered the Underworld via the cave system to complete his twelfth labor. Greek travel writer Pausanias observed, "On the promontory is a temple like a cave, with a statue of Poseidon in front of it. Some of the Greek poets state that Heracles brought up the hound of Hades here."[74]

The ruins of a temple dedicated to the sea god Poseidon can be found on the hill directly above the cave entrance to the Underworld. This temple was converted to a Christian place of worship by the Byzantines, and it is still used for religious services to this day.[75] The caves at Cape Tainaron are partially below the water level, but it is still possible to visit the caverns by boat to view the natural beauty of its stalactite and stalagmite formations.

Invitations to Practice

Invoke Hades Eubuleus for advice on moving forward (not looking back), bringing a sense of mercy and compassion to a situation, identifying what the concept of arete means for you, and for taking steps to move your life in that direction. Symbols and correspondences that resonate with the energy of Hades in this aspect are his single black tear, the Mediterranean cypress tree, dittany of Crete, and keen-sighted bats.

Hymn to Hades Eubuleus

The following hymn can be spoken or sung to connect with Hades Eubuleus. It contains a humble petition for Hades' consolation and perspective. Try reciting this hymn to Hades in times of difficulty or loneliness, when you want his advice on how to align your actions and words with your values, or when you are seeking a big-picture perspective on a situation.

Who will give me counsel in this lonely hour?
Who will walk with me in the depths of darkest night?
Who will hear my cry echoing through hollow halls, my feet pacing the floor?

74. Pausanias, "Description of Greece," in *Complete Works of Pausanias*, trans. W. H. S. Jones (Hastings, East Sussex, UK: Delphi Classics, 2014), 3.25.4–5.

75. Atlas Obscura and Darmon Richter, "Cape Matapan Caves," Atlas Obscura, accessed November 19, 2022, https://www.atlasobscura.com/places/cape-matapan-caves.

I petition thee, Eubuleus, the Good Counselor,
You who hold the heart's vigil through seasons of separation,
You who remain steadfast in the desolation of hope,
You who never forget.
I offer praise to thee, Hades Eubuleus, and humbly ask
For your assistance: please lend your attention
To my mortal woes, please comfort my spirit
With your eternal perspective.
Your wisdom is rich as the fertile earth.
Your counsel is precious as silver and gold.
It falls like tender, beautiful chords upon my weary ears.

Working with the Gods: Evocation and Invocation

When it comes to working with the gods in a magical or ritual sense, there are three key concepts to understand: evocation, invocation, and correspondences. I cover the topic of correspondences in chapter 1, in regard to creating an altar to Hades, and expand on it in chapter 3 when discussing khthonic offerings and seasonal veneration. As you progress in your relationship with Hades, you may want to *evoke* his presence in ritual, or *invoke* his blessing for a magical operation (such as a spell). For purposes of clarity, let's break down these two terms.

The English words *evocation* and *invocation* are very similar and oftentimes used interchangeably. According to *Merriam-Webster*, both words are derived from Latin and share a common root in that language (*vocare*, meaning "to call"). Invoke comes from *invocare* ("to call upon") and evoke from *evocare* ("to call forth").[76] When it comes to magical praxis, however, these two terms refer to different kinds of operations.

Evocation, in the magical sense, is the calling forth of the presence of a god or other spirit being into your ritual working. In other words, to evoke is to summon. In ancient Greece, *epiklesis* described the epithet used to evoke the desired aspect of a deity during religious ceremonies. Epiklesis specifically refers to a surname used to evoke an aspect of a deity in a religious context, in contrast to the more general or casual use of an epithet as a character descriptor in poetic contexts. This same term was adopted into the Christian

---

76. *Merriam-Webster*, "Is It 'Invoke' or 'Evoke'?," Merriam-Webster Online, accessed January 14, 2023, https://www.merriam-webster.com/words-at-play/is-it-invoke-or-evoke.

sacrament of the Last Supper, also called the Eucharist. In the Eucharist, the epiklesis is the evocation of the Holy Spirit to consecrate and transform bread and wine into the flesh and blood of Jesus Christ. When evoked in ritual, a god or spirit can come forth to bear witness, to lend you some of their energy for your rites, to perform a magical act of blessing or transformation, or even to communicate with you through divination or scrying. Offerings for the god are usually included on the ritual altar. Some magical practitioners also like to have a designated object or container for the god to inhabit for the duration of the ritual, such as a flame, fluid condenser, or statue. Proper etiquette is to thank and release the god(s) when the ritual is complete.

Invocation, on the other hand, is a bit more complex. Invocation, in essence, is an invitation. For instance, you can invite Hades to bless an invisibility spell by reading a hymn or poem invoking the Unseen One as part of the spellcasting (many of the hymns shared throughout this book can be used for this purpose). But the term *invoke*, in the magical sense, can also refer to an invitation for a deity to enter into the magical practitioner's physical body. I like to use the term *trance possession* (rather than invocation) to describe this more advanced magical skill. Almost anyone can learn trance possession, but it is advisable to seek out a teacher adept in this technique before attempting it yourself. Trance possession workings require a lot of emotional, spiritual, and psychological preparation.

With an understanding of these three concepts—evocation, invocation, and correspondences—you have the building blocks to work with Hades in magic and ritual. In the next chapter, I'll discuss the fundamentals of circle casting, warding, and energetic protection techniques.

Magical Praxis: Crafting Fluid Condensers

In European-descended magical traditions, fluid condensers are made by infusing water with metals, herbs, stones, and other materials. The condenser serves as a medium for spiritual or etheric energy to coalesce and relies on the principle of magical correspondence. The theory and technique behind my method for crafting compound fluid condensers is based on the work of the Hermeticist Franz Bardon (1909–1958). The process of making a fluid condenser is relatively simple:

1. Start with spring water (preferably) or filtered tap water. Pour approximately 2 cups of water into a small pot and set it on a heat source, such as your stove top.

2. Gather the items you will use to empower the purpose of the condenser—corresponding metals, herbs, stones, etc. Place them in the water. Only use a pinch of each herb.

3. Bring the water to a boil, slowly, as you feed energy to the water. You can sing, pray, chant, or send energy through the palms of your hands (be careful not to touch the pot or the water itself, to avoid burns). When the boiling point is reached, remove the pot from the heat source, setting it aside to steep and cool for a minimum of 20 minutes.

4. Once the water is cooled so as not to burn you, filter out the herbs and other ingredients, until you have a tea-like fluid remaining. Take care removing stones and metals, as they have a tendency to retain heat.

5. Your condenser is made! You can store it in a refrigerator for a short period of time if you are not planning to use it right away. I suggest only 2 to 3 days maximum—the energy will start to wane.[77]

Here are a few suggestions for crafting fluid condensers aligned with Hades. Keep in mind that you don't have to include all these ingredients, or even one of each type—your condenser can be crafted exclusively from herbs, for example. I like to layer in number magic when choosing ingredients: I typically choose three, six, or nine correspondences for Hades. I consider which aspect, or epiklesis, I am trying to summon. Over time, you will discover what formulas work best for your magical practice. Keep a record of your experiments—note the date, ingredients, and purpose for each condenser you craft.

Herbs: Mint, thyme, dittany of Crete, rosemary
Metals: Small piece of pure gold or silver, such as a ring or pendant—you may find it resonates to designate one piece of your personal jewelry for this specific purpose, so that it becomes your energetic signature in every condenser you make.

---

77. Franz Bardon, *Initiation into Hermetics: The Path of the True Adept* (Salt Lake City, UT: Merkur Publishing, 2014), loc. 198–201, Kindle.

Stones: Clear or smoky quartz, amethyst, black obsidian. Be sure to rinse any stones used in your condenser under cold running water to remove dirt, dust, or other residues.

To use the condenser for ritual evocation, pour the fluid into a shallow glass or metal bowl in which a significant amount of the fluid's surface area will remain exposed. For now, cover the condenser with a lid or piece of fabric, and place the bowl on your altar as you set up your ritual space. After your circle is cast and warded (see chapter 5), when you are ready to perform the evocation, remove the covering and lift the vessel in both hands. Recite a hymn or chant to call the god you are summoning into the circle and, specifically, into the condenser. When you feel the subtle energy shift, they have arrived. Acknowledge their presence aloud, such as by saying, "Khaire Hades." You can return the condenser to the altar for the remainder of the ritual, but leave it uncovered.

During ritual, you can imbibe the condenser if you want, to further physically embody the energy of the deity or your magical working. However, use caution: not all herbs are safe to ingest, and some nontoxic herbs are contraindicated for certain conditions, such as pregnancy, high blood pressure, or heart conditions. Not all stones can be safely boiled, for reasons of toxicity, structural integrity, or trace metals in their composition. You will want to research your ingredients with due diligence before deciding to imbibe. If working with fluid condensers is new to you, just try a sip or two at first—the energy infused into the condenser is often quite amplified, having been fed by both your magic and the presence of an etheric entity.

When the primary working of your ritual is complete, *devoke* the god you have summoned before you release your wards of protection and boundary circle. Devocation is the opposite action of evocation. To perform the devocation, lift the fluid condenser in both hands again, speaking words of gratitude and farewell. This might sound something like, "Thank you, Hades, for presiding over these rites. I release you now and bid you farewell." Scatter the energy from the condenser with a long, intentional exhale or, if you are outside, by placing it on the ground. After the close of your ritual, dispose of any remaining liquid in a respectful way by offering it to a tree, a plant, or your garden.

CHAPTER 5
THE UNBREAKABLE

Hades speaks:

The sun sets as I walk among the dead on the smoking battlefield of Pylos. Such disregard, so many precious mortal lives ended, all for the sake of a family drama. I wonder, did the Moirai know in advance that these threads were to be cut at this hour? These people, the Pylians, victims of the whims of the gods. My siblings, my nephew. I feel responsible for their suffering. I came with all haste to my people's defense, but we were overcome. I walk among them now, stopping to touch my thumb into the dust and ashes, marking each of their foreheads. Even without an obol, Kharon will know to ferry them to our home. Elysium will welcome them with laughter and honey.

Is this truly the land of the "living"? All I can see are corpses, dented shields, broken arrows. Broken dreams. There is nothing more I can do on this grim day, so I make ready to leave. And suddenly, pain—incredible pain— an arrow is lodged deep in my shoulder. I turn, crouching, searching for the arrow's source. Who has the audacity to try to wound me? Then I see him: Herakles. He's still holding his bow, intently focused in my direction. I stand; he startles when he sees my face and bolts to join his men. Some hero, that one.

Herakles' arrows are all tipped in the poisonous blood of the Hydra. The poison won't kill me, but it will make the next few hours very uncomfortable. I take one final glance at the fallen Pylians, my heart grieving for the waste of it all. My shoulder aching, I grudgingly face the prospect of another trip to Olympus, to have the poisonous arrow extracted and my wounds healed. I make the journey, wishing all the while for the khthonic solitude of my halls. I've already decided to let Kerberos sleep in front of my fire tonight, and perhaps I'll even give him an extra bone. He's a good dog and I am glad to have him back home.

Adamastos: Hades the Resolute

The epithet *Adamastos* is derived from the Greek word *adámas,* meaning unalterable, unbreakable, or untamed. *Adamant* is an archaic form of the word *diamond*; the modern English word *diamond* is ultimately derived from *adámas,* by way of the Late Latin word *diamas* and Old French *diamant.* Today we use the English word *adamant* as an adjective to describe a refusal to be persuaded or to change one's mind.

"For Hades gives not way, and is pitiless, and therefore he among all the gods is the most hateful to mortals."[78] This is the description of Hades given by Agamemnon, King of Mycenae, in Homer's *Iliad.* In this instance, as well as many others, the epithet Hades Adamastos clearly alludes to the inevitability of death. However, although it's not a direct translation, I like to use the word *resolute* to describe the adamantine aspect of Hades' character. Someone who is resolute is purposeful, determined, unwavering, and steadfast. Hades Adamastos is resolute in fulfilling the duties of his office—even when going toe-to-toe with his Olympian siblings or their demigod children.

Hades and Herakles

Herakles was the son of the god Zeus and the mortal Alcmene. (If you're keeping track of the twists and turns of this immortal family tree, this means that Hades is Herakles' uncle.) The birth of this semidivine child enraged Zeus' wife, the goddess Hera, so much that she launched a lifelong vendetta against Herakles. This vendetta eventually led to Herakles being challenged to complete ten (which later grew to twelve) impossible labors in servitude to Eurystheus, king of the Mycenaean city of Tiryns.

Herakles' twelfth and final labor was to kidnap Kerberos, the monstrous three-headed guard dog of the Underworld, and bring the beast before King Eurystheus. To prepare for his descent to the Underworld, Herakles first participates in the Eleusinian Mysteries. After picking up some tips and tricks from a priest, he journeys through the land of the dead, raising quite a ruckus as he makes his way to the Halls of Hades. Herakles steals and slaughters one of Hades' immortal black cattle, enraging Menoites the cattle-herd and provoking a wrestling match. He encounters the heroes Theseus and Pirithous, firmly

---

78. Homer, *Iliad,* 9.158–59.

stuck to stone chairs, still in the midst of their imprisonment for attempting to kidnap the Dread Queen Persephone to serve as Pirithous' wife. Herakles is able to free Theseus, but when he tries to free Pirithous, the ground begins to rumble and shake. Hades, it seems, considers Pirithous a permanent resident. The heroes are forced to leave him behind.

Herakles eventually finds the Halls of Hades and is granted an audience with his uncle. Accounts detailing the conversation (or in some instances, the confrontation) between Hades and Herakles vary, particularly over the request to "borrow" Kerberos. One of the most well-known accounts is that of Pseudo-Apollodorus, in which Hades tells Herakles that he can take Kerberos back with him to the land of the living, but there is one stipulation: Herakles must overpower Kerberos without using any weapons—only his own strength and cunning. From *Library*, the account of Pseudo-Apollodorus: "When Hercules asked Pluto for Cerberus, Pluto ordered him to take the animal provided he mastered him without the use of the weapons which he carried. Hercules found him at the gates of Acheron, and, cased in his cuirass and covered by the lion's skin, he flung his arms round the head of the brute, and though the dragon in its tail bit him, he never relaxed his grip and pressure till it yielded."[79]

Unlike other monsters that crossed paths with Herakles, three-headed Kerberos eventually returned, unscathed, to resume his guard duties in the Underworld. Hades' stipulation against using weapons most certainly helped keep the beast safe.

The Battle of Pylos

The story of the Battle of Pylos is not well known. In the fifth book of the *Iliad*, the Titaness Dione relates an anecdote in which Hades is injured by an arrow in battle. She tells this story to the goddess Aphrodite, who has been injured, to soothe and comfort her as Dione heals her wounds: "Hades the gigantic had to endure with the rest the flying arrow when this self-same man [Herakles], the son of Zeus of the aegis, struck him among the dead men at Pylos, and gave him to agony; but he [Hades] went up to the house of Zeus and to tall Olympos

---

79. Apollodorus, *The Library, Volume 1: Books 1–3.9*, trans. James George Frazer, Loeb Classical Library 121 (Cambridge, MA: Harvard University Press, 1921), 2.5.12.

heavy at heart, stabbed through and through with pain, for the arrow was driven into his heavy shoulder, and his spirit was suffering."[80]

This passage refers to Herakles, that same hero of the twelve labors, leading an expedition to the city of Pylos. The Pylos referred to in the *Iliad* could be a city located either in the region of Messenia or near the city of Elis in the region of the same name (this distinction becomes important later). Herakles travels to Pylos to ask King Neleus to cleanse him of a blood debt. The king refuses his request. In retaliation, Herakles leads an army against Neleus and his twelve sons, destroying their city and killing all of them except for Nestor. In the midst of this battle, Herakles launches an arrow that strikes Hades in the shoulder. Tipped in the poisonous blood of the Lernaean Hydra, the arrow has the power to affect even the immortal Hades, "heavy at heart, stabbed through and through with pain."[81] Hades must leave the battle and travel to Olympus to have his wound healed.

Hades is not known to involve himself in wars or heroic exploits. In general, he remains quite distant from mortal affairs. So why was Hades present at the Battle of Pylos? There are three prevailing theories. First, the passage in the fifth book of the *Iliad* states that Hades was struck "among the dead men at Pylos."[82] It could be inferred from this passage that Hades was walking among the dead on the battlefield, perhaps assisting them to the Underworld or performing some other duty related to his office, when he was struck by an arrow. Dione's account does not specify whether the arrow was aimed at him or merely an unfortunate accident.

According to the second theory, Hades joined in the Battle of Pylos because he was irritated with his nephew's cavalier behavior and entitled attitude while in the Underworld. After all, Herakles killed one of Hades' cattle, wrestled one of his daimons, freed the blasphemer Theseus, and succeeded in kidnapping Kerberos. When the siege erupted at Pylos, Hades sided with his Olympian siblings Hera and Poseidon against Herakles, entering the fray to burn off some pent-up anger.

---

80. Homer, *Iliad*, 5.394–400.

81. Homer, *The Iliad*, 5.399.

82. Homer, *The Iliad*, 5.397.

The third theory concerns the people of Elis, and Hades' extant cult there. The region of Elis was located on the western-most point of the Peloponnese (southern mainland Greece). Ancient Greek travel writer Pausanias claims that a fight between Hades and Herakles happened at Pylos in Elis, where Hades stood up for the Pylians because he was worshiped there.[83] Pausanias goes on to note that even in his time, centuries after the events described in the *Iliad* were purported to have occurred, the Eleans still quoted Homer's lines because they considered the myth an important part of the origin story of Hades' cult in the area. Strabo, Greek geographer, philosopher, and historian (ca. 64 BCE–24 CE), confirms this in his *Geographica*. The Eleans, seeing themselves as allies of Pylos against Herakles (who also happened to sack Elis en route to the siege at Pylos), re-founded their cult for Hades.[84]

In her book entitled *Underworld Gods in Ancient Greek Religion*, present-day historian Ellie Mackin Roberts also concurs that the most well-known cult honoring Hades was in Elis. Roberts explains that the name *Pylos* gives us important clues regarding Hades' worship in this area: "Pylos comes from the Greek πύλος, meaning 'in the gateway' and sometimes explained as the entrance to the gates of Hades, and it is at the western point of the Greek mainland, that is, the direction of the setting sun."[85] Recall that in some accounts, the Underworld is described as lying just beyond Oceanus to the west, past the setting sun.

At Pylos and Elis, Hades is worshiped as the Ruler of the Dead—not by any of his other kinder epithets, related to his wealth, fertility, or relationship with Persephone (such as Klymenos or Plouton). This fact is noteworthy in and of itself, but to also see Hades cast in the role of community defender is quite exceptional.[86]

---

83. Pausanias, "Description of Greece," in *Complete Works of Pausanias*, 6.25.2.

84. Karolina Sekita, "Hades and Heracles at Pylos: Dione's Tale Dismantled," *The Classical Quarterly* 68, no. 1 (May 1, 2018): 1–9, https://doi.org/10.1017/S0009838818000216.

85. Ellie Mackin Roberts, *Underworld Gods in Ancient Greek Religion: Death and Reciprocity* (Abingdon, UK: Routledge, 2020), loc. 47, Kindle.

86. Diana Burton, "Worshipping Hades: Myth and Cult in Elis and Triphylia," *Archiv für Religionsgeschichte* 20, no. 1 (March 28, 2018): 224, https://doi.org/10.1515/arege-2018-0013.

Exploring the Lore

Hades Adamastos is resolute. As he shows us at the Battle of Pylos, to be resolute is also to be resilient, able to experience wounds and setbacks, but ultimately impossible to subdue or defeat. He comes to the defense of those who worship him. He is grievously injured, forced to retreat to Olympus to have his wound healed. When the battle concludes, Pylos is destroyed. If, however, we are to believe the accounts of Pausanias and Strabo, the Eleans pick up the torch, reestablishing Hades' cult center in honor of the fallen Pylians. His temple is rebuilt. His worship is restored. Hades may have been wounded, but his relationship with the people of the region remains unaltered.

Reframing Masculinity

Greek mythology is full of heroes like Herakles, Theseus, and Pirithous. The hero's journey is a common template for stories involving a hero who goes on an adventure, is victorious in a pivotal crisis, and comes home changed or transformed. This framework was popularized by Joseph Campbell (1904–1987) in his 1949 book entitled *The Hero with a Thousand Faces*: "A hero ventures forth from the world of common day into a region of supernatural wonder (x): fabulous forces are there encountered and a decisive victory is won (y): the hero comes back from this mysterious adventure with the power to bestow boons on his fellow man (z)."[87] In the years since its first publication, Campbell's work on this so-called monomyth has been criticized—deservedly so—for source-selection and privilege bias, misogyny, and other reasons. However, uplifting the figure of the conquering hero as the ideal representation of masculinity and human achievement is a tendency that persists in our culture to this day.

"What about a society which has had enough of war and death? Not everyone identifies with the active, conquering hero archetype, who sets off on a grand adventure and returns to save the world. What about the men who stay home, and make things work?"[88] This is the question posed by mythologist Sharon Blackie in discussing the necessity of reenvisioning and reframing outdated masculine archetypes. Viewed through this lens, the god Hades is a foil to

---

87. Joseph Campbell, *The Hero with a Thousand Faces* (Novato, CA: New World Library, 2008), 23.

88. Sharon Blackie, "The Mythic Imagination," online course, 2016, https://sharonblackie.net/.

aggrandized heroes like Herakles, providing a more balanced, grounded representation of masculinity, one more suited to moving toward a post-heroic age.

Murphy Robinson is a transmasculine wilderness guide, activist, and magic-weaver who has worked with Hades over the past several years. In an interview conducted for this book, they shared some of their personal experiences of working with him: "Speaking as someone who has been on a journey of embracing masculinity over the course of my whole life, Hades is compelling because he's masculine but not macho. His energy feels much more elegant and balanced than other male deities. The gods are interested in what is alive and vital in us, and Hades has always been very affirming of my masculinity and helping me express it."[89] Murphy goes on to explain that it can be difficult to navigate the competing narratives of masculinity in today's culture, but working with Hades can help. They observe, "On one hand, those of us who identify as masculine want to be good, supportive feminists and help dismantle the patriarchy. On the other hand, we're encouraged to be bold and confident [in our masculinity]. How can we be all these things at once? Hades presents a relatively functional model on how to accomplish that."[90]

Hades does not instigate wars or heroic exploits, opting instead to tend to the Underworld, its denizens, and guests. He cultivates a stable environment for the shades of the dead. His approach to his duties focuses less on himself as an individual and more on sustaining balance for the whole. Hades does not micromanage his realm. He models collaborative leadership that allows others to utilize their skills and abilities, spreading responsibility among the collective: Kharon the Ferryman, Kerberos the Guard Dog, the avenging Furies, and more. He trusts the expertise of his three judges and the Dread Queen Persephone to help with hard judgment calls. He is reliable and steadfast in fulfilling his responsibilities—Hades is the Host of Many, not the conquering hero on a quest. Hades is a stronghold, rather than a savior.

Symbols of Hades: The Bident

In surviving art and literary fragments, Hades is often depicted with a staff or bident as a symbol of his rulership. Some depictions show him holding a staff

---

89. Murphy Robinson, interview with the author, January 4, 2023.

90. Robinson, interview, January 4, 2023.

tipped with a golden bird, but the image of Hades grasping a bident is far more common. A bident is a two-pronged metal implement similar to a pitchfork. As an agricultural tool, the bident is used for breaking up dirt that is rocky and hard.

Similar to Zeus' single-point lightning bolt and Poseidon's three-pronged trident, Hades' bident serves as a symbol of his authority over the third realm, the Underworld. Since Hades' dominion also includes the fertile soil under Earth's surface, the bident—a tool for working soil—is a fitting symbol of his sovereignty. Hades Adamastos is here to defend, cultivate, and sustain, and he's brought the right tool for the job.

In His Dark Garden: Aconite and Adamant

Aconite and adamant are as dangerous as they are beautiful. As plant and mineral allies, aconite offers powerful protection and reinforcement of boundaries, while adamant helps to cultivate strength, fortitude, and clarity.

ACONITE

Species: *Aconitum napellus*
Other Common Names: Hekate, knight's helmet, monkshood, witchflower, wolfsbane
Toxicity: Highly toxic (never ingest, and use caution when handling)
Keywords: Baneful magic, boundaries, glamoury, protection, witchcraft

Aconite is a deciduous perennial plant with primarily vivid, purplish-blue flowers, although some ornamental cultivars can display white blooms. All parts of aconite are extremely toxic, and it has been used as a poison since ancient times. This herb makes a dramatic appearance in the story of Medea, infamous sorceress and priestess of the khthonic goddess Hekate, who serves wine laced with aconite to the hero Theseus in an attempt to poison him and prevent him from usurping her son's inheritance. According to Ovid, Kerberos is central to the origin story of this herb: "For his destruction Medea mingles the wolfsbane [aconite], which she once brought with her from the shores of Scythia. This, they say, sprang from the teeth of the Echidnean dog. There is a gloomy cave, with a dark entrance, *wherein* there is a descending path, along which the Tirynthian hero [Herakles] dragged away Cerberus resisting, and turning his eyes sideways from the day and the shining rays *of the Sun*, in chains formed of adamant; he, filled with furious rage, filled the air with triple barkings at the same moment, and sprinkled the verdant fields with white foam. This, they suppose, grew solid, and, receiving the nourishment of a fruitful and productive soil, acquired the power of being noxious."[91]

The folk names "monkshood" and "knight's helmet" refer to the shape of the flowers. These folk names, in addition to the plant's connection to the Underworld guardian beast Kerberos, reveal much about its protective properties and magical uses. According to plant essence practitioner Nicholas Pearson, "Like the hood or helmet it resembles, this flower protects during spiritual endeavors, allowing the crown and third-eye chakras to open wide without worry of interference."[92] Include aconite in workings of protection or glamoury or to fortify physical and energetic boundaries. The dried flowers can be added to ritual incense, but use caution to burn this baneful plant in a well-ventilated area. Do not add aconite to fluid condensers that you intend to drink—you should never ingest any part of the plant. Many skilled flower essence practitioners offer monkshood or aconite essences that have been diluted to less than a microdose; always refer to the practitioner's instructions before using flower essences internally.

ADAMANT
Mineral Content: Carbon
Other Common Names: Diamond
Keywords: Clarity, fearlessness, fortitude, invincible, unbreakable

Adamant, or diamond, is a solid form of the element carbon, with its atoms arranged in a specific structure called diamond cubic. It takes the earth roughly 1 to 3.5 billion years of high temperature and intense pressure to make a diamond. Under these conditions, pure carbon trapped in the earth's mantle (about 100 miles beneath the surface) is heated and compressed into the solid mineral structures we know as diamonds. Much more recently (only hundreds to tens of million years ago), these same diamonds were reborn in fire—carried to the earth's surface via volcanic eruptions and subsequently deposited in igneous rock formations known as kimberlites and lamproites. Diamonds

91. Ovid, *The Metamorphoses of Ovid*, 7.402–423. Translator's italics.

92. Nicholas Pearson, *Flower Essences from the Witch's Garden: Plant Spirits in Magickal Herbalism* (Rochester, VT: Destiny Books, 2022), 366.

are the hardest known natural material on both the Vickers and Mohs scales of measuring hardness.

Diamonds are mined all over the world, but most diamonds on today's market come from Africa. Be aware that there are ethical issues associated with diamonds: many diamond mines use child labor, and this expensive commodity is often sold to fund wars and genocide—these stones are referred to as "blood diamonds." If you are interested in acquiring adamant for your own magical practice, look for diamonds that are certified as ethically sourced, or better yet, shop around at local jewelry and antique stores for a secondhand piece of diamond jewelry. Alternatively, Murphy Robinson suggests that you can easily and cheaply buy a diamond file or sharpener (used for sharpening blades) online or at knife stores. Diamond files are made of ground-up bits of industrial-grade diamonds, and pocket versions cost under twenty dollars.

Remember that you also have the tools to work with adamant without having a physical specimen of the stone. You can use trance journey to commune with the spirit of the mineral in the Otherworld, draw it meditatively, or create a collage of diamond images for your altar.

Khthonic Bestiary: Three-Headed Kerberos

Kerberos, also known as Cerberus, was one of the offspring born to the monsters Echidna and Typhon. There are several competing descriptions of Kerberos in primary sources, with the number of his heads stretching anywhere from one to one hundred, but later writers almost always portrayed Kerberos as having three heads, a serpentine or dragon-like tail, and various smaller snakes writhing from different parts of his body.

Kerberos lives in the Underworld, loyal to Hades and Persephone, who give him the duty of guarding the gates to their realm. Hesiod describes Kerberos' role: "There, in front, stand the echoing halls of the god of the lower-world, strong Hades, and of awful Persephone. A fearful hound guards the house in front, pitiless, and he has a cruel trick. On those who go in he fawns with his tail and both his ears, but suffers them not to go out back again, but keeps watch and devours whomsoever he catches going out of the gates of strong Hades and awful Persephone."[93]

---

93. Hugh G. Evelyn-White, trans., *Theogony*, in *Hesiod, the Homeric Hymns, and Homerica* (London: William Heinemann, 1914), 135.

Faithful guardian, companion, and protector, Kerberos takes his duties very seriously. However, according to myth, Kerberos loves honey cakes and can be distracted or lulled to sleep with a sweet baked-goods bribe. In the next chapter, you'll find two recipes for offering cakes that will appease Kerberos, helping you make friends with this fearsome Underworld canine. Just remember to watch out for that poisonous, deadly drool.

Finding Hades in the Landscape: Archaeological Site of Elis

The archaeological site of Elis, located 60 kilometers north of Olympia in Greece, is home to the ruins of the largest ancient city in the northwestern Peloponnese. According to the UNESCO World Heritage Centre, "The city thrived in the early historical period (11th to 10th centuries BC), during the late Archaic and early Classical periods (6th to 5th centuries BC), and in the Roman period (2nd century BC to early 3rd century AD). Elis was responsible for the organisation of the Olympic Games and according to regulations, the athletes would stay in the city to train in its sporting facilities a month before the Game[s'] beginning."[94] The archaeological site is extensive. Visitors can explore the ancient *agora* (marketplace), theater, acropolis, residential sector, cemeteries, and unexcavated gymnasiums.

This site may have been near the Battle of Pylos described in Homer's *Iliad*, wherein Herakles wounded Hades with a poison arrow. Ancient Greek travel writer Pausanias claimed that the fight between Hades and Herakles happened at Pylos in Elis, where Hades stood up for the Pylians because he was worshiped there.[95] Pausanias also notes another instance of Hades worship less than 16 kilometers to the east of Elis, and 55 kilometers to the south, the geographer Strabo mentions a temenos dedicated to Hades at Triphylia.[96]

94. UNESCO World Heritage Centre, "Archaeological Site of Elis," accessed January 31, 2023, https://visit worldheritage.com/en/eu/archaeological-site-of-elis/5f1f5051-f0d2-494a-8eed-c46269f483f1.

95. Pausanias, "Description of Greece," in *Complete Works of Pausanias*, trans. W. H. S. Jones (Hastings, East Sussex, UK: Delphi Classics, 2014), 6.25.2.

96. Strabo, *The Geography of Strabo*, trans. H. C. Hamilton and W. Falconer (London: George Bell & Sons, 1903), 8.3.15.

Invitations to Practice

Invoke Hades Adamastos for setting and defending your boundaries, remaining steadfast under pressure, resiliency, strength, and fortitude when pursuing long goals or undergoing extensive growth processes. Symbols and correspondences that resonate with the energy of Hades in this aspect are the bident, aconite, adamant (diamond), and three-headed Kerberos.

Hymn to Hades Adamastos

The following hymn can be spoken or sung to connect with Hades Adamastos. This is a helpful hymn to recite when you need to stand up for yourself, remain steadfast in your convictions, or bolster your determination. Hades' adamantine qualities will come to your aid.

> *Adamant, Unyielding, Resolute—*
> *I sing of Hades the Unconquerable,*
> *Hades Adamastos, the indestructible stronghold,*
> *Khthonic king who is like a priceless gem*
> *Honed by heat and pressure, ruling from his onyx throne.*
> *Lend me your strength and determination,*
> *Adamastos, so that I may uphold my convictions,*
> *That I may honor my commitments,*
> *That I may stand in integrity.*

No Stray Arrows: Energetic Protection Techniques

In ancient Greece, a *temenos* was a grove, cave, grotto, or parcel of land set aside and dedicated to a god. It was considered sacred ground, with all things within its boundaries belonging to that god. Oftentimes the boundary of the temenos was demarcated with stones, a fence, or a wall. Ancient Greeks who sought sanctuary within the confines of the temenos were under the protection of its tutelary god and could not be harmed or moved against their will.

Psychologist Carl Jung (1875–1961) would later equate the concept of the temenos with the magical circle—the energetic boundary line that practitioners of magic cast for protection and containment of rituals and other workings.[97] Similar to sheltering inside a temenos, using a few of these simple energetic protection techniques will help shield you from unwanted or harmful influences.

Circle Casting and Warding

To prepare for a ritual or other magical operations, select a quiet space that allows for clear focus. You should feel safe and comfortable in this space. The space can be indoors or outdoors, but it's best to try to limit distractions. Set up the altar and any supplies you will be using for your activities. Purify yourself and the area with khernips.

When you are ready to begin, start by casting a circle. The purpose of casting a circle is to clearly delineate a physical and ethereal boundary to encapsulate you while engaging in vulnerable spiritual or energetic work. Standing in the center of your space and pointing outward with your right index finger, slowly turn in a clockwise circle to cast an energetic barrier around you, your altar, and any supplies. Leave enough room inside the boundary of the circle for you to move freely and to perform your planned activities. The intention is to create a workspace in which you can concentrate freely and safely.

Once you have turned a full circle, the next step is to place a sign of warding and protection at each of the four cardinal directions (east, south, west, and north), as well as in the center of the circle. Once again, you can draw this sign with your right index finger, empowering it with the intention of protection. The pentagram, or five-pointed star, is a great warding sign for magic and rituals incorporating Greek deities, due to its history of use in the Pythagorean mystery cult. However, feel free to use another sigil or symbol of protection that has meaning for you. Begin in the east and move clockwise around the circle, finishing with the direction of center.

Now you're ready to do the work: your ritual, divination rites, trance journey, spellwork, or other magical operation. Once the working is complete, speak some words of conclusion, such as "It is done." Thank and release your wards in the opposite direction that you set them (center, north, west, south, and finally east). Take down your circle by walking its boundary counterclockwise,

---

97. Carl Gustav Jung, *The Collected Works of C. G. Jung,* vol. 12, *Psychology and Alchemy,* ed. William McGuire, Herbert Read, Michael Fordham, and Gerhard Adler, trans. R. F. C. Hull (Princeton, NJ: Princeton University Press, 1980), 87–113.

opposite of the direction you cast it. You can also sweep the boundary away as you walk, using an actual broom or with a sweeping hand motion.

How to Stay Grounded

Magic and ritual with the gods can be powerful stuff. Afterward, you might feel unusually hyperactive, lightheaded, or like your energy is spinning off into the stratosphere—even if you've been working with khthonic gods. Grounding your energy will help you return to yourself in the moment; committing to a consistent daily or weekly grounding practice can lessen these aftereffects even further.

One of the most common grounding visualization techniques is to imagine yourself as a tree. Close your eyes. Envision your feet becoming roots that anchor you deep into the ground; see your arms and hands reach and stretch as branches touching the sky. Feel into the solidity and strength of your trunk in the midsection of your body. Pause inside this tree visualization until your breath returns to its resting pace and your mind begins to slow. Once you're feeling grounded, slowly imagine pulling your roots back up into your feet, your branches back down into your hands and arms. Open your eyes, blink, and move slowly until you have fully returned from the visualization. Repeat if necessary.

Physical cues are also extremely helpful for grounding. Here's a short list of some of my favorite grounding activities:

- Touching a tree, walking on the earth with bare feet, or lying down in the grass
- Lying down under a heavy blanket or, if not available, covering yourself with a sweater or jacket. In warmer weather, this could be a towel or light sheet.
- Petting an animal, touching an animal pelt, or snuggling a plushie
- Utilizing grounding stones: jet (my personal favorite for grounding), smoky quartz, obsidian, brown or black tourmaline
- Humming to reset your parasympathetic nervous system
- Wrapping your arms around your shoulders or middle for a self-hug
- Eating grounding foods: milk, cheese, nuts, salty foods (such as jerky or potato chips)

Reinforcing Personal Energetic Boundaries

How do you know what's "you" versus "not you"? Finding, rooting into, and reinforcing the boundaries of your personal energy field is key to feeling centered within yourself. Many magical practitioners experience heightened sensitivity and empathy; being centered in yourself allows you to discern and set aside things that do not belong to you (someone else's emotions, ritual residue, etc.). Arming yourself with a list of personal reality checks as part of a self-care protocol can help you sort through the different energetic inputs—those stray arrows—that you may be receiving moment-to-moment. Such self-reflective questions might include the following:

- How do I feel physically in this moment? Am I tired? Do I need a snack or drink of water?
- What is unsettling, annoying, or worrying me?
- Do I recognize these feelings within myself?
- Is something activating my self-preservation instincts? What is it?
- Are my feelings a proportionate response to what is happening right now?
- Where can I lean into expansion and curiosity in this moment?
- What do I need to help me feel centered, safe, and grounded in this moment?

Visualizing an etheric shield can also help reinforce personal energetic boundaries. To engage in this technique, imagine yourself surrounded by a protective shield of energy. This shield can take many forms, depending on the situation and your preferences: a ball of light, a reflective mirrored surface, a thorny rose or blackberry bramble, or a thick steel garage door, for example. Personally, I like to imagine my etheric shield as a dense, infinite pink fog constantly emanating from my energetic field—allowing all my compassion, love, and empathy to flow outward into the world, yet still able to filter out any harmful energies before they can reach me.

Moreover, here are a few easy psychic defense strategies you can add to your daily routine, utilize when on-the-go, or employ anytime you want to feel refreshed and centered:

- Intentionally wash your hands.
- Splash water on your face and neck.
- Brush your hair or dry brush your body.
- Take a 1:1:1 cleansing bath: dissolve equal parts sea salt, baking soda, and Epsom salt (about ¼ cup, of each) into bathwater and soak comfortably for 20–60 minutes.
- Protect the back of your neck—stray energies love to sneak in at this vulnerable spot. You can use a few drops of protective oil or wear a protective necklace, bandana, or scarf.
- Use silk as an energetic insulator. You can veil your head in a silk scarf, drape a piece of silk around your neck, or wear silk underclothes. A great way to ethically source silk is by hunting thrift stores, garage sales, and estate sales. You can wash, purify, and consecrate secondhand silk for your protection after you acquire it. This organic material works wonderfully to insulate the wearer from outside energies.

CHAPTER 6
THE HARROWING JOURNEY

Hades speaks:

A temple dedicated to Apollo sits high upon a sun-drenched hill in the ancient city of Cumae. The sea below sparkles in the sunlight while wildflowers sway and bend in the breeze. The air is scented with salt, sea grass, and poppy flowers. Far down the hillside, beneath the shining terrace of the temple complex, lies a mystery: the dark entrance to the cave of the Cumaean Sibyl.

From deep within this khthonic sanctuary, the Sibyl reaches forward a thousand years, scribing her prophecies on oak leaves. She releases the leaves at the entrance of her cave, to drift and scatter freely on the afternoon wind. Her prophecies swirl and twist in the Mediterranean breeze, rearranging themselves, dancing back and forth like the wandering lines of the meandros. Kings and heroes come here seeking her audience, not only for her powers of prophecy, but because she knows something they do not: how to travel to and from the Underworld.

Mistletoe grows high in the branches of the oak trees surrounding her cave. Its green leaves are camouflaged now, but come winter, the bare branches of the tree will reveal its golden flowers and pearl-like fruits. I wonder, did the plant teach the Sibyl its secrets? For the golden bough is like a key, providing safe passage, unlocking my gates. To reach the golden bough takes patience, skill, and courage—the qualities you will need to traverse my realm. The bough of Aeneas has begun to fade, and I would like another to grace the arched entrance to my halls. Will you bring me one?

Katabasis: The Harrowing Journey

Katabasis is the Greek term for making a trip to the Underworld. This word is usually associated with Greco-Roman mythology, but it is also used in other mythological and spiritual traditions as a general term to describe any journey to the realm of the dead. Katabasis is different from instances of necromantic visitation, wherein one might experience an unbidden vision of the Underworld or its denizens, primarily because katabasis involves an intentional physical (or metaphysical) journey. In previous chapters, I've discussed three examples of katabasis in Greek mythology: Odysseus and his men sailing to the Underworld to consult the seer Tiresias, Orpheus traveling to the Underworld to retrieve Eurydice, and Herakles descending to capture Kerberos.

Why travel to the Underworld? In *Underland: A Deep Time Journey*, author Robert Macfarlane observes: "What these narratives [in mythology and folklore] all suggest is something seemingly paradoxical: that darkness might be a medium of vision, and that descent may be a movement towards revelation rather than deprivation. Our common verb 'to understand' itself bears an old sense of passing beneath something in order fully to comprehend it."[98] In other words, mythology tells us there are boons for those who dare to make the harrowing journey.

When we visit the Underworld in trance journey, we can talk to shades of the dead. We can interact with Hades and his retinue. We can uncover insights, innovations, and paradoxes hidden deep underground, waiting for us in the dark like sparkling gems. We might even get to scratch Kerberos behind the ears—as long as we remember to bring him honey cakes. In an essay entitled *Wrestling with Thanatos*, author Iona Miller states it beautifully: "Our answers come from the heart of life itself and the dance of mortality. In engaging the imaginal [in the Underworld] we are not struggling with ways to become superhuman or immortal but with becoming more fully human in a deeply connected, more-than-human world. It makes living more conscious."[99] As we travel to khthonic depths, katabasis provides us with opportunities to expand our courage, curiosity, and awareness in equal measure.

---

98. Macfarlane, *Underland*, loc. 16, Kindle.

99. Iona Miller, "Wrestling with Thanatos: A Mythological Study," in *Host of Many: Hades and His Retinue*, ed. Terence P. Ward (Orlando, FL: Bibliotheca Alexandria, 2020), 193.

Psychopompós: Guide of Souls

The Greek word *psychopompós* means "guide of souls." The role of the psycho-pomp is not to harvest or judge the deceased, but simply to guide them on the way to their next home—in this context, the Underworld. Kharon, Khthonic Hermes, and Hekate are three notable psychopomps from Greek mythology; if you're planning to engage in regular travel to and from the Underworld, becoming familiar with these guides is a good idea. Each of them brings a unique set of skills and know-how that can assist travelers on their katabasis.

Kharon the Ferryman

Reliable Kharon is the skilled, weathered daimon eternally tasked with ferrying the shades of the dead across the River Styx (or Akheron), onward to the gates of the Underworld. In ancient funerary art, he is depicted with a wild beard, wearing the laborer's attire of a short red tunic called an *exomis* and a conical felt hat called a *pilos*.[100] Kharon's fee for the ferry is one obol—this coin was to be placed in the mouth of a corpse upon burial, so that its shade would be prepared to pay the fee. The ferryman can seem a bit gruff at first, but I've learned to bring him a bit of chocolate, a flower, or a candy to sweeten his mood. As we float across the river, I ask Kharon about his day and if he has any good gossip to share (he usually does).

If I know I am headed to the Underworld in a trance journey, I slip my reusable ferry token in my pocket before leaving my HQ. It was Hades who originally provided me with this reusable token, which happens to take the form of a barn owl feather. You could use a coin, a ring, or any other portable object as a reusable token—but I recommend getting Hades' blessing to use the object for this purpose. If you have an actual physical representation of your token, you can wear it, hold it, or place it near your body while you trance journey. I hand the feather over to Kharon each time I need to cross the river. He holds the token while I am in the Underworld, returning it once he ferries me back across the border.

---

100. Sabouroff Painter, *Terracotta Lekythos (Oil Flask)*, ca. 450 BCE, terracotta, white-ground, Metropolitan Museum of Art, New York, NY, https://www.metmuseum.org/art/collection/search/251043.

Khthonic Hermes

Hermes is the only Olympian to regularly travel back and forth from the Underworld. The trickster god of communication, gambling, thievery, athletics, the marketplace, commerce, and travel, Hermes is a natural extrovert able to adapt to any situation with ease. He is depicted as an athletic young man wearing a winged helmet and sandals and sometimes with a traveler's cloak and purse. Hermes carries a staff called a *caduceus*, featuring a pair of wings and two intertwined serpents. In his khthonic psychopomp aspect, Hermes gathers up the shades of the dead, guiding them to the shores of the River Styx to await transport across the water on Kharon's ferry.

Hermes is also a god of boundaries and liminal spaces. Stone cairns or square pillars called *herms* were used to mark the midway point between villages on ancient roadways, and placed outside homes as symbols of protection, community, and fertility. As a psychopomp, khthonic Hermes straddles the boundary between life and death. Call on swift-footed Hermes if you need a translator, a guide to the borderlands, or a partner for Underworld game night. When not in the realm of the dead, try finding him in the marketplace or at the gym.

Hekate

Hekate is a fearsome and ancient Titaness who sided with Hades and his siblings in the Titanomachy. Although she traverses many realms, Hekate still spends a good portion of her time in the Underworld. A venerable goddess in her own right, Hekate has an impressively broad purview, including magic, witchcraft, ghosts, the moon, and the night, but it is within her role as Underworld torchbearer and guide that she joins the ranks of the psychopomps. Ancient art depicts Hekate wearing saffron robes, carrying a torch in each hand, accompanied by a black she-dog.

It is Hekate who guides the Dread Queen Persephone to and from the Underworld each year. Hekate knows all the secret passageways in and out, shortcuts, scenic routes, and locals-only hidden gems and hideouts in the realm of the dead. Find yourself in need of directions? Hekate is your Underworld GPS. With her sacred torches, lantern, or flashlight in hand, she will help illuminate your path. As the Lady of the Ways, Hekate can usually be found at a triple crossroads.

Best Practices for Traveling to and from the Underworld

You can always ask Hades, Persephone, or any of the other denizens of the realm to meet you somewhere else in the Otherworld (although there is no guarantee that they will do so). However, I find that I learn much more about someone when I visit their home. What kind of decor do they like? What books are on their shelves? Does their home have a particular smell? What is the general feeling of their environment? Visiting someone's home can provide more context and insight into their character, but katabasis is not metaphysical tourism. If you want to journey to the Underworld successfully and often, it's a process of building relationships and rapport. Taking the time to be a good guest, one who follows established protocols and etiquette and comes bearing considerate gifts for their host, is a sign of goodwill and respect. Here are some guidelines to help you develop a skillful katabasis practice.

Preparing for Your Trip

Allow enough time and space for preparation, trance journeying, and fully returning to yourself—abruptly switching from the Otherworld to the ordinary world can be jarring, especially after returning from khthonic depths. Prepare water and a grounding snack before you journey so that sustenance is close at hand when you return. Anticipate that you may return in a slightly open, vulnerable state, more sensitive to (or less tolerant of) people and outside energies than usual. This is completely normal. Grant yourself the time you need to get centered and find your edges again.

If you're feeling stressed out, ill, or overwhelmed, it's probably not a beneficial time to engage in katabasis. Check in with yourself before you journey. Just before traveling to the Underworld, I like to journal a quick paragraph or two or make a bullet point list to formulate my intention and make sure my focus is clear. There is no rush—you can always make the journey another day.

Practicing Safely

When you are ready, begin with the basics. Whether or not your katabasis is part of a ritual, it is a best practice to cast a circle around yourself, setting wards of protection in each of the cardinal directions, including the center.

If you trance journey often, you may want to enliven or enchant a set of physical wards that you can partner with for these workings. For example, I have a set of five selenite crystals that are wards for all my rituals and various other magical operations. If I ever need to amplify their warding abilities, I also have five clear quartz crystals that pair with the selenite crystals for a power boost. I have developed a protocol for waking them so that they know it is time to work, as well as a protocol for releasing them back to a state of rest. I keep them stashed in a silk sleeping bag (drawstring pouch) when they are not in use.

Use the Buddy System

Just like in primary school, remember that you can always use the buddy system. Otherworldly guides can be good allies for exploring unfamiliar territory. During katabasis, they can help you make safer choices, reinforce your boundaries, and provide companionship. They might even help you process information by interpreting signs and symbols.

You may find it helpful to have a guide to show you the way from your HQ to the banks of the River Styx, for example, and wait there for your return. Moreover, you could ask for a psychopomp or denizen of the Underworld to guide and accompany you within its borders; in this case, they might meet you as you step off Kharon's ferry.

Eating and Drinking

This is a very common, important, and somewhat controversial question: Should you eat or drink anything while in the Underworld? Hades or other denizens may offer you something to eat or drink during your katabasis—after all, hospitality is firmly ingrained in the culture of the Underworld. Mythologically speaking, the answer is no: Persephone's experience tells us that eating the food of the Underworld has the potential to irrevocably bind you to the land of the dead. However, from my own experiments with katabasis, I will simply advise you to use caution. Let me explain.

When I first started traveling to and from the Underworld, I was quite wary of eating anything. At that time, I would ask one of my trusted spirit guides to help me pack a safe snack bag at my HQ, which I then took along on my journey to the Underworld. Thus prepared, I was able to enjoy feasting with Hades and his retinue without actually having to eat anything harvested in the realm of the dead. I even shared my snacks with them, which they found delightful! After some time, however, I became a little more comfortable and began trying some of the food that was offered to me.

You might find it beneficial, depending on the type of ritual or magical working you are doing, to ingest something that is offered to you in the Underworld. Before eating, ask your guide(s) for their opinions. Perhaps try politely refusing the first few times, and notice if or when the offering is extended again; this may be a clue to its value and meaning for you. I have never seen any of the denizens of the Underworld become angry or offended by a polite, respectful refusal. To this day, I have never been offered pomegranate—and I am not sure I would accept it, should the opportunity present itself.

I will also share with you that I do not drink any water during katabasis. At this time in my practice, when presented with a vessel of water in the Underworld, I don't have a good method for identifying exactly which source (i.e., river or pool) it comes from. I'm not willing to take a chance on losing my memories (Lethe) or returning with a terrible case of heartburn (Phlegethon). This is an example of how waking-world common sense and street smarts can serve you well in the Underworld, too—I liken it to the very good advice of never accepting a drink at a party or bar that you haven't seen made with your own eyes.

You are your own spiritual authority. You are the best person to make the decision whether or not you will eat or drink anything in the Underworld. Just remember that choices made during trance journey can ripple outward, affecting your life in the waking world, too. Choose your adventures wisely.

Gifts and Offerings for Your Hosts

In Virgil's *Aeneid*, the Cumaean Sibyl advises Aeneas that he must collect the "bough with leafage and pliant shoot all of gold" that grows nearby before he can enter the Underworld. The golden bough is a gift for Persephone: "But to him only who first hath plucked the golden-tressed fruitage from the tree is it given to enter the hidden places of the earth. This hath beautiful Proserpine [Persephone] ordained to be borne to her for her proper gift."[101] When shown to Kharon, the golden bough grants the pair passage on his ferryboat across the River Styx. Upon reaching the Halls of Hades, Aeneas places the bough above

---

101. Virgil, *The Aeneid of Virgil*, trans. J. W. Mackail (London: Macmillan and Co., 1885; Project Gutenberg, 2007), 6.124–57.

the arched doorway. What can we learn from this anecdote? That it's polite protocol to bring a gift for your host(s), similar to when attending a house party or other type of get-together.

During katabasis, you will receive many gifts: insight, advice, energetic healing, and friendships or mentorships are just a few possible examples. While the gods may greatly appreciate your daring spirit, they also speak the language of reciprocity. Are there gifts you can gather at your HQ to bring to the Underworld? Is there a song you'd like to sing to them or a joke or story you'd like to share? Your guide(s) may have some ideas, too. Once you've made your first trip, you can ask Hades, Persephone, and any other denizens you meet what they might like you to bring next time.

Hades (or someone else) may ask you to make a specific offering or complete a certain task—on the metaphysical plane or once you return to the waking world—that you are not entirely sure about. It is up to you whether or not you agree to the request. It is completely and absolutely acceptable to courteously refuse any request you are not comfortable with, even if it is a deity doing the asking. You can negotiate with them to clarify or modify their request, suggest an alternative, or respectfully decline.

Returning

As with all trance journeys, remember to return in reverse of the way you traveled, fully crossing over the border of the Underworld (and back to your HQ, if that's where you started out) before letting your consciousness drift back to its waking state. Crossing the border—whether it is the River Styx or some other threshold or boundary line—is a very important cue for your subconscious mind. It clearly delineates that you started out here, then visited there, and now you are back here again. If you feel discombobulated upon your return, consider these:

- Sprinkle yourself with khernips, rue-infused water, or fresh spring water.
- Try some activities to calm your parasympathetic nervous system: deep breathing, humming, singing, snuggling under weighted blankets or coverings, physical exercise (like walking or dancing), eating, and enjoying social cues of safety (such as hugs and laughter).

- Engage in self-reflection: refer to your list of reality-check questions (from chapter 5) to discern what's you versus not you in this moment.
- If you should ever find yourself in serious mental or emotional distress after a trance journey, please seek professional psychological help. It's not a common occurrence, but traumatic events experienced on the metaphysical plane are still trauma and should always be taken seriously.

Stowaways

What happens if you return with an energetic stowaway? Again, this is not a very common experience in katabasis, but it can occur. If you feel unsafe, unusually depressed, emotionally disconnected, lonely, or drained, or if you have a lingering sense of scarcity or lack, you may have returned with a greedy, uninvited guest. There are precautions you can take to prevent this from happening:

- When your energetic field is already well-tended and healthy, it is extremely difficult for anything else to stick to you. Engage in daily grounding and centering practices as routine self-care. If daily practice is too much at first, try for an initial goal of two to three times each week.
- Be sure to cast a boundary circle and set wards before entering the trance state.
- Remember that you can deploy psychic shielding techniques in the Otherworld, too.
- Ask your guide(s) to give you an energetic touch-up at your HQ. Your guide can sweep your energetic field for any psychic gunk, gently cleansing and refreshing it for you before your return.

If you do suspect an uninvited entity is sucking your energy or emotions, here are some suggestions for sending the intruder packing:

- Open all the windows and doors in your home. Ring a loud bell, clatter pots and pans together, or make some other extremely loud, obnoxious cacophony of sound while speaking strong words to banish the entity. Move the sound around your body, passing through your energetic field several times, and throughout all the areas of your home (including stairways, attics, fireplaces, basements, garages, cabinets, and closets if you have them). If your home has more than one level, begin at the top and work your way down. Once you have completed these actions, and the noise has faded, revisit each area with khernips to purify it and reset the energy.

- Get naked outdoors: skinny dip in fresh, freely flowing creek, stream, river, or ocean water.

- Take a 1:1:1 cleansing bath as described on page 102. Oftentimes this combination alone does the trick—but if you find yourself needing extra cleansing power, try adding a few pinches of dried rosemary or bay laurel leaves to your bath. Dried rue works really well for this, too, but be aware that some people have skin sensitivity to rue. Be sure to dunk your head and fully immerse each part of your body. Step completely out of the tub before you drain the water.

- Ask a brown or black tourmaline to partner with you to remove the entity. For this magical operation, you'll need a small dish of salt water and the crystal. Sit holding the stone in your hands, or lie down placing the stone on your chest. Relax. Imagine the stone sucking every impurity out of your energetic field. Once the tourmaline feels "full," place it in the dish of salt water. Visualize the tourmaline transferring anything it has collected into the salt water, neutralizing it. Once this feels complete, take the dish outside to dispose of the salt water on the earth or by pouring it into moving water. Thank the tourmaline and give your stone friend a little rinse under cold running water before putting them away.

- Reach out to a trusted friend, mentor, or spiritual practitioner for support. You might just need to speak your feelings aloud to neutralize negativity. If you feel you are out of your depth, a vetted spiritual or magical practitioner (such as a Reiki master, Pagan priest/ess/x, rootworker, etc.) can help you diagnose the problem and clear your energetic field.

You may also experience vivid dreams upon your return, which could be related to your katabasis. It can be helpful to keep paper and a pen at your bedside in case you need to jot something down in the middle of the night. Expect insights, signs, and symbols collected on your journey to continue unfolding and revealing more about their meanings in the days, weeks, and maybe even months, to come.

Memento Vivere: Remember to Live

In the days immediately following your katabasis, do something enjoyable and life-affirming. Eat your favorite foods, wear your favorite clothes, play with children or animals, engage in fun physical activities. Stroll through a marketplace. Watch a comedy. Drink lots of water. Smile. Many people have heard of the Latin phrase *memento mori*—"remember you must die"—but they are not aware that it is only the first part of the saying. The full saying is *memento mori, memento vivere*: "remember you must die, so remember to live."

Exploring the Lore

Have you tried a few trance journeys and thought to yourself, "Am I just making all of this up? How do I know that any of this is a real experience?" If so, you are not alone. Many magical practitioners go through a phase, usually near the beginning of their studies, when they train themselves to intentionally suspend their disbelief in experiences, influences, and outcomes outside of ordinary reality, and simply focus on being present in the trance journey as it unfolds.

In "Mundis Originalis, or the Imaginary and the Imaginal," philosopher Henry Corbin describes the existential phenomenon that occurs when disbelief is suspended: "Strange as it may seem, once the journey is completed, the reality which has hitherto been an inner and hidden one turns out to envelop, surround, or contain that which at first was outer and visible.... Spiritual reality envelops, surrounds, contains so-called material reality."[102] When it comes right down to it, reality is subjective. Unlike facts, which can be established through empirical evidence, reality can only be established through existential evidence. Every individual experiences a different version of reality. Whether or not the information you are receiving in trance journey is useful or productive and enhances your life and understanding is a far more relevant concern than proving your experiences in the Otherworld are real.

It is important to record any information, observations, lessons, and questions you may have each time you trance journey; this practice will aid you in the effort to suspend disbelief. You can do this by describing your trances longhand in your journal, recording yourself recounting the journey, capturing

---

102. Henry Corbin, "Mundis Originalis, or the Imaginary and the Imaginal," trans. Ruth Horine, *Colloquium on Symbolism* 6 (1946): 4, http://www.bahaistudies.net/asma/mundus_imaginalis.pdf.

a bulleted list of the highlights, or sketching images and impressions. Choose the technique that best supports your efforts to track your experiences. As you record your observances, avoid passing judgment on their validity. At some point, you will receive a surprising snippet of information in trance journey—something unique and noteworthy that your conscious mind would be unlikely to have encountered in your day-to-day life—like a word that is unfamiliar to you, or a symbol you've never seen before. This is your first clue that the information is meaningful—and quite possibly coming from a source outside yourself. Synchronicities between ordinary reality and experiences in trance journey are another clue: events or details that are significantly related to one another but that have no causal connection. A third clue is commonality of experience, such as when you chat about your trance journeys with other practitioners and are amazed to find that they have come across information and experiences similar to your own.

With each katabasis, the journey becomes easier. Like a muscle memory that allows you to dial a phone number without thought, over time, the path from your HQ to the Underworld will become more ingrained, more instinctual. Trust your gut and have faith that you are your own best spiritual authority.

Symbols of Hades: The Meandros

Often referred to as the Greek key or Greek fret pattern, the *meandros* is a stylized pattern of continuous, interlocking spirals used to decorate the border of anything from clothing to jewelry, pottery, mosaics, and more. The popularity of this ancient motif persists even today.

Meandros in Linear and Circular Forms

The Greek word *meandros* is related to the modern English word *meander*, meaning "to wander." It resembles a labyrinth in linear form. Although not specifically linked to Hades or the Underworld, the meandros is thought by some to represent the unending spiral of life—and possibly the wandering, or transmigration, of the soul.

In my own practice, the meandros reminds me that my understanding of Hades and the Underworld grows with each katabasis. And as I ride the twists and turns of each year, through the spiral of the seasons, the winding path of the meandros also helps me remember that although I may find myself revisiting some of the same themes again and again, I have gained more cognizance, compassion, and agency along the way.

In His Dark Garden: Mistletoe and Rue

Mistletoe and rue are two solar-aligned plants that make great traveling partners for katabasis. Precious mistletoe captures the bright energy of the sun, humming with the vibrancy of life from its home high in the treetops—a fitting gift for a queen who travels between two worlds. Bitter, beautiful rue is a powerful protector against unwanted energies as well as a potent ally for strengthening the third eye.

MISTLETOE

Species: *Viscum album*

Other Common Names: Birdlime, golden bough, herbe de la croix, kissing bough, mystyldene

Toxicity: Somewhat toxic—use caution. Consult a professional herbalist before ingesting, and always keep mistletoe out of reach of children and pets. Ingesting mistletoe is contraindicated for pregnant people.

Keywords: Fertility, fidelity, higher knowledge, safe passage

Mistletoe is an evergreen, hemiparasitic plant that attaches itself to trees, receiving part of its nutrients from photosynthesis and part from its host. Mistletoe leaves sometimes turn from green to grayish-yellow in the winter months. Honey-gold mistletoe flowers also bloom in the winter, being eventually replaced by white berries. During this time, mistletoe can be clearly spotted high in the bare branches of the host trees it inhabits—this is likely why the plant was dubbed "the golden bough." Aeneas, mythological ancestor of the Romans and protagonist of Virgil's *Aeneid,* brings a golden bough with him on his journey to the Underworld to seek the counsel of his deceased father. According to Pliny the Elder, mistletoe was also very sacred to the ancient Druids. It was allegedly prized as a source of fertility and inspiration associated with the winter solstice: "The Druids—for that is the name [the Gauls] give to their magicians—held nothing more sacred than the mistletoe and the tree that bears it.... It is the belief with them that the mistletoe, taken in drink, will impart fecundity to all animals that are barren, and that it is an antidote for all poisons."[103] To this day, we still pause to kiss under the mistletoe in December, echoing the traditions of those who preceded us.

The golden bough is difficult to harvest, which contributes to its value as an offering or gift; indeed, the advice of the Cumaean Sibyl teaches us that this plant is a precious, fitting gift for the Dread Queen Persephone. In trance journey, you may want to experiment with ways of partnering with mistletoe for the purposes of gifting and safe passage. If working with the spiritus viridis of mistletoe resonates with you, try adding the leaves and berries to your altar, using their scent as a trance induction cue, or including them in a small pouch to wear during your journeys.

RUE

Species: *Ruta graveolens*

Other Common Names: Ruta, herb-of-grace, herbygrass, mother-of-herbs, witchbane

Toxicity: Rue is generally safe if consumed in small amounts as an herb to flavor food. However, it can interfere with liver function if consumed in large amounts. Ingesting rue is contraindicated for pregnant people. Some people have skin sensitivity to the plant's oils (causing contact dermatitis and/or photosensitive blisters), so a small patch test is recommended if you plan to use rue in a bath or asperge.

Keywords: Protection, purification, second sight

Rue is an evergreen herb native to southeastern Europe, with fuzzy, silverish stalks and leaves, and four-petaled yellow flowers. Records stretching back to the early modern period describe bunches of dried rue hung in doorways and win-

---

103. Pliny the Elder, *The Natural History,* 16.95.

dows to repel pests, plagues, and the evil eye. This custom was especially prevalent in southern Europe and the Mediterranean. Beginning sometime around the eighteenth century, Italians crafted protective amulets called *cimaruta* from tin or silver to resemble the tops of rue. Each metal branch was adorned with a symbol of fertility or good luck. Phalli, horns, solar disks, crescent moons, fish, hearts, and keys were popular choices.

As a folk remedy, rue has a reputation for healing and supporting eyesight. Renaissance painters purportedly ate sandwiches of watercress and rue to boost their ability to see colors. A single rue leaf could be placed on the forehead to cure a headache caused by poor eyesight. Because of this association with the eyes, as well as the mind's eye (third eye), rue is considered a magical ally in developing the psychic "second sight."[104]

Rue's reputation for protection and purification persisted through the centuries, making its way across the Atlantic Ocean, showing up again in the folk magic practices of settlers in the Appalachian and Ozark regions of North America. Rue water is used in a similar manner to khernips for purifying people and animals. It can be prepared in large batches and used as a floor wash to protect a home or other structure. Rue is a somewhat bitter herb, and from my own gnosis, I think this may be part of the reason why it makes such a good spiritual repellent. To put it simply, rue tastes bad. Here's a simple recipe for making your own rue-infused water.

RUE WATER
- 1 gallon spring water, filtered tap water, or fresh rainwater if you have the means to capture it
- 1 cup fresh rue leaves or ½ cup dried leaves
- Large glass or stainless steel container for brewing
- Cheesecloth
- Rubber band or cook's twine
- Large glass jar, or several small glass jars, with lids for storage

Pour water into the container you are using for brewing. Add fresh or dry leaves, covering the top of the container with cheesecloth. Use a rubber band or cook's twine to secure the cheesecloth tightly—you will be draining the water through

---

104. Pearson, *Flower Essences from the Witch's Garden*, 412.

this cloth later, so you don't want it to slip off. Take the container outside to infuse in the sunlight, similar to brewing sun tea. Leave the container in bright, direct sunlight for 3 hours, preferably during the time the sun is highest in the sky. The bright, fiery energy of the sun complements and boosts the protective nature of this herb. After brewing, drain the rue-infused water into a large jar or several small jars, capping tightly with the lid(s). Store the jar(s) in a refrigerator for up to 1 week, until you are ready to use the water.

Khthonic Bestiary: Cakes for Kerberos

In Virgil's *Aeneid*, the Cumaean Sibyl is guiding Aeneas to the Underworld when they encounter Kerberos at the gates. Prepared for this obstacle, she "throws a cake made slumberous with honey and drugged grain."[105] Kerberos gobbles up the sweet loaf and falls asleep, allowing Aeneas to sneak past and enter Hades' realm. Another mention of honeyed cakes occurs in the bawdy mythological work *The Golden Asse*, written by the philosopher and rhetorician Lucius Apuleius in the second century CE. In Apuleius' work, we encounter the story of Cupid and Psyche, in which Psyche is given a series of quests to complete—some of which require her to travel to the Underworld. In preparation for her katabasis, Psyche is advised to take two coins for Kharon (so that she can make a return trip back across the Styx), as well as barley cake sops (bread or cake drenched in milk) to distract Kerberos.[106]

Food blogger and YouTube content creator Just a Fat Boi has researched historical recipes for this over two-thousand-year-old baked treat.[107] They have identified two ancient recipes that might make loaves or cakes similar to those mentioned in mythology: *maza* and *aliter dulcia*. From descriptions in the lore, we know that the honey cakes in the story of Cupid and Psyche are made with barley. Barley was considered a less desirable type of grain in ancient Greece and Rome; the rich who could afford wheat preferred it over barley for its glutenous texture and lighter color. *Maza*, cakes made with barley, were a staple

105. Virgil, *The Aeneid of Virgil*, trans. J. W. Mackail (London: Macmillan and Co., 1885; Project Gutenberg, 2007), 6.404–437.

106. Lucius Apuleius, *The Golden Asse*, trans. William Adlington (London: Thomas Harper, 1639; Project Gutenberg, 2022), 6:16–20.

107. Just a Fat Boi, "Cerberus's Honey Cakes: 2000 Year Old Recipe, Myth and History," Just a Fat Boi, accessed January 14, 2023, https://justafatboi.com/cerberuss-honey-cakes/.

food for everyday Athenians. Just a Fat Boi bases their maza recipe on a description of barley cakes in a seventh-century medical encyclopedia written by the Byzantine Greek physician Paulus Aegineta.

Just a Fat Boi also suggests that the ancient Roman recipe for an unnamed *aliter dulcia*, which translates to "another dessert," could be similar to those used to make the cakes mentioned in mythology. They have adapted a recipe found in *Apicius*, one of the Western world's oldest surviving cookbooks, for baking this dessert in the modern kitchen. Rue was commonly used in ancient versions of the recipe, but Just a Fat Boi suggests rosemary for the modern palate. Almonds and hazelnuts were also incorporated into the dough to create a delectable honeyed yeast cake.

Maza (Honeyed Barley Cakes)

- 1 cup barley
- ½ cup water
- 3 tablespoons honey
- 2 tablespoons olive oil

Toast the barley until lightly browned. Toasting the barley before milling it gives the finished cakes a bit more flavor and depth. Once toasted, blend or mill the barley into a fine flour. Mix the flour with remaining ingredients until the consistency is workable. Transfer the mixture to a refrigerator and chill for 30 minutes. Once chilled and dry, shape the dough into 6 rounds using your hands or a cookie cutter. Bake for 15 minutes in a preheated oven at 350 degrees Fahrenheit (180°C).

"Aliter Dulcia" (Ancient Roman Honey Cakes)

- 1 teaspoon cinnamon
- ¼ cup chopped almonds
- ¼ teaspoon ground rosemary
- 1 cup spelt flour (white flour can be substituted for spelt)
- ¾ teaspoon instant dried yeast or 1 teaspoon baking powder
- 2 tablespoons sweet raisin wine such as Passum, Passito, or Vin de Paille
- 1 egg
- 2 tablespoons honey, plus an extra ½ tablespoon if using yeast, and more for garnishing

- 6 tablespoons milk
- Chopped hazelnuts or filberts, as desired

Preheat your oven to 350 degrees Fahrenheit (180°C). Combine the dry ingredients (cinnamon, chopped almonds, rosemary, yeast or baking powder, and flour) in a mixing bowl. Combine the wet ingredients (sweet wine, egg, honey, and milk) in a second mixing bowl. Gently fold the wet ingredients into the dry mixture, taking care not to overwork the dough, or gluten will start to form. Let the dough rise at room temperature for 10 minutes. Once it has risen, place the dough into a well-oiled cake pan or muffin tin. Bake for 30 minutes. Once cool, garnish the cakes by drizzling honey and sprinkling the chopped hazelnuts on top. This recipe yields 6 muffin-size portions.

Finding Hades in the Landscape: Antro della Sibilla

The Antro della Sibilla, or Cave of the Sibyl, is part of the Parco Archeologico di Cuma located near the town of Cuma, Italy. The Sibyls of the ancient world were always linked to a particular place—famously described in Virgil's *Aeneid*, it was the Cumaean Sibyl who guided Aeneas to the Underworld. According to tradition, the Cumaean Sibyl would sing her prophecies or transcribe them onto oak leaves, which she left at the mouth of her cave. If the prophecies were scattered by the wind, she would not help reconstruct them. The Cumaean Sibyl also appears in the works of Ovid, on the ceiling of the Sistine Chapel (painted by Michelangelo), in Dante's *Inferno*, and in the poetry of T. S. Eliot.

The Antro della Sibilla at the Parco Archeologico di Cuma cave was uncovered in 1932 by the archaeologist Amedeo Maiuri, who also excavated Pompeii and Herculaneum for many years. Experts now think the cave passage, with its many entrances, side galleries, and cisterns, was likely later in origin than the events of the *Aeneid*, cut into the rock around the sixth century BCE.[108] However, a plaque by the entrance to the Antro della Sibilla still labels it as the cave of Virgil's Cumaean Sibyl. On the cliff above the cave are the ruins of a temple dedicated to Apollo, with a stunning view of the Bay of Naples.

---

108. Annetta Black, "Cave of the Sibyl—Antro Della Sibilla," Atlas Obscura, December 31, 2009, https://www.atlasobscura.com/places/cave-of-the-sibyl-antro-della-sibilla.

Invitations to Practice

Invoke any of the psychopomps for journeying to the Underworld: Kharon, for safe passage over the River Styx; Khthonic Hermes, for clear communication, borderland guidance, and travel protection; and Hekate, to light your way in darkness and to provide orientation or directions when you feel lost. Correspondences and offerings that resonate with katabasis are the meandros, mistletoe, rue, and cakes for Kerberos.

Hymn to Kharon

The following hymn can be spoken or sung to connect with Kharon. This is a helpful hymn to recite just before trance journeying because it offers praise and adoration to the daimon who will safely convey you across the watery boundary of the Styx, to and from the Underworld. If you prefer, you can memorize this hymn and recite it to him in person when you meet in trance journey.

> *Skillful Kharon, ferryman of the River Styx,*
> *Are your arms tired? Do you grow weary of your task?*
> *Take heart, Kharon, for I sing praises to thee!*
> *Deft navigator of currents, rapids, rocks, and eddies,*
> *Ensuring safe passage, once the obol has been paid.*
> *Stay fast to your duty, dear Kharon!*
> *With calloused hands and the taste of the river on your tongue,*
> *For all mortals must reach the other side*
> *And your skill is our succor.*

Trance Journey: Katabasis

This guided trance journey is a katabasis. You can read through the text before you journey, and let your memory of it guide your experience in the Otherworld. Alternatively, you can record yourself reading the text aloud (on your phone, for example) and play it back as you journey. To begin, ease into your preferred method for inducing the trance journey state and land at your Otherworld HQ.

> *It is late afternoon when you arrive at your headquarters. Take a few deep breaths. Notice what the air is like today. Also notice that there is a small satchel or bag here and three items placed near it, awaiting your arrival. The*

*first item is a bowl of fruit—fresh, ripe, delicious. You select four or five pieces
of fruit and place them in the satchel. The second item is an envelope. Breaking the seal, you find a note and a token object inside. The note reads, "Good
for one round trip to and from the Underworld." You slip the note and the
token back into the envelope, and then place it in your satchel with the fruit.
The third item is a bouquet of flowers and herbs, tied with a silky black ribbon. Lift them to your nose, inhale their scent. Take note of the plants in the
bouquet—can you identify them, either visually or just by "knowing"? Place
the bouquet in your satchel. Take a moment to make any other preparations
you'd like, and when you are ready, slip the satchel over your shoulder and
cross the threshold of your HQ.*

*The sun is setting in the west. You head toward the sunset, taking note of
your surroundings as the light continues to wane. The beautiful, liminal color
and quality of sunset twilight descends just as you reach a river and a quiet
wooden dock. A figure in a boat drifts toward you. As the boat meets the dock,
you realize this figure is Kharon, the ferryman of the River Styx. Introduce
yourself and hand Kharon the envelope from your satchel. Wait patiently as
he reads the note and pockets the token. At his nod, climb into the boat.*

*The trip across the river is smooth. The surface of the water reflects
the twilight sky. Below the surface, its waters are murky and inscrutable. If
you listen closely, you can hear the faintest wisp of sound coming from the
water—voices, speaking in many different languages, making promises. The
boat glides across the water to the far riverbank, where you disembark from
the ferry onto another simple wooden dock. Thank Kharon and offer him one
of the pieces of fruit from your bag.*

*Before you is a triple crossroads. The road to the left leads upstream, to
what appears to be the gateway to the Underworld. Many shades are gathered
there, on both sides of the river. You spot Hermes arriving with a few more
shades, dropping them off at the border. The road to the right leads to a large
structure. It's hard to make out any details from your vantage point, but it has
the look of a castle or mansion—it must be the Halls of Hades. In the road
just before you, the center road, another figure is waiting. Note the details of
this figure's appearance. What are they wearing? How old do they appear to
be? What is your general impression of their energy? If it feels right, introduce*

yourself and ask this figure to accompany you as a guide while you explore the Underworld.

You follow the middle path up and over a hill. From the top of this hill, you can see rolling green grass, flowers, and fruit trees. You can smell honey and hear laughter. These are the Elysian Fields, a place filled with beauty and peace. Sit on the hillside and observe your surroundings. If a guide is with you, offer them a piece of fruit from your satchel and enjoy one yourself. As you sit in quiet contemplation, your Host approaches.

Hades climbs the hill to sit next to you. Greeting him, you offer him the fourth piece of fruit from your bag. He accepts and clearly enjoys tasting the offering you have brought. He invites you to visit his halls. Gather your things and follow Hades down the hillside.

On your way, before reaching the Halls, you pass through the Asphodel Fields. This place feels different from the last—more transitory, less colorful. It is not a frightening place, but it definitely gives you the feeling of being some-where "in between." Keep following your host, noting your route and sur-roundings, until you reach the Halls of Hades.

Inside the halls you are guided to a room containing a large table, long enough to seat at least thirty or so guests, walls lined with shelves of books bound in leather, and an enormous stone fireplace. There is a bright, roaring fire. Hades offers you a chair near the warmth of the fireplace. He turns to the shelves, pulls a book, and takes a seat next to you. "There is something I have marked to show you," he says, handing the book to you.

You run your fingers over its cover, noting its color, aspect, and the feel of the leather. Perhaps you even lift the book to your nose to take in its scent. There is a ribbon marking a specific page of the book. You open it to that page. Note what you see there. Is there text on the page? Pictures or illustrations? Symbols? Once you've absorbed the contents of the page, hand the book back to Hades. Thank him and present him with the bouquet that you brought as a gift.

Sit in companionship by the fire as long as feels right. When you are ready to take your leave, thank Hades one last time. If you'd like to ask him to give you a reusable token for visiting the Underworld, you can do that now. He may hand you an object as you depart, or it may appear later at your HQ.

Travel back to the wooden boat dock via the same route. Head back through the Asphodel Fields, over the sunny hillside in the Elysian Fields, down the middle path to the riverside. If you've been traveling with a guide, thank them for accompanying you. Kharon is waiting for you at the dock, and once more, he smoothly and efficiently ferries you back across the River Styx. Express your gratitude and head east to your HQ. Stash your trusty satchel at your headquarters and prepare to return to the waking world.

CHAPTER 7
SHADOW
AND DESIRE

Hades speaks:

Mortals assume I know nothing of the stars. Tonight there is a full moon, an eclipsed full moon, in the constellation of Scorpio. I have traveled to the far edges of the Underworld, to the domain of Erebos, to watch the shadow of Earth fall across the moon.

Erebos is everywhere. He is the darkness that envelops, the space between stars and atoms, the darkness that fills all the hollow places of the earth. As I approach, he is caught up in an embrace with his lover, Nyx, the goddess of night. I avert my eyes as he adjusts the opaque cloak on her shoulders, kissing her deeply. "Hello Hades," he laughs, and I am caught. An unintentional voyeur. Nyx waves to me, departing to trail her cloak of night across the sky.

During an eclipse, Earth is an obstacle. Shadows can only be seen by illuminating obstacles. Too often, I see mortals try desperately to remove any and all obstacles from their lives. What I wish they would understand is that sometimes it is not the obstacle that needs to be removed but their resistance to the obstacle. Obstacles create tension. Some obstacles can be a beneficial kind of tension, with the power to reveal hidden passions, desires, gifts, and yearnings—through revealing the forms and shapes of their shadows.

Wanting is essential. Desire is essential. As the astronomers teach, for small creatures such as us, the vastness of the universe is bearable only through love. How can we claim to understand love if we perceive nothing of its shadow? I watch as the moon darkens and turns red, eclipsed by Earth's shadow, glowing like fire. Earth is too big to comprehend from my perspective, and yet, I can know the shape of her. She is round. I know because I see her shadow.

Paradox and the Underworld

The Underworld is a place of paradox. In the Underworld, the sacred and the profane intermingle, and the lines between them become blurred. Death and decay are not despised in this realm; here they are acknowledged and treated with respect. Souls are given a safe place to rest between lifetimes. Paradoxically, death becomes regenerative. Decay leads to growth. Paradox is the creative opposite of contradiction, as Jungian analyst Robert Johnson observes: "Contradiction is barren and destructive, yet paradox is creative. It is a powerful embracing of all reality.... While contradiction is static and unproductive, paradox makes room for grace and mystery."[109] To embrace paradox is to open yourself up to the idea that multiple, and even competing truths, can exist at the same time.

Hades himself is paradoxical, too, being simultaneously the intimidating Ruler of the Dead and the wealthy, gracious provider of the rich soil that ensures a bountiful harvest. Hades is a notorious kidnapper, and by all reports, he's also a dedicated, loving husband. The Host of Many is no stranger to heartache, fear, or difficulty; just like us, Hades has both benevolent traits and shadow aspects in his personality. Our *shadow* is that part of ourselves of which we may not be consciously aware, and it can comprise many things. Sometimes there are aspects of ourselves that are too painful to recognize, so we keep them deeply buried, locked tight and hidden in shadow. In other instances, our shadow may hold the mirror opposite of our most benevolent outer traits: for example, someone who is wonderfully giving and generous on the outside may secretly struggle with intense jealousy. Exceptionally creative and generative parts of our personality may be relegated to shadow, too, if they do not easily fit into the mold cast by the dominant culture. Have you ever held back a unique opinion, gift, or talent because you were afraid of being "too much" or "too big" for some people? Have you ever suppressed a genuine, heartfelt desire because you felt it would be judged as harmful or unacceptable to others? You may have unintentionally consigned these powerful gifts and longings to your shadow.

---

109. Robert A. Johnson, *Owning Your Own Shadow: Understanding the Dark Side of the Psyche* (New York: HarperCollins, 1991), 75.

Facing your shadow can be difficult, especially if you have a tendency to judge and evaluate parts of yourself as either acceptable or unacceptable, or label them as good or bad. Learning to embrace paradox, however, allows space for your whole self to exist, including the shadowy aspects. Due to their own paradoxical natures, Hades and the denizens of the Underworld are uniquely suited to help us more skillfully encounter, understand, and work with the paradoxes within ourselves.

Desire, Darkness, and Shadow

Something I've observed over and over in public rituals and trance possession work with Hades is that the king of the dead is attractive—and I don't mean just his physical appearance. Hades' energy is mysterious and alluring. He's not domineering, yet his presence tends to take over any room that he enters. People queue up to speak with him. They whisper their secret queries and lay bare their most painful, hidden wounds. He listens intently and has a wonderfully blunt, ironic sense of humor. He may sometimes comfort or advise petitioners, but a question he often asks them is "What do you desire?"

This is another one of the great paradoxes of the Ruler of the Dead: he is insatiably curious about what makes us feel truly alive. Hades is virile in a way that seems antithetical to being a death god, and he has a deep understanding that desire is a vital, essential component of who we are as humans. Recognizing what we truly want, and sharing it with other people, is an incredibly vulnerable act. Our desire to express our authentic self can sometimes seem like it is in direct competition with our desire for acceptance and love, so we relegate it to shadow. We ignore or downplay our deepest longings out of fear that they will harm us or others; rejection hurts, so we opt for safety instead. If you choose to work with him, know that Hades will tease out your desires—it's part of his inexplicable appeal. Hades is not afraid of dark or shadowy places, and as the Host of Many, he's privy to the entire scope of human experience.

Speaking of darkness, within Western culture there is an extremely harmful habit of equating darkness with evil—with anything considered dangerous, threatening, or subversive or with anything worthy of disregard, disdain, and avoidance. In addition to its unhealthy limiting effects on our psyche, this ideology also has a direct, continuous, and intensely destructive impact on Black, Indigenous, and other people of color in our communities. It is beyond time that we stopped using the words *dark* and *darkness* as synonyms for evil. In my experience, the Underworld and its denizens offer a refreshing perspective on darkness. From their point of view, darkness is not something to be feared. In fact, primordial darkness encircles the entire Underworld, in the form of the god Erebos. Darkness is not a state of absence, such as the absence of light, but instead a state of *presence*.

In ancient Greek mythology, Darkness and Night have many children. Among them are the twin brothers Hypnos and Thanatos, the daimons of Sleep and Peaceful Death. These siblings are responsible for giving mortals peace and respite at the end of each day and the end of life, respectively. There are many facets to the gods and daimons of darkness and death. Spend some time getting to know them, and they may help you shift your perception of the shadows.

Erebos, God of Darkness

Erebos is the primordial god of darkness, one of the *Protogenoi* who emerged at the dawn of creation. Erebos is elemental, being the substance of darkness, rather than an anthropomorphized god. Erebos encircles the Underworld, and his darkness fills all the hollow places under the Earth's surface. Have you ever visited a cave, and experienced the complete and utter darkness when your tour guide turns off the artificial lighting? That thick, viscous, impenetrable darkness is Erebos.

Nyx, Goddess of Night

Nyx is the primordial goddess of night. Her home is the Underworld, which she leaves each evening to trail her opaque cloak across the sky. Like her consort Erebos, she is more elemental than other goddesses—she is the night itself, the veil of darkness that descends to block out the daylight. In ancient art, Nyx was represented as either a winged goddess or charioteer, with dark skin, and often with a corona of inky mist encircling her head. She is accompanied on her nightly journey by her son Hypnos, the daimon of sleep.

Hypnos, Daimon of Sleep

Personally, I love daimons as mythological figures, and magical allies, because they are beautifully and unapologetically in-between. Daimons are not gods, not humans, and not quite monsters—yet they have elements of all of these. Why be just one type of being, when you can have elements of them all? Moreover, they are something larger than the mere sum of their parts, because they represent complex ideas and concepts.

Hypnos is the daimon of sleep. He travels from his home in the Underworld each night with his mother, Nyx, granting rest to mortals. He is depicted carrying a poppy stem, a horn of sleep-inducing elixir of opium, or a small vessel of water from the river Lethe (or any combination of the three). The respite of the "small death" Hypnos grants to mortals each night is an echo of his twin brother, Thanatos, the daimon of peaceful death.

Thanatos, Daimon of Death

The black-winged daimon of death, Thanatos is the supernatural being who brings a peaceful end to life. The son of Erebos and Nyx, brother to Hypnos, he reports more directly to Hades than the rest of his family. Thanatos is the death that most of us hope for: a simple, untroubled ending after a long, fulfilling, well-lived, and well-loved life. His touch is said to be similar to that of his twin brother Hypnos—gentle and just like falling asleep. In Roman art, Thanatos was depicted symbolically as a laurel wreath encircling a butterfly, symbolizing his respectful caretaking of the souls of the dead.

Exploring the Lore

Carl Gustav Jung (1875–1961) was the founder of analytical psychology and the first to introduce and popularize the concept of the shadow—that part of ourselves of which we may not be consciously aware. Jung made many incredible contributions to the field of psychology over his lifetime and remains enormously influential to this day; however, one can occasionally come across outdated or problematic ideas in his work. Modern readers should approach him with a critical eye. Key to navigating Jung's concept of shadow is understanding the conscious versus unconscious mind and the distinctions between ego, shadow, and persona. In case some readers are not familiar with the legacy of Jung's work, I'll give a quick overview of the differences between these terms and share why understanding how they operate is important.

Ego, Shadow, and Persona

Simply defined, consciousness is the state of awareness—of being aware of external objects or something within oneself (as in introspection). The conscious mind drives our experience of the ordinary waking world. Within this domain lives our ego: that part of ourselves of which we are consciously aware. However, this is just one part of our whole self. The unconscious, on the other hand, consists of mental processes that occur automatically and are not usually available for introspection. The unconscious mind is the home of suppressed memories, desires, interests, and motivations, as well as unmet needs. We access the unconscious through the extra-ordinary world (such as in dreams, meditation, ritual, or trance journey). Within this domain lives our shadow: that part of ourselves of which we may not be consciously aware.

To create the persona we show to others, we continually evaluate our environment and—similar to changing our clothes—change our personality and behaviors to suit its conditions. Our bodies constantly regulate temperature, pulse, breath rate, release of hormones, and many other precise chemical and physiological processes; just like the rest of our body, our psyche also aims for equilibrium. Some parts of our whole self are considered acceptable; these parts are integrated into our ego. Other parts of our whole self are refused, but these parts do not disappear—they are integrated into our shadow. Over the long term, casting out and ignoring undesirable or unwanted parts of ourselves becomes ineffective and unsustainable. We continue to unconsciously store and accumulate shadow until our psyche reaches a tipping point. What happens then? Jungian analyst Robert Johnson explains: "Unless we do conscious work on it, the shadow is almost always projected; that is, neatly laid on someone or something else so we do not have to take responsibility for it.... Projection is always easier than assimilation."[110]

Projecting our shadow is problematic on both a personal scale and a collective scale. When we are unaware that a certain emotion or reaction actually originates from a deeply hidden part of ourselves and consequently project those feelings onto something or someone else that has triggered us, we damage relationships, miss opportunities for growth, and fall victim to misunderstandings. On the collective scale, the potential for harm intensifies.

---

110. Johnson, *Owning Your Own Shadow*, 31–32.

Throughout history we can observe innumerable instances of war, racism, colonization, intolerance, hate crimes, inequality, and injustice wherein humans justified their actions by assigning blame onto someone else—another nation or a different group of individuals. This divisive, large-scale projection of collective shadow still occurs. It takes steadfast courage and deep commitment to honest self-reflection for us to explore and own our shadow—personally and collectively.

Symbols of Hades: The Soul Fire

Empedocles of Sicily (ca. 494–34 BCE) was a Greek pre-Socratic philosopher, poet, and mystic whose far-reaching impact can still be seen in medicine, chemistry, biology, astronomy, cosmology, rhetoric, and religion. In fact, much of our modern magical understanding of the five elements (earth, air, fire, water, and spirit) originated from the teachings of Empedocles.

Similar to the Orphics and other mystery cults, Empedocles utilized poetry and code words in his teachings in order to obscure their meanings to the uninitiated. Central to his philosophy is the theory that two primal and opposing forces exist in the universe: love and strife. According to Empedocles, these two forces act upon four basic elements—aither, fire, earth, and water— causing them to interact and form the material universe. Aither does not refer to our modern concept of the element of air, but rather to the Classical notion of an ineffable spiritual substance filling all the regions of the universe above the surface of the earth. Empedocles used mythical code words, full of subtle meaning, for each of these elements: he referred to aither as Zeus, fire as Hades, earth as Hera, and water as Nestis.[111]

Empedocles' deliberate choice of code words points to Hades as the custodian of souls, or more specifically, the caretaker of the fiery light at the very core of all souls. "Considering that Empedocles used Hades as a code word for fire, it is clear that the light-fire entering the aither at birth is the soul of the living being," writes Johan August Alm in *Tartaros: On the Orphic and Pythagorean Underworld and the Pythagorean Pentagram*. He continues: "Before the material body is born, this soul of fire exists in Hades-Tartaros [the Underworld] as a fiery light, and after the death of the material body (which is not a destruction,

---

111. Empedocles, "Empedokles of Akragas," in *Early Greek Philosophy*, trans. John Burnet (London: Adam and Charles Black, 1908; Project Gutenberg, 2022), 240.

but merely a separation of the elements) this soul-fire returns to Hades."[112] This explanation correlates with some of my own visions of the Underworld, in which I have seen a bright light glowing inside each shade of the dead.

In Western magic, the element of fire represents heat, passion, and transformation. Fire is life and light in the darkness. Working with Hades can help us tap into the elemental energy of fire as well as the very soul fire inside ourselves, to connect with our vitality, creativity, and desire.

In His Dark Garden: Datura and Fig

Shadow and desire often accompany one another. Mysterious and enticing, datura and fig are two sensuous, heady plants with the power to draw us deeper into the perplexity of our true selves. What secret longings and desires are hiding in your shadow? Working with these plant allies will help you unearth them.

DATURA

Species: *Datura stramonium*

Other Common Names: Devil's trumpet, hell's bells, jimsonweed, moon-flower, thornapple

Toxicity: Highly toxic (never ingest, and use caution when handling)

Keywords: Death and rebirth, hidden mysteries, intoxication, soul retrieval, trance journey

Datura is a genus of highly poisonous, vespertine-blooming plants belonging to the nightshade family. Datura's large white or purple flowers open in the evening, imbuing the air with an intoxicating floral smell. Due to its large, spiny fruit, datura earned the folk name *thornapple*. Initially, archaeobotanists thought datura was native to the Americas and only introduced to Europe in the sixteenth century CE. Recently reevaluated Arabic medical texts mention datura as early as the tenth century CE; however, leading researchers to believe that the plant was present in the Old World much earlier, even if its range or usage was not yet widespread.[113]

Historically, datura was used medicinally as a narcotic, nervine, hallucinogenic, and purgative, and the rolled leaves were smoked like cigarettes to

---

112. Alm, *Tartaros*, 64.

113. Occvlta, "Thornapple," *Materia Venefica* 7 (March 2022): 4, https://www.occvlta.org/.

induce transcendental states and provide relief from the symptoms of asthma. However, all species of datura are now known to be highly toxic and should always be handled with extreme care. No part of the plant should be ingested, smoked, or used to create fluid condensers. For the highly sensitive, simply touching the plant can be intoxicating. Limit your skin exposure and always be sure to wash your hands after handling datura.

Datura's manner of unveiling its velvety blooms at night, hiding its dangerous nature behind an intensely alluring smell, reveals its potency for shadow work. Similar to unearthing parts of ourselves hidden in shadow, one must work with great care to access the seeds resting inside datura's thorny fruit. Once dried, the spiked seed pods can be strung over doorways or used in witch bottles for protection. In trance journey, following datura's spiritus viridis may lead you down unknown and unnerving paths; however, illumination awaits for the courageous practitioner. To initiate a relationship with this formidable ally, I recommend simply sitting in the presence of the plant or its image a few times to get a sense of its energy before seeking it out in trance journey. When you feel ready to contact datura in the Otherworld, ask a trusted guide to accompany and support you. Remember to clear your mind and energetic field of datura's intoxicating influence once you return—you can use khernips, rue water, or a salt bath to purify yourself.

FIG TREE
Species: *Ficus carica*
Other Common Names: Common fig, ficus
Toxicity: Non-toxic to humans (but toxic to cats, dogs, and other animals).
  All parts of the fig tree contain latex sap, which is especially concentrated in the white sap produced when unripe figs are harvested early. People who are allergic to the latex sap of the rubber tree (*Hevea brasiliensis*) should be aware of the potential for cross-allergic reactions.
Keywords: Potency, protection, sex, vitality

The fig is a species of small flowering tree native to the Mediterranean and western Asia. It has been widely cultivated for its fruit and ornamental beauty. Its sweet fruit is tear-shaped and may ripen from green into a deep purple or brown color. The fruit contains a plethora of small, crunchy seeds, and has been consequently linked to sex, potency, and fertility since ancient times.

The *figa*, or more precisely the *mano fico*, is a centuries-old Italian (or possibly even Etruscan) talisman believed to ward against the evil eye and bring protection to its wearer. *Figa* is a euphemistic slang term for fig. The figa is composed of a closed fist, with the tip of the thumb extending through the index and middle fingers; the gesture is meant to represent a vulva and the act of sex. The figa is a not-so-subtle evocation of the vitality of life against any forces that would attempt to harm us.

Some magical practitioners believe that the figa gesture is useful for protecting oneself on the metaphysical plane as well as the physical—if you ever feel threatened in the Otherworld, try throwing a figa. Just keep in mind that this gesture, like many others, is not universally accepted as positive around the world. You may want to do some research before publicly wearing a figa pendant or throwing a figa gesture in some countries.

Khthonic Bestiary: The Scorpion

Scorpions are predatory arachnids with eight legs, a pair of large, grasping pincers, and a segmented tail that is most often carried in a recognizable, characteristic forward curve over its back, ending with a sharp stinger. Scorpions primarily live in desert climates but have adapted to a wide range of environmental conditions and can now be found on all continents except Antarctica. One of the more unique characteristics of scorpions is that their exoskeletons contain fluorescent chemicals that glow under ultraviolet light; this natural fluorescence may explain how scorpions are able to hunt so efficiently in extreme low light. Scorpions utilize their strong front pincers to restrain and kill prey or to defend against their own predation. The scorpion's venomous sting is also used for offense and defense. Scorpions are generally not considered a threat to human populations, however, since only 25 species of scorpions (fewer than 1 percent of the total species count) contain venom capable of killing a human.

Scorpio is the eighth astrological sign in the Western zodiac, named after the constellation of Scorpius, a grouping of stars well known to the ancient Greeks, whose hooked shape reminded astronomers of the curved tail of a scorpion. Pluto is the modern ruling planet of the astrological sign of Scorpio, and yes, this planet is named after Hades' Roman counterpart. In astrology, Pluto is "the great renewer," representing the idea that destruction must sometimes precede renewal and that long-buried needs, drives, and desires must eventually rise to the surface to be expressed, even at the expense of the existing order. Pluto rules over sex, death, absolutes, power, transformation, intensity, and anything that requires delving under the surface to bring the truth to light. Interestingly, the discovery of the planet Pluto in 1930 coincided with the birth of modern psychoanalysis, the time period when Sigmund Freud and his protégé, Carl Gustav Jung, began to explore the depths of the unconscious.

Astrological Symbol for Scorpio

Finding Hades in the Landscape: Lake Avernus

In Virgil's *Aeneid*, the hero Aeneas enters the Underworld at Lake Avernus via the cave of the Cumaean Sibyl, located in southern Italy. The Antro della Sibilla is near other caves in the area that lead to Lake Avernus, including the Crypta Romana and the enormous Grotta di Cocceio, a tunnel dug through the mountain that is large enough to accommodate a chariot. But in reality, however, Aeneas would have needed to use one of these other caves to get to the lake, as the Antro della Sibilla itself does not provide direct access.

Lake Avernus is a volcanic crater lake located near the volcanically active region of Italy known as the *Campi Flegrei*: the "Phlegraean Fields" or "Fiery Fields." The Campi Flegrei are part of the caldera of an active volcano that is the twin of Mount Vesuvius—the infamous volcano that destroyed the ancient Roman city of Pompeii.[114] Despite its natural dangers and associations with the Underworld, ancient Romans established villas and vineyards all around Lake Avernus. Deus Avernus, the tutelary spirit of the lake, was venerated in lakeside temples. Visitors to this site today can walk the perimeter of the lake, which measures only 1.3 miles (2 km), in about the space of an hour.

---

114. Mike Dash, "The Unsolved Mystery of the Tunnels at Baiae," *Smithsonian Magazine*, October 1, 2012, https://www.smithsonianmag.com/history/the-unsolved-mystery-of-the-tunnels-at-baiae-56267963/.

Invitations to Practice

Invoke the primordial gods Darkness, Night, and their children for assistance with works of magic and ritual involving shadow: Erebos for comfort and safety in total darkness; Nyx for navigating the night, whether it be nighttime, or the dark night of the soul; Hypnos for restful and restorative sleep; and Thanatos for peaceful death (both physical and metaphorical). Symbols and correspondences that resonate with shadow praxis are the transformative element of fire, mysterious datura, the fig tree and *mano fico*, and the scorpion.

Hymn to Nyx and Shadow

The following hymn is dedicated to Nyx and shadow. Recite this hymn in conjunction with rituals or magical operations involving shadow work, to express gratitude to aspects of yourself hidden in shadow, or to connect more deeply with your desires.

To my shadow, thank you for carrying
Those precious parts of myself that I dared not see.
Thank you for holding them close to your heart,
Cherishing them, sheltering them—
Thank you for placing them in the arms of the Night Mother,
Who tenderly wraps them in robes of night and starlight.
Venerable Nyx, Lover of Darkness,
Night Mother, gather your son and ride your chariot across the sky!
It is time to dream my desires,
To dream more of myself into being.

Learning to Embrace the Whole Self

When I first began my magical studies, I thought the goal of spiritual or magical practice was evolution—and in order to evolve, I readily embraced the notion that I would have to visit some shadowy and uncomfortable places in my psyche. I thought that once I was able to confront the unwanted detritus in my soul, I could easily bag it up and set it on the curb like last week's garbage. After all, the object of the game was self-improvement, and hanging onto shadowy imperfections would only weigh me down. Forcing myself onward, I spent years chasing the mirage of a higher, more enlightened self.

Friends, it was an illusion. Spoiler alert: there is no higher or lower self. There is only the whole self—and all parts of it are necessary, vital, and worthy of grace and love. Both my understanding of how magic works and my spiritual goals have shifted significantly since those early days. I have discovered that ecstasy, not evolution, is the goal of my magical practice. I am able to experience spiritual ecstasy through merger and connection with something larger than myself. Learning to embrace my whole self, just as I embrace the paradoxes in the stories of the gods I love, supports me in this endeavor.

Mikayla Ricks is a death doula, healer, poet, and author of a thought-provoking newsletter entitled *The Shadow Space*. In an interview for this book, she eloquently explained why working with your shadow helps to reveal your whole self, leading to acceptance: "Shadow work allows you to see everything as it is. Oftentimes, when looking at ourselves, it's like looking into a broken mirror. There are fractures and cracks, and you are not able to see a true reflection of yourself. When we do shadow work, we start to repair some of those cracks. The true picture of who we really are starts to emerge."[115] In addition to having a fractured perspective, keeping all the aspects of your shadow self hidden and suppressed uses up a tremendous amount of personal energy. By exploring and consciously working with your shadow, you may begin to uncover the outmoded ideas, perceptions, restrictions, and ways of thinking and being that no longer resonate. You can then reclaim these energies, transmute them, and infuse them with another purpose. You may also grow to trust the uniquely healing gifts that your shadow has to offer and figure out new, more beneficial ways to work these aspects of yourself into your life.

Shadow Transmutation Ritual

Shadow is paradoxical in nature: baneful and beneficent, it can both harm and heal. As magical practitioners, we have the capability to engage directly with our deep psyche by connecting inner transmutation with outward symbolic action—that's why ceremony and ritual are some of the most powerful ways to work shadow magic.

Before embarking on any type of shadow work, it is important to understand that this is extremely weighty, profound, and nuanced magic. Facing your

---

115. Mikayla Ricks, interview with the author, December 14, 2022.

shadow has the potential to be very challenging and emotional. It's a good idea to check in with yourself to see if you are in a stable, supported place before you begin—physically, mentally, emotionally, and spiritually. This self-assessment is especially critical if you want to work with a piece of your shadow, or the collective shadow, that has been touched by trauma.

Step One: Identifying Shadow Aspects

When you are ready to ritually acknowledge and transmute an aspect of your shadow, start by identifying some aspects of yourself that you tend to deny or keep hidden. This can be as simple as making a list of personality traits, values, motivations, or trigger behaviors or as involved as engaging in trance journey to seek out and speak directly with your shadow. Choose one aspect of your shadow that no longer resonates with you, with whom you want to change your relationship. For example, I know I have a tendency to hold parts of myself back, making myself smaller so as not to take up too much space or attract censure from others. Secretly, I long to let loose all my boldness and confidence—but I keep this desire hidden in my shadow, where it feels less risky, more safe. In this example, I choose to ritually acknowledge this longing, so my desire to be bold and confident feels valued instead of rejected, worthy rather than dangerous. I also choose to transmute my relationship with it, so that rather than living in fear of drawing negative attention, I feel free to work on letting my confidence shine.

Step Two: Shadow Transmutation Ritual

The next step is to plan and execute a ritual that serves as a safe space for this aspect of your shadow to be acknowledged and expressed, as well as a container for you to symbolically transmute your relationship to it. The magic of this ritual takes place in three central parts: creative expression, transmutation, and outward symbolic action.

In the first part of the ritual, you will engage the chosen aspect of your shadow through some means of creative expression, acknowledging it and bringing it into the light of consciousness. Your method of creative expression should feel satisfying, but do no harm to yourself or others. For example, if you are working with anger that is hidden in your shadow, you could give your anger a safe place to play out through ecstatic, frenzied dancing or by vocalizing loud noises and screams. Alternatively, it may resonate for you to draw, sculpt, or paint this aspect of your shadow, to write a story or poem about it, or to make a simple dolly to represent it. Or maybe your shadow wants to be expressed through physical means of movement or sound, such as acting, tumbling, singing, or martial art forms. Once you've decided on a vehicle for expression, collect the supplies you will need (such as paper, watercolors, and brushes if you will be painting, or your Bluetooth device and speakers if you require music), and gather them up with any other materials you wish to include on your ritual altar. Remember, altars work on the principle of correspondence. You may want to source items or images that will draw corresponding energies useful for shadow work to your altar: in this instance, perhaps a black altar cloth, with an image of datura, a few black figs, and a toy scorpion. An image or small statue of Hades is always welcome, too.

In the second part of the ritual, you will use the element of fire as a vehicle for transmutation. Try to choose a ritual space that is private but also near an indoor fireplace or an outdoor fire pit. If this type of setting is not accessible to you, simply gather a small candle and fire-proof container, such as a cast-iron cauldron. For practical safety purposes, remember to have a bucket of water or sand nearby to put out the fire if necessary.

In the third part of the ritual, you will commit to one outward symbolic action that you will take in the next week to seal this magical working. For my own example, transmuting my relationship with confidence, this might look like choosing a date for a dinner party and inviting a group of friends, or submitting an article to an online publication that I admire. In the example of working with hidden anger, this might look like organizing a protest in your hometown, harnessing your passion to catalyze change.

Read through the following framework to plan your own shadow transmutation ritual, making note of the details you need to customize: invocation, statement of intention, words of transmutation, and commitment to outward symbolic action. This ritual is best performed at night, or at a time that you will not be disturbed for one to two hours.

1. Purification: Purify the floor or ground where your ritual will take place with khernips. Set up your altar and supplies. Next purify your altar, materials, any offerings, and yourself with khernips. Check to

make sure you have all the materials needed to carry out each step of the ritual, and start the fire for your ritual. If you are using a candle, wait to light it until after you have cast your boundary circle and set wards.

2. Circle Casting and Warding: Using your preferred method of demarcation, cast a clockwise circle encompassing the entire ritual area, including yourself, your altar, and the fire if you have one. Beginning in the east and moving clockwise, ward your circle with a sigil of protection in each of the four cardinal directions, finishing with the fifth direction of center.

3. Invocation and Welcome: Invoke any gods you wish to bless your ritual, such as Hades, Erebus, or Nyx. You can read one of the hymns from this book, sing a chant of your choosing, or create a special invocation for this occasion. After the invocation is complete, welcome any other Unseen Ones who may also have gathered with you for this ritual: denizens of the Underworld, ancestors, spirits of place, guides, familiars, elementals, plant spirits, and so on.

4. Consecration: Read aloud a statement of intention to consecrate this ritual. This may sound something like, "I consecrate this ritual as a safe space for (insert aspect of your shadow) to be acknowledged and expressed, as well as a magical container for me to transmute my relationship to it."

5. Creative Expression: Engage your chosen shadow aspect through creative expression. Using the materials you gathered in your ritual preparations, stay in the moment of creative flow, letting the energy naturally wax and wane. This piece of the magic is about self-expression, not perfection. Take your time and be as messy as needed. You are creating a heartfelt and precious offering for your shadow. When this feels complete, acknowledge this aspect of your shadow by naming it aloud once more. You can also offer your shadow words of gratitude if you like.

6. Transmutation: Place your creative offering in the fire, or use the candle flame to light it before placing it in a firesafe container, releasing it to the elemental power of the flames. If your creative offering is something nonphysical like a song or dance, focus on sending its

essence and energy into the flames. Explain aloud that you are now reclaiming the energy tied up in this aspect of shadow, transmuting it, shifting your relationship to this aspect of yourself. For my earlier example, this might sound something like, "I am now reclaiming the energy previously tied up in making myself smaller. I choose to transmute my relationship with my hidden desire to let loose my boldness and confidence, so that rather than living in denial and fear of drawing negative attention, I let my confidence shine brilliantly. In fact, I will let it shine so bright that it inspires others and gives them permission to shine, too!"

7. Outward Symbolic Action: Once your offering has been consumed, speak aloud what you are now inviting into your life. With this step, you are connecting with your desire. You are inviting something desirable and constructive to fill any void left behind by the energy you just reclaimed. Name aloud one outward symbolic action that you will take in the next week to seal this magical working.

8. Gratitude and Farewell: Thank the Unseen Ones who gathered for the ritual, offer gratitude for their witness, and bid them farewell. Thank the god(s) you invoked for the ritual, offer gratitude for their blessing, and bid them farewell.

9. Ward and Circle Release: Release your wards by thanking and bidding farewell to them in the opposite direction they were raised: center, north, west, south, and east. Release your circle by sweeping it away counterclockwise, with a broom or a sweeping motion of the hands. Once this motion is completed, announce out loud, "It is done."

Step Three: Ritual Aftercare and Follow-Up

After your shadow transmutation ritual is complete, do not keep the ashes left from your fire. Once they are cooled, scatter them in freely moving water or wind. Ground yourself post-ritual by relaxing with nourishing food and a nonalcoholic beverage. You may also want to capture some of your initial impressions from the ritual in your journal. Drink lots of water and be sure to get adequate sleep during the following week—more revelations about working with this aspect of yourself may reveal themselves through dreams or synchronicities.

And, last but not least, don't forget about completing the outward symbolic act you committed to in ritual.

While engaged in shadow work, also consider scheduling periodic check-ins with a trusted mentor or friend to support you through the process and to prevent feelings of isolation. Sometimes it can be tempting to give in to guilt, shame, or other self-deprecating emotions when we face up to aspects of our shadow self, but don't get too bogged down in these feelings—once you have completed some deep excavation and transmutation, remember to balance it out with rest, fun, and connection. You may also want to add another devotional, grounding, or centering practice to your daily routine during this time, to help restore and sustain you.

CHAPTER 8
THE GOOD DEATH

Hades speaks:

Persephone is absent at this time of year. The halls feel too big without her. Sometimes I fall asleep and forget she is gone, until I wake and she is not beside me. Her clothes hang haphazardly in our wardrobe, her pyxis sits open on the bedroom dresser, its lid not quite in place. I don't straighten her clothes—their disarray reminds me of my wife, as if she is still there in the next room, having dressed quickly to start her busy day. I run my index finger along the rim of her pyxis, the earthenware pottery exquisite and beautiful, as befits my queen. Inside are a few crushed fragments of a flower petal and a single earring. Did she lose the other? I will ask her about it when she returns. Perhaps she will want a replacement. I pick up the lid and set it gently back into place.

If she were here, I would tell her about our daughters. I would boast of Makaria tending the Elysian Fields, of her honey production, which has such a bountiful yield this year that we will be able to provide ambrosia to the Isles of the Blessed for at least a decade. I would tell her how all the shades who dwell there are happy and that I can hear their laughter on the evening breeze.

I would also tell her of Melinoe, half light and half darkness, our child of two realms. Sometimes I fear Melinoe is too much like me, given to melancholy, sunk deep into the responsibilities of her role. I check on her often, by the shores of the Kokytos, where she keeps company with restless souls. Too often, in fact, as she has begged me to stop lurking in her domain. I cannot help myself—a father worries for his daughters. So I still look in, but I stay invisible. Sometimes I leave a stack of blankets by the icy riverbank. It is one of the rare times I see her smile, as she wraps them around her companions.

I wish she would speak to me of her experiences in the realm of the living, when she rides the night winds with her retinue of hungry shades, demanding propitiation so that they can move on. Perhaps Persephone can get her to talk. I will ask her about it when she returns.

Yes, when she returns. In the world above, the summer solstice has come and gone; the nights grow longer, minute by minute, with each day that passes. Death knows no season, my duties continue, but I sense that the time for harvest is coming soon. So I will save my stories and questions, to enjoy at our leisure, together. When Persephone returns.

Death and Burial Customs in Ancient Greece

Take a moment to think about this fact: we are only alive because of the dead.

To live, we need a few critical things: fresh water, restful sleep, clean air, and nourishing food. Whether you're vegan, vegetarian, omnivore, carnivore, or otherwise, a plethora of plants and animals regularly give their lives so that you can consume the food you need to live. Dead and decaying matter—leaves, fungi, insects, animals, even humans—are forever composting into soil, which will in time grow the plants we harvest for our tables, or feed to the animals that we slaughter for food. Death is truly among us, every moment of the day, whether we are cognizant of its presence or not.

For the ancient Greeks and Romans, being dead was actually the default condition of humanity. "Humans, essentially, are like the gods—immortal and indestructible. The body might die (and it frequently does), but the spirit it contains cannot be destroyed. At any given time, most of the human race dwells among the shadows of the Underworld," explains historian Philip Matyszak in *Ancient Magic: A Practitioner's Guide to the Supernatural in Greece and Rome.*[116] Hades has multiple epithets linking him to death and burial rituals, such as *Hades Adesius* (Hades of the Grave) and *Hades Nekrodegmon* (Hades Receiver of the Dead). Completion of the proper death and burial rituals was viewed as an essential ending to a virtuous life, and it was the sacred responsibility of living individuals to ensure that these rites were carried out.

The ancient Greeks believed that the soul left the body at the moment of death on a little breath or puff of wind—this may be why butterflies, bats,

---

116. Matyszak, *Ancient Magic,* 14.

and birds, with their ability to fly, often represented the soul in ancient art. Immediately following death, the body of the deceased was washed and laid out by the women of the family. This laying out of the body was called *prothesis*. The body would be anointed with oil and herbs to cover up the smell of illness or decomposition. Additional herbs, such as rue or oregano, may have been tucked underneath the body to ward off harmful energies and magical attacks. An obol was placed under the tongue to pay Kharon for passage to the Underworld. During prothesis, friends and relatives of the deceased would come to pay their respects. Author and Classics professor Sarah Iles Johnston notes: "The traditional length of *prothesis* was one day; this would fit with the fact it was on the third day after death (counting inclusively) that the body was carried out to the place of burial (*ekphora*). The swiftness of burial reflects not only the obvious need to remove a decomposing corpse quickly but also the perception that the individual no longer belonged amongst the living."[117]

During the *ekphora*, or funeral procession, the dead were carried to their place of burial by family members and sometimes accompanied by other mourners, singing laments. Funeral rites included offerings of ritual libations called *khoai* and a *deipnon*, or supper, for the deceased. During these rites, the dead were described as *eudeipnoi*, "those who are content with their meal."[118] This euphemistic word seems to imply that once the dead were offered libations and a meal, they would be propitiated. Offerings at the time of burial sometimes also included jewelry, flowers, and everyday objects such as cosmetics, swords, toys, and mirrors.

A grave marker called a *sema* or *stele* was added after the burial. According to Johnston, these markers were decorated with ribbons, myrtle branches, and even hair—it was common for the living to cut and offer some of their hair to the dead. Scholars debate the meaning of the hair offering; some have suggested it may have been a symbolic human sacrifice, or perhaps it was an outward way to signify to society that the living were in a state of mourning.[119]

---

117. Sarah Iles Johnston, *Restless Dead: Encounters between the Living and the Dead in Ancient Greece* (Berkeley, CA: University of California Press, 2013), 40.

118. Johnston, *Restless Dead*, 41.

119. Johnston, *Restless Dead*, 42.

Offerings continued to be made at the gravesite on certain days after the funeral (on the third, ninth, thirtieth days, and possibly also after one year). These rites were seen as necessary for settling the spirit of the deceased. The dead may return to haunt their family members if the proper offerings were not observed. Some evidence also suggests that offerings were made on important dates, such as birthdays and anniversaries, and when family members wished to invite the dead to participate in significant events such as weddings.[120]

The Daughters of Hades

Primary sources vary widely in their opinions on whether or not Hades has any offspring and, considering that he is the Ruler of the Dead, whether or not he can even father children at all. Among the mythological figures that Hades is reported to have possibly fathered are Makaria, Melinoe, Zagreus, and the Erinyes. When it comes to working with death in a ritual or magical sense, Hades' daughters Makaria and Melinoe are of particular importance.

The goddess Makaria is the embodiment of blessed death—when the soul is settled, happy, and at peace in the Underworld. Melinoe, on the other hand, is the goddess of unsettled ghosts and spirits, the restless dead, and those who haunt the living because they are unable to cross over to the Underworld.

Makaria

The primary source reference to Makaria is found in the *Suda*, an encyclopedic Byzantine Greek lexicon containing approximately 30,000 entries, likely compiled by several authors working together sometime around the tenth century CE. The translated entry reads: "[A way of referring to] death. [Makaria was] a daughter of Hades. And [there is] a proverb: 'be gone into blessedness,' meaning into misery and utter destruction. Or 'begone into blessedness' [is said] by euphemism. Since even the dead are called blessed ones."[121]

The name of Makaria's other parent is unknown. Makaria rules over the Elysian Fields, sometimes called Elysium, the region of the Underworld separated from the rest of the realm of the dead by the River Lethe. You may recall from chapter 2 that the Elysian Fields are pleasant: sunny, warm, and

---

120. Johnston, *Restless Dead*, 42–43.

121. Suda and Katina Ball, trans., "mu,51." Suda On Line: Byzantine Lexicography, ed. David Whitehead and Catharine Roth, last modified April 28, 2013, http://www.cs.uky.edu/~raphael/sol/sol-entries/mu/51.

abundant with food, drink, and conversation. In my personal practice, Makaria has expressed to me that she loves offerings of watered-down, anise-flavored Greek liquors such as Ouzo. Adding water to liquor frees up aroma molecules to evaporate into the nose—since appreciation of flavor happens in the nose as well as on the tongue, watered-down spirits can actually seem more flavorful to the drinker. The sweet, licorice-scented taste of this beverage is reminiscent of the sweetness to be found in the Elysian Fields.

Melinoe

Melinoe, the daughter of Hades and Persephone, is described by the Orphics as half light and half shadow; representing both darkness and light, one half of her body is deepest black while the other half is stark white. Personally, I love this depiction of her appearance because it embodies a paradoxical, nonbinary expression of life in death, and death in life. Although Melinoe does not rule any particular region of the Underworld, she is said to have been conceived by the mouth of the icy River Kokytos and can often be found there among the wailing shades of the restless dead.

The name *Melinoe* is unusual and intriguing. Etymologically speaking, it may derive from the Greek words *melinos*, "having the color of quince," and *melon*, "the tree fruit." The quince tree was quite common in ancient Mediterranean orchards, along with fig, olive, apple, and pomegranate. The quince fruit's yellowish-green color may have reminded ancient peoples of the pallor of illness or death; etymological evidence supporting this interpretation is that a name derived from *melas*, meaning "black," would typically begin with *mela-*, not *melin-*. However, many people interpret her name to mean "dark-minded" or "propitiation-minded," stemming from a combination of the Greek words *melas* (black), *meilia* (propitiation), and *noe* (mind). The term *meilia* was widely used to refer to offerings made as an act of appeasement to the spirits of the dead, and Melinoe was the goddess invoked to bless these offerings and bring them to the Underworld.[122]

It can be very unnerving for mortals to encounter Melinoe and her attendants. When propitiations for the dead are neglected, Melinoe leads their restless shades from the Underworld back to the land of the living to seek justice.

---

122. Clark, "Hades Daughter: Everything You Must Know About Her Story," Ancient Literature, September 20, 2022, https://ancient-literature.com/hades-daughter/.

She can take the form of an ethereal mist or nightmarish apparition, with a milieu of ghosts trailing in her wake. It is said that her aspect and retinue have the power to induce madness. In my personal practice, Melinoe has expressed to me that she loves offerings of rusty water, most especially rusty water made from soaking iron coffin nails in spring water under the light of the full moon. In case you are not familiar with this term, historic coffin nails were hand-forged one-to-two-inch (2.5–5 cm) iron nails with a square head that tapered to a point. They were made specifically to fasten wooden coffins; their shape causes the wood fibers to push downward and wedge against the nails, making it extremely hard to remove them. They are less common today, since most people opt for burial in decorative caskets instead of plain wooden coffins. However, replica coffin nails can be purchased online from casket- and coffin-making supply companies, and the authentic historical version can sometimes be spotted in antique shops or flea markets.

Exploring the Lore

The dead and the living are forever, intimately intertwined. Learning about the community participation, reverence, and catharsis of ancient death and burial rituals is inspiring. In much of the modern Western world, we have very little exposure to the process of death and dying, and this lack can be problematic. Death doula Mikayla Ricks observes, "We've been removed from death as a society since the introduction of embalming. By no longer needing to care for the dead bodies of our loved ones, we don't get to see or participate in the full death process."[123] Considering the limited amount of time and outlets modern society provides for healthy grieving, our nervous systems are often not able to cope with the pace of change that death can bring. As a result, collective, trauma-born reluctance to deal with death continues to grow.

The Death Positive Movement

The Order of the Good Death was founded in 2011 by Caitlin Doughty, a funeral director from Los Angeles. According to its website, "The Order is about making death a part of your life. That means committing to staring down your death fears—whether it be your own death, the death of those you

---

123. Mikayla Ricks, interview with the author, December 14, 2022.

love, the pain of dying, the afterlife (or lack thereof), grief, corpses, bodily decomposition, or all of the above. Accepting that death itself is natural, but the death anxiety and terror of modern culture are not."[124] This growing community of funeral industry professionals, academics, and artists would expand internationally over the next decade into the Death Positive Movement, a term coined by the Order. "People who are death positive believe that it is not morbid or taboo to speak openly about death. They see honest conversations about death & dying as the cornerstone of a healthy society," clarifies the team at orderofthegooddeath.com.[125]

However, in its attempts to destigmatize death, some death industry professionals feel the Death Positive Movement may have swung too far in the opposite direction. Mikayla Ricks shares her thoughts: "Sometimes it can feel like people are giving death a sunny, capitalist rebrand. Much of the Death Positive Movement is led by white women, who don't necessarily see all the things I [as a Black woman] have to go through when it comes to dealing with death. I think the Death Positive Movement is being made in good faith, but it needs to be more realistic."[126]

Ricks goes on to observe that some of our accepted social attitudes and cultural mores around death, as well as the spectrum of human reactions to it, need to be recognized and questioned. She offers a recent example from world news headlines: "Part of white supremacy culture is to not make a scene, not cause any disruptions. We see this play out in the phrase 'Don't speak ill of the dead.' We can, and we should, speak out about the reality of someone's impact. We should speak out against abusers, colonizers, and other harmful figures. A lot of people were not prepared for the recent death of Queen Elizabeth. It was a divisive moment; some people celebrated, while others cried out for respect for her memory. I wonder, do those people crying out for respect realize that they were really mourning the death of colonization, the face of colonization?

---

124. Order of the Good Death, "Our Story," accessed January 28, 2023, https://www.orderofthegooddeath.com/our-story/.

125. Order of the Good Death, "Death Positive Movement," accessed January 28, 2023, https://www.orderofthegooddeath.com/death-positive-movement/.

126. Ricks, interview, December 14, 2022.

What does that say about us as a society? I want to see more death industry workers talking about this."[127]

Ricks also thinks that de-sensationalizing death can help strike a balance between avoiding the subject entirely and painting it in too positive a light: "Suffering always gets attention. In de-sensationalizing death, I want to show others the truth of death, without relying on only the worst or most traumatic examples to provoke a response. As a death doula, I've seen the good in death and the bad in death. But I've also been able to see death just as it is, as something that just happens to us. Death is not our enemy. It is not punishment. It is not something to try to escape or overcome."[128]

In an online article entitled "What Death Positive Is NOT," the Order of the Good Death founder Caitlin Doughty addresses some of the misunderstandings around the Death Positive Movement. She points out: "Yes, our organization is called The Order of the Good Death, and we encourage discussion on how to achieve the good death. But a huge part of that discussion is the structural inequality that makes it more difficult for certain groups to obtain the death or funeral they might desire. Not all deaths are created equal. Openly acknowledging this allows us to place our focus on this reality and work to change it."[129] The Order lobbies for legalization of greener death technologies such as aquamation, advocates for expanded end-of-life options for terminally ill patients, and fights against bills that would prohibit families from keeping the bodies of their deceased at home for more than forty-eight hours. Doughty continues, "We don't believe that we should accept bad deaths, especially in our current political climate, as a fixed condition. We should be allowing communities to define what a 'good death' means to them, the very real barriers that exist to realizing a good death, and examining and dismantling those barriers. This discovery is a key part of the death positive movement."[130]

So what is the good death? In my opinion, there is no definitive or universal good death. The good death is a concept worthy of examination and discussion, but one best determined by each individual, family, and community for

127. Ricks, interview, December 14, 2022.

128. Ricks, interview, December 14, 2022.

129. Caitlin Doughty, "What Death Positive Is NOT," the Order of the Good Death, accessed January 58, 2018, https://www.orderofthegooddeath.com/article/what-death-positive-is-not/.

130. Doughty, "What Death Positive Is NOT."

themselves. We all have the opportunity to explore this concept right now, by reflecting on how the good death looks in our own lives. Here are some topics and self-reflective questions to get you started:

Relationships: How do I give romantic relationships, friendships, partnerships, jobs, and other interactions a good death? What do I need to feel a sense of closure for myself, regardless of what the other party may be willing or able to provide? Am I still grieving any relationships? How am I moving through any grief processes that may be ongoing?

Habits: How do I give outdated, undesired, or unnecessary habits and ways of thinking or being a good death? What feels like the right way to say goodbye? How can I compost them into fertile soil, ready for new growth?

Death Planning: Have I considered what a good death would entail for me? Do I have preferences regarding my own death vigil, funeral, or celebration of life and what will be done with my body? What about any possessions or resources I want to gift to others? Have I made time to put these desires down in writing? Have I talked about it with my loved ones?

Symbols of Hades: The Lekythos

A *lekythos* (plural *lekythoi*) was a narrow vessel used by the ancient Greeks to store oil and, in particular, the precious olive or perfumed oil set aside for purposes of ritual anointment. The body of the lekythos was typically slender, with a single handle attached to its elongated neck. Most ancient lekythoi utilized the "white ground" technique of vase painting, which was far too delicate and fragile for a jug or pitcher employed in normal, day-to-day use. In this painting technique, a thin layer of kaolinite slurry was applied to the vessel before it was painted; this white background layer made colors appear more brilliant, but it could potentially chip or flake if not handled with care. Lekythoi were only brought out for special occasions—such as ritually anointing a bride's skin on the eve of her wedding or the respectful preparation and laying out of a deceased loved one for prothesis.[131]

Many lekythoi have been uncovered in ancient graves. Images decorating these funerary lekythoi depict daily activities, religious rituals, funeral rites,

---

131. *Encyclopaedia Britannica Online*, s.v. "lekythos," accessed March 23, 2016. https://www.britannica.com /art/lekythos.

themes of loss or departure, or scenes of the afterlife. At the time of burial or interment, the lekythos used to anoint the body of the deceased was left behind at their graveside or sometimes placed with the body inside a tomb. The remainder of the precious oil in the lekythos was considered a sacred offering for the newly dead or for Hades, Persephone, and the denizens of the Underworld.

In His Dark Garden: Rosemary and Quince

Rosemary and quince are both associated with remembrance, propitiating the dead, and helping calm restless ghosts and spirits. These plants make wonderful offerings, ritual centerpieces, and in the case of rosemary leaves and quince blossoms, pleasing additions to aromatic incense blends.

ROSEMARY

Species: *Salvia rosmarinus*
Other Common Names: Dew of the sea, compass weed, rose of Mary
Toxicity: No reported toxicity. Ingesting rosemary is contraindicated for those with hypertension.
Keywords: Fidelity, remembrance, purification, protection from ghosts and nightmares

Beloved rosemary is an aromatic evergreen shrub with spikes of needle-like leaves and small blue or purplish flowers. Prior to 2017, this herb was known by the scientific name *Rosmarinus officinalis*. Rosemary is native to the regions of the Mediterranean and Asia but is now grown widely for its hardy beauty, distinctive scent, and use as a culinary herb. In ancient Greece and other areas of the Mediterranean, rosemary was extensively utilized for purification, festivals, weddings, and funerals.[132] It could be burnt as an offering or aromatic, used to season food, crafted into wreaths for celebrants to wear or to decorate statues of the gods, or used as a funerary herb to mask the scent of decomposition.

In folklore, rosemary has long been associated with remembrance. Drinking a cup of rosemary tea or tucking a sprig of rosemary behind the ear is said to stimulate the mental faculty of memory. In Shakespeare's *Hamlet*, Ophelia's

---

132. Mallorie Vaudoise, *Honoring Your Ancestors: A Guide to Ancestral Veneration* (Woodbury, MN: Llewellyn Publications, 2019), 164.

sentiment echoes this belief: "There's rosemary, that's for remembrance; pray you, love, remember."[133] A small bouquet of rosemary sprigs left at the grave of a loved one is a customary token of remembrance. In *Flower Essences from the Witch's Garden*, author Nicholas Pearson theorizes that rosemary's resonance with memory can also extend to awakening our ancestral or cellular memory, as well as memories of past lives.[134]

Due to its exceptional powers of purification, rosemary can also help guard against unwanted nightmares and ghosts. Tuck a sprig of rosemary under your pillow or bed, or include it in a sachet with mugwort, hops, and lavender for easement of nightmares. To discourage unwanted ghosts or spirits, burn rosemary in your home or other space, fumigating it by wafting the smoke of the smoldering herb throughout each room.

Quince Tree

Species: *Cydonia oblonga*
Other Common Names: Cydonian pomme, golden apple
Toxicity: No reported toxicity. However, humans and animals should only eat the fleshy fruit and not ingest the seeds, leaves, or stems, like with pears and apples.
Keywords: Offerings, propitiation of the dead

Quince is a flowering deciduous tree that bears hard, aromatic, yellowish-green fruit somewhat similar in appearance to a pear. Quince fruit is seldom eaten raw because of its tough skin and hard flesh, as well as its unpleasant tart, astringent taste. However, quince fruit can be roasted, cooked, and processed into delicious treats such as quince paste, jam, or pudding and also used to make alcoholic brandies. In ancient Greek mythology, quince fruit may have been the Golden Apple of Discord, the fruit Eris, the goddess of strife, inscribed with the words "to the fairest" before tossing it onto the Olympians' table during the wedding feast of Peleus and Thetis, parents of the hero Achilles. The inscription allegedly provoked a fight between the goddesses Hera, Athena, and Aphrodite that led to the Trojan War.

---

133. William Shakespeare, *Hamlet*, ed. Charles John Kean (London: Bradbury and Evans, 1859; Project Gutenberg, 2009), 4.5.199–201.

134. Pearson, *Flower Essences from the Witch's Garden*, 407.

Before bearing fruit, the quince tree produces delicate pink flowers. In a nod to one of the interpretations of Melinoe's name, "having the color of quince," I have had success using quince flowers to evoke her presence. The fresh or dried flower petals seem to work just as well as the fruit itself, and they have the added benefit of exhibiting a softer, gentler energy than the tart fruit. I find that this softer approach helps calm and focus Melinoe's restless nature, as well as that of any attending ghosts, so that propitiations, rituals, and other works of magic can be more fully received.

Khthonic Bestiary: Snakes and the Ouroboros

People tend to have very polarized feelings about snakes—they are either fascinated by them or completely petrified of them. Snakes move without limbs, appear suddenly from underground hiding places, stare with unblinking eyes, and swallow their prey whole. The venom of venomous snakes is paradoxically a deadly killer and an antidote, with other helpful medical uses such as pain control and slowing of hemorrhage.[135] "There has been a tendency to classify snakes among the strange and supernatural in societies around the world; everywhere, in fact, where snakes are part of the local fauna," writes Patricia Fourcade in *Snakes: A Natural History*. She continues, "They have been seen either as demons, monsters, gods, ancestors, or sacred protectors, according to the civilization in question.... One discovers that there is an ambiguity and plurality of the snake's image, which represents opposite values, or serves as a link between them."[136] A snake wrapped around a staff is the symbol of Asklepios, ancient Greek god of medicine and healing arts; two snakes coiled around a winged staff is the symbol of Hermes, swift-footed messenger of the Olympian gods and bearer of departed souls to the Underworld.

Snakes continually shed their skins as they grow, reminiscent of khthonic themes like death, regeneration, rebirth, and eternity. Rather than being a mythological snake of a particular civilization, the snake known as the *Ouroboros* is a symbol that spans many ancient cultures. The Ouroboros features a snake eating its own tail, simultaneously devouring and giving birth to itself.

---

135. Burton, *The Meaning of Myth*, loc. 101, Kindle.

136. Patricia Fourcade, "Mythology," in *Snakes: A Natural History*, ed. Roland Bauchot (New York: Sterling Publishing, 1994), 184.

The snake's ability to renew its skin through molting is at the root of this concept. It is a vision of the infinite cycle of life and the transmigration of the soul.

Ouroboros

Death happens on multiple levels: in our personal lives, in our communities, and in that which is larger (on a global or existential scale). As it is not only a physical ending, we can also experience the death of relationships, careers, and outmoded ways of thinking, being, or doing—just to name a few types of death that may be encountered within a human lifespan. Like the ouroboros, we continually die and give birth to ourselves, right down to the cellular level. Perhaps this is why Hades was sometimes depicted with snakes, silently undulating, bellies connected to the ground. Snakes have much to teach us about endings *and* beginnings.

Finding Hades in the Landscape: Nekromanteion at Baiae

The ancient Roman city of Baiae is located along the Bay of Naples in Italy. In an article for *Smithsonian Magazine*, reporter Mike Dash writes, "Two thousand years ago, Baiæ was a flourishing spa, noted both for its mineral cures and for the scandalous immorality that flourished there. Today, it is little more than a collection of picturesque ruins—but it was there, in the 1950s, that the entrance to a hitherto unknown antrum was discovered by the Italian archaeologist

Amedeo Maiuri. It had been concealed for years beneath a vineyard; Maiuri's workers had to clear a 15-foot-thick accumulation of earth and vines."[137]

The entrance to the antrum at Baiae is a tight squeeze—a mere sliver of a tunnel, carved from the surrounding rock, disappearing into the hillside near the ancient ruins of a temple. The cramped space is uncomfortably hot and filled with fumes, so the site remained relatively unexplored until it came to the attention of Robert Paget in the early 1960s. Paget was an amateur archaeologist who excavated as a hobby; he and colleague Keith Jones pressed their way through the narrow opening to find themselves inside a close, confined tunnel, 8 feet (2.4 m) tall but only 21 inches (53 cm) wide.[138] Paget and Jones, working in difficult conditions with only a small group of volunteers, would spend the next decade clearing and exploring the intricate man-made tunnel system they found. They eventually concluded that the tunnels were a Nekromanteion, specially designed by priests to mimic a visit to the Underworld of Greek mythology.

The claims made by Paget and Jones have been subject to much critique over the years, and the site is still pending reinvestigation by trained archaeologists. A local guide can be hired to lead intrepid visitors into the antrum at Baiae, but be forewarned that the ancient tunnel system remains extremely narrow and difficult terrain.

Invitations to Practice

Invoke Hades Adesius (Hades of the Grave) when it becomes necessary to give a good death to relationships, habits, or outdated ways of thinking and being. Call upon Hades Nekrodegmon (Hades Receiver of the Dead) as appropriate during funeral rites, celebrations of life, or burials and interments. Correspondences and symbols that resonate with the energy of Hades in these aspects are lekythoi filled with olive or perfume oil, rosemary, and the infinite ouroboros.

Hymn to Makaria

The following hymn is dedicated to Hades' daughter Makaria. Recite this hymn to invoke Makaria's blessing when working with the concept of the good death,

---

137. Mike Dash, "The Unsolved Mystery of the Tunnels at Baiae," *Smithsonian Magazine*, accessed October 1, 2012, https://www.smithsonianmag.com/history/the-unsolved-mystery-of-the-tunnels-at-baiae-56267963/.

138. Dash, "The Unsolved Mystery of the Tunnels at Baiae."

remembering beloved ancestors, or making annual offerings for those who have passed. Makaria enjoys libations of sweet beverages flavored with anise or honey.

I sing of thee, Makaria, Daughter of Hades,
Walking the fields of Elysium,
Tending groves of ripe fruit and hives heavy with honey.
You, with gentle footsteps, offer mortals
Respite, contentment, and rest,
The taste of your gifts sweet on my tongue,
The sound of your voice soothing to my ear.
I offer honor to thee, Makaria, called Blessed
Companion of the River of Forgetting,
As I burn precious manna and hang lanterns in the cypress tree.
Let me not forget that all things must be laid to rest well and in their own time,
So that I, too, may rest well,
Knowing I have lived this life fully
When I lift the cup of Lethe to my lips.

Hymn to Melinoe

The following hymn is dedicated to Hades' daughter Melinoe. Recite this hymn to evoke Melinoe's presence when propitiating the restless dead or to ask for her assistance when dealing with ghosts and hauntings. Melinoe appreciates offerings of bitter herbs, ice, and quince fruit or flowers.

I sing of thee, Melinoe, Ethereal Daughter
Of the Host of Many and Queen Persephone,
Your veil spun of tears,
Your garment woven from the fabric of ghosts and shades.
Neither shadow nor light,
You wander the borderlands,
Haunting, haunted, haunting.
I offer honor to thee, Melinoe, called Propitiator,
A moonlit plate of quince fruit,
An altar to my ancestors, earnest prayers sung
For the restless dead,

So that they may no longer need to drink from the River of Tears,
So that they may no longer be thirsty,
So that they may, finally, be at rest.

Magical Praxis: Symbolic Rite of Good Death

This simple rite of sympathetic magic incorporates three ancient Greek funeral traditions: honoring the dead with an organic wreath, providing an obol for Kharon, and propitiating the dead with khoai. Use this magical rite to give relationships or habits a good death, so that they do not come back to haunt you.

For the funereal herbs, try to procure fresh plants, either store-bought or harvested, so that the leaves and stems are still tender enough to be woven into a circle. Many of these plants are also culinary herbs, and two to three small bunches (such as the presorted bunches sold in markets and grocery stores) will provide enough organic material for you to work with. If you do not have access to fresh plants, you can draw a wreath of herbs on a piece of paper.

MATERIAL SUPPLIES

- Funereal herbs such as rosemary, oregano, parsley, thyme, or mint to construct a small wreath
- 2–3 feet (approximately 1 m) of twine or ribbon
- Scissors
- 1 coin for Kharon. Any denomination is fine—it just needs to be a metal coin.
- Khoai for the dead. In ancient Greece, acceptable libations were either olive oil, a mixture of milk and honey, or a mixture of wine and water.
- Salt or rue-infused water (see page 117)

Directions for the Rite

1. Prepare for your symbolic death rite by digging a shallow "grave" in which to bury your wreath. Gather the material supplies on a central altar, cast a boundary circle around the grave and your workspace, and set wards of protection in each of the five directions.

2. Create your wreath by weaving or braiding together the herbs you have selected, reinforcing the structure of the wreath by tying knots at 3-to-4-inch (7–10 cm) intervals with ribbon or twine. Use the scissors

to trim the loose ends of your knots. If you like, you can recite a
hymn, sing, or pray while you construct the wreath. The wreath can
be any size, depending on your supplies, but 12 to 14 inches (30–35
cm) should suffice. Complete the wreath with one final knot that
binds the beginning and end together, forming a circle.

3. Once your wreath is complete, approach the grave with it in hand. As
    you place the wreath into the earth, speak aloud that you are giving
    something a symbolic good death. Add the coin for Kharon to the
    grave and pour out your khoai.

4. Fill in the grave with dirt, making sure to cover the wreath and offer-
    ings, and toss a pinch of salt or sprinkle of rue-infused water onto the
    soil. In sealing the grave with salt or rue water, you help ensure that
    any residual energy from this symbolic funeral rite does not cling to
    you.

5. Release your wards and your circle. Once they have been released,
    announce out loud, "It is done." Purify yourself with khernips before
    returning to normal activities.

Trance Journey: Two Pathways in the Cave

This guided trance begins at the mouth of a cave in the Otherworld, wherein
you will have the chance to speak with Makaria or Melinoe. You can read
through the text before you journey and let your memory of it guide your
experience in the Otherworld. Alternatively, you can record yourself reading
the text aloud (on your phone, for example) and play it back as you journey. To
begin, ease into your preferred method for inducing the trance journey state,
and land at your Otherworld HQ.

*Find your way to the mouth of a cave. There is rich, dark packed earth beneath
your feet, forming a clear path into its depths. The world around you is still
and silent; the only sound is the beating of your own heart. You feel compelled
to move forward down the earthen path and pass through the threshold of the
cave's entrance.*

*Your way is lit by the soft glow of oil lamps. They shine from small divots
carved directly into the walls of the cave, the handiwork of ancient stone artisans. Stalactites and stalagmites lean toward each other like lovers. You can
hear water dripping in the distance, the sound of an underground spring or*

river in another area of the caverns. The oil lamps provide a small amount of warmth, but the air around you remains slightly chilled. You pause and notice goosebumps skating across the surface of your skin. Upon looking forward again, you find that the path before you diverges.

Two altars, heralding two distinct choices, now greet you. The altar on the right is filled with crisp apples and luscious honeycombs; the altar on the left, with overripe quince fruit and stalks of rue. There is a small charcoal brazier on each altar and a dish of incense. Pilgrims passing this way before you have added a dash of incense to the braziers; now that you see these items, you recognize the faint scent of their offerings in the air around you.

Which path will you choose? At which altar will you make your offering?

Should you choose the altar to the right, redolent with sweet apples and honey, you will meet Makaria, She of the Blessed Death. A pinch of manna is your offering for her brazier. Moving past the altar, down the right-hand path, you come into her presence. Take a moment to notice how she appears. What is she wearing? What are her features and facial expression? What sensory cues and perceptions do you pick up in her presence? Introduce yourself and your purpose for this visit. If you have a specific question in mind, such as how to give something or someone a good death, gain her consent and ask. If you don't have any specific questions for Makaria, simply ask what she may wish to share about herself, her Underworld family, or the nature of the good death in general.

Should you choose the altar to the left, foreboding yet compelling, you will meet Melinoe, She of Ghosts and the Restless Dead. A pinch of aromatic funerary herbs are your offering for her brazier. Moving past the altar, down the left-hand path, you come into her presence. Take a moment to notice how she appears. What is she wearing? What are her features and facial expression? What sensory cues and perceptions do you pick up in her presence? Introduce yourself and your purpose for this visit. If you have a specific question in mind, such as how to feed hungry ghosts, gain her consent and ask. If you don't have any specific questions for Melinoe, simply ask what she may wish to share about her mythology, her Underworld responsibilities, or the restless dead.

When you are finished speaking, make a gesture of gratitude and offer your thanks for this meeting. If the goddess fades into the dark of the cave before you are finished asking questions, it simply signals that this interview is over. You can come back another time to continue the conversation. Again, offer your thanks before turning to leave. Leave the same way you came, heading back up the path to the altar. Gently touch the altar where you made your offering as you pass, acknowledging the spirits who live in and maintain this place.

At the fork in the path, you leave both altars behind. Retracing your way to the mouth of the cave, the oil lamps flicker, and you can once again sense the world outside of this dark, earthen womb. The knowledge and experiences gained here travel with you, solidifying with each step you take. You pass over the threshold of the cave and return to your Otherworld HQ.

CHAPTER 9
WHEN GODS COME CALLING

꡶꡶꡶꡶꡶꡶꡶꡶꡶꡶꡶꡶꡶꡶꡶꡶꡶꡶꡶꡶꡶

Hades speaks:

Many things were different in the past. Mortals rarely ever approached my temples, sacred groves, or precincts. On the few occasions they made sacrifices or offerings, supplicants turned their backs to me, afraid to catch even a fleeting glimpse of my face. Mortals avoided sharing libations with me. They hardly spoke my name, Hades, until recently. And even now, my name is more often spoken with revile than gratitude or adoration. If only the living could see the power of their veneration, of their earnest offerings and acts of devotion: the Halls of Hades gleam brighter. Underworld rivers are renewed and pools refilled. The denizens of my realm are nourished, replenished, and ready to continue carrying out their tasks. This is the impact of their devotion. Why would they not want to see the home of their ancestors thrive?

How many thousands of years have passed since then, I do not exactly know, for I am deathless and have lost count over the millennia. But I can tell you what gifts I have received from interacting with mortals and their shades for so long: determination, compassion, and perhaps, acknowledgment. I know firsthand how important it is to provide a place for souls to rest between lifetimes; having encountered many souls more than once and witnessed their progress, I am determined to remain resolute in the fulfillment of my duties. I came to understand compassion by watching mortals be kind to one another, oftentimes kinder than required, and observing how their souls glowed brighter as a result. Compassion is growth and expansion. I have expanded my sense of self to embrace both stoicism and compassion—because I learned these two traits are not incompatible.

The last of these gifts, acknowledgment, is what I desire. Not approval, but acknowledgment of my place in the eternal cycle of life and death, and of my contributions to the collective. I will always be a god apart, Ruler of the Dead, seemingly separated from the living by both time and space. But I seek kharis with mortals, and for me, reciprocity means acknowledgment. Acknowledge me by reading my hymns. By pouring libations. And by speaking my name: Hades. If you feel called, look upon my face and pursue my mysteries. I am waiting.

Kharis: Devotion and Reciprocity

At the heart of ancient Greek religion was the concept of *kharis*. Loosely defined, kharis is an offering made in the spirit of reciprocity: "I give, so that you may give." It can also refer to a sense of grace, good fortune, or providence that is felt on behalf of the giver and the receiver. Kharis speaks to sacred give and take, to the idea that mortals and gods can engage in reciprocal relationships with mutual benefit.

To the ancient Greeks, kharis was fostered through sacrifices, libations, observance of seasonal festivals, and other devotional practices. Gods who received sacrifices and offerings were understood to have a vested interest in mortal affairs; consequently, in the case of Hades, this meant the Ruler of the Dead received little veneration. Classics scholar Diana Burton explains, "Although other instantiations of the god such as Plouton or Klymenos are the recipients of cult [sacrifices and devotional practices], the god under the name of Hades is not. This lack of cult is confirmed by the dearth of evidence, epigraphic [inscriptions] or otherwise, for cult in Hades' name throughout the Greek world. Greek religion is based upon reciprocity, and it is an aspect of Hades' isolation that he receives nothing from worshippers as he has nothing to offer in exchange."[139] The only known exceptions to this were Hades' cult at Elis and in the surrounding area.

Considering Hades received so little recognition and devotion in the ancient world, does that limit our ability to build meaningful relationships with him? Is he a stranger to kharis? No, most definitely not. In my experience, Hades is very much open to the idea of participating in short-term working

139. Diana Burton, "Worshipping Hades: Myth and Cult in Elis and Triphylia," *Archiv für Religionsgeschichte* 20, no. 1 (2018): 212, https://doi.org/10.1515/arege-2018-0013.

relationships, supporting devotees with his patronage, and even to accepting oaths of dedication. Ancient peoples may have ignored or resisted building relationships with Hades because they feared death or because they felt he had little to offer to the living. Modern Hades devotees, however, realize that he has much more to offer than material and agricultural wealth. We have only to look at his other epithets to realize the many ways in which having a relationship with Hades could benefit our lives: Polydegmon for matters of hospitality, for example, or Eubuleus for wise counsel, Adamastos for resolve, or Agesilaos for building leadership skills.

When Gods Come Calling

When it comes to friendships, romantic partnerships, and other types of relationships, sometimes we may find ourselves to be the initiators—making the first move, casting the first tentative line—and sometimes we may find ourselves on the other side of the equation, the ones who are being courted. Devotional relationships with the gods can be very similar. You might feel called to initiate a relationship with a certain god because you are drawn to their energy and mythos, or maybe because you want to invite some of their qualities into your life. In other instances, a deity may reach out to you in a distinctive way—perhaps unexpectedly—and it feels more like they are pursuing you. Both of these experiences, and anything along the spectrum in between, are equally valid.

Cultivating relationships with deities feeds my soul and remains a cornerstone of my magical praxis and life. I've nurtured relationships with gods from a few different pantheons over the years: Mary Magdalene, Mary the Mother of Jesus, Branwen, Ceridwen, Arianrhod, Bhuvaneshwari, Saraswati, Kali-Ma, Artemis, and more recently, Hades and his Underworld retinue. Some of these relationships were temporary, while others have stayed with me for decades. From my experience, devotional relationships offer many beautiful possibilities: inspiration, aid and assistance, mentorship, spiritual ecstasy, divine union, and a bone-deep sense of acceptance and belonging.

So, did I choose Hades, or did he choose me? Admittedly, I've always been attracted to the more shadowy side of magic, mythology, and folklore. Tales of death rituals, ghosts, and hauntings have fascinated me for all my life. In books and movies, I root for the misfits, misunderstood villains, and antiheroes. So it's not too surprising that I am intrigued by the mystery, complexity, and the taboo nature of shadowy gods like Hades. But, honestly, I think the story of Hades and me began far before I even knew his name; it began when I was a child, suffering from insomnia and night terrors.

My Story: An Unmistakable Presence

For over a decade of my childhood, I regularly averaged about four hours of sleep each night; sometimes a couple more hours, other times less. When I did sleep, my dreams were vivid and scary, fraught with impending doom. Killer bees, earthquakes, fear of life after death, mononucleosis, doomsday prophecies, velociraptors, encephalitis—the list was long and varied. My parents consulted our family pediatrician, but the doctor was not able to identify anything physically wrong with me. He concluded that I was simply a very precocious young person, bright and observant, and prone to worry about grown-up problems that I did not yet have the emotional maturity to process. Frustrated and out of ideas, my parents advised me to deal with my nighttime struggles by saying a bedtime prayer and trying to think of something happy. I don't resent my folks for this period in my life—they loved me, and like most parents, they were doing the best they knew how to do at the time. Later, as an adult, I would be accurately diagnosed with generalized anxiety disorder. As anyone with an anxiety disorder can attest, it is nigh impossible to escape troubling thought-loops without the proper coping skills; as an undiagnosed child, I felt alone and misunderstood in my struggles. So I found another way to self-soothe my fears through the long nights: I became a voracious reader.

My parents quickly caught on and bought me a reading lamp that clamped onto the headboard of my bed. I haunted libraries and always had a plentiful amount of books on standby—my two favorites were *Charlotte's Web* by E. B. White and *Black Beauty* by Anna Sewell. I read them so many times that their spines cracked and their pages grew loose. To be honest, the words of these beloved literary companions offered a succor I could not find in the bedtime prayer I so desperately whispered each night. As I grew into my twenties, the insomnia began to fade. Perhaps my emotional maturity, with its ability to process fear and overwhelm, had finally caught up. Or perhaps it was simply moving away from home for the first time, attending college, and engaging in all the distractions of young adulthood. The scary dreams, however, stuck around. To this day my dreams are still very intense. But over the years I have developed the ability to lucid dream; I can now recognize when I am dreaming, and oftentimes I can control the narrative of my dreams. It quells the fear. And it helps me discern when my heightened emotions are tied to a dream, not any sort of real danger.

How do these experiences fit into my Hades devotion story? Two explanations come to mind. First, since I spent so many nights in the company of death and fear, I became well acquainted with these particular shadows—shadow work is an essential component of my relationship with Hades. In fact, an astrologer interpreting my birth chart once told me that my childhood insomnia experiences were likely "early onset Hades," which made me chuckle. Second, there were many times in the middle of those nights when I felt a comforting presence in my room; I even remember a vague impression of dark, curly hair. I did not know who or what it was at the time, but the presence was not scary or alarming. It helped me feel less alone. It was not until decades later, when I experienced Hades' energy and personality first-hand through ritual trance possession, that I realized I already knew him. His presence is unmistakable: I had met Hades as a child.

Working Relationships with Gods

Just like human relationships, partnerships with deities and spirits involve varying levels of commitment. Some relationships may be short-term for a specific purpose or need, while others may last many years, and still others can land somewhere in the middle. Relationships with deities and other beings are one of the topics Murphy Robinson and I teach about in our Way of the Weaver magical studies program. Murphy was the one to coin the phrase *working relationships* to describe transactional contracts or bargains with the gods. We've been refining our thoughts around this concept since launching the program in 2019.

Working relationships with the gods are similar to the Roman custom of *vota*. In ancient Roman religious practices, a *votum* (or vota, plural) was a vow or promise made to a deity, but it also referred to that which fulfilled a vow: the actions, offerings, statues, or temples that were promised. Vota represented contractual agreements between mortals and gods. This practice may have looked a bit more transactional than the Greek concept of kharis in its execution, but it still functioned on the supposition that if mortals delivered their end of the bargain, the gods would deliver theirs. Vota were indicative of the Latin phrase *quid pro quo*, "something for something" or "a favor for a favor." As you may have guessed, the Latin word *votum* is the origin of the modern English word *vow*.

When you approach a god for a working relationship, or if one approaches you with a specific request, be extremely clear when negotiating the terms of your agreement with them. Refrain from making open-ended bargains. Clearly state when the service you are offering will be considered complete and your understanding of what you will receive from them in the exchange. The ways of the gods are not always copacetic with human ethics, morality, and cultural understandings. You may have to initiate conversations to help them understand concepts like consent, for example, but remain firm and stand your ground. If a deity—or any other being, for that matter—refuses to respect your boundaries, you have every right to refuse to engage in a relationship with them.

It is not necessary to adopt a god as your patron or consider yourself their devotee, in order to have this type of contractual working relationship with them. For example, I had a short-term working agreement with the Greek goddess Artemis in 2016. I was looking for opportunities to hone my skills as a community ritualist, and the goddess offered to mentor me in these efforts. Artemis connected me with teachers and events that helped me stretch and gain confidence in my abilities. As her boon, she requested that I conduct a large community ritual in her honor. Using the skills I learned that year, I created and led a successful (and fun!) Rites of Artemis ritual with over 200 people in attendance. Upon delivering that ritual, our agreement was complete.

Adopting a Patron God

A patron or matron is a god whom you invite into your life for a longer period of time; your involvement with them is something more than just engaging them for one ritual, for example, or calling on them to empower the odd spell every now and then. A god can be the patron of one part of your life— for instance, Hades might be your patron of financial planning—or of your life in general. I like to use the word *devotee* to describe my role in these types of relationships, such as, "I am a devotee of Ceridwen, and she is my matron goddess of poetry and storytelling." If you prefer to use a gender-neutral term for this relationship, you can call them your benefactor, prime, mentor, or zatron. *Zatron* is a gender-neutral term that was suggested by Sage Elwyn, one of the participants in our Way of the Weaver program. Can you think of more creative terms? I encourage you to try them out and see what your gods respond to.

Choosing to adopt a god as your patron is oftentimes a natural result of performing acts of devotion; over time, you begin to resonate with them more and more. You find their presence in your life to be beneficial in some way. You might even feel a sense of existential or transcendent love for them. In my own experience, this type of relationship is very similar to having a beloved, close friend: you enjoy each other's company, have similar interests, spend a lot of time together, do nice things for one another, and celebrate holidays and significant life events together.

Patronage relationships tend to be open-ended, with a natural ebb and flow of attention and activity. They wax and wane organically; it is the generous quality of kharis that feeds these partnerships. People may have more than one patron god in their life at a time or over the course of their lifetime. If your life or desires change, you are not required to continue honoring a god as your patron if you've not made any formal promises or commitments to them. However, just like with human relationships, plan your exit strategy with gratitude and respect.

Exploring the Lore

Know thyself is an ancient Greek aphorism—a principle or observation concisely stated. According to travel writer Pausanias, this aphorism was inscribed in stone: "In the fore-temple at Delphi are written maxims useful for the life of men, inscribed by those whom the Greeks say were sages.... These sages, then, came to Delphi and dedicated to Apollo the celebrated maxims, 'Know thyself,' and 'Nothing in excess.'"[140] Before consulting the Pythia in the inner sanctum of the temple, ancient visitors would have had time to pause, and perhaps reflect, on these statements.

Inner reflection often seems like an indulgence in our too-busy, digital-technology-driven, fast-paced modern world. But sometimes it can be helpful to check in with your inner desires and longings, as well as your fears and inhibitions—especially when embarking on new relationships. Many people

---

140. Pausanias, "Description of Greece," in *Complete Works of Pausanias*, 10.24.1.

find long-hand stream of consciousness journaling to be a helpful tool to separate and organize their thoughts. If that's not quite your thing, you can try collaging, drawing, dancing, mind-mapping, or simply making a list of your thoughts. Maybe even take a self-reflective walk, or find a natural setting in which to sit quietly for a few contemplative moments?

However you choose to engage with your inner dialogue, here are twelve prompts to help you reflect on initiating a devotional relationship with Hades. Choose one prompt a day, one prompt a week, or one prompt a month. Or sit down and answer them all at once! Do what works best for you. Your answers can help craft your intent and guide your steps.

- What does the concept of devotion mean to me?
- What do I desire from a devotional relationship with Hades?
- What is my favorite bit of Hades' mythology, and how might that guide my devotion?
- How will I approach him to gain his consent? How will I give mine?
- What am I willing to offer in the spirit of kharis, in reciprocity?
- Is there anything specific I would like to receive in return?
- What are my unique talents, skills, gifts, and abilities?
- What are my boundaries around time, finances, and accessibility?
- What are my safety and privacy requirements?
- What are my fears around involving Hades in my life in a larger capacity?
- What support, if any, do I need in terms of accountability?
- How will I know if it might be time to move on and devote my energy elsewhere?

Symbols of Hades: The Cornucopia

The cornucopia, sometimes also called the horn of plenty, is a large horn-shaped basket overflowing with vegetables, fruits, flowers, and nuts. Often associated with fertility and agricultural prosperity, the cornucopia is a symbol of blessings and abundance. In ancient art and iconography, Hades is depicted in his guise of Plouton, the Wealthy One, with a cornucopia to symbolize the wealth of nourishment that comes from the rich, fertile soil of his domain. According to Diana Burton, "The cornucopia is not specific to Hades, but it is predominantly his.... In those images in which the cornucopia appears, it is often the only really distinctive thing about him. And it is very distinctive: it is usually large, often fully half his height, and full of leaves or fruit or both."[141]

The contents of cornucopias depicted with Hades are not always consistent. However, art historians have observed many instances of small, round objects that could represent pumpkins, pomegranates, or poppy seed heads tumbling from Hades' cornucopia—all foods that can be consumed, but that also carry Underworld connotations. Burton continues, "To regard Plouton as *solely* a god of fertility risks omitting an important aspect of his character. Hades' wealth, from which he draws his epithet Plouton, is not only composed of the fertility drawn from the earth but also refers to the wealth of souls he holds underneath the earth. Wherever Plouton, or Hades, is, and whatever he does, he brings with him a faint but pervasive reminder of mortality."[142] The cornucopia at its most utilitarian is a tool used to collect and carry harvested vegetation—thus emblematic of a bountiful yield. At the same time, however, the gifts of Plouton's cornucopia also remind us that death may sometimes be necessary for nourishment.

In His Dark Garden: Violet and Thyme

Working with violet and thyme can feel like inhaling a deep breath of fresh, clean spring air after a long winter spent indoors. Delicate violet resonates with the tender pull of heartfelt devotion, while the vibrant energy of thyme purifies and bolsters courage. Call on these plant allies to invite sweetness, fortitude, remembrance, and easy transitions into your life.

VIOLET
Species: *Viola odorata*
Other Common Names: English violet, sweet violet, wood violet
Toxicity: No reported toxicity
Keywords: Beauty, devotion, honoring the beloved dead, springtime, sweetness

---

141. Diana Burton, "Hades: Cornucopiae, Fertility and Death," 32nd Australasian Society for Classical Studies Conference, 2011, 2, https://www.ascs.org.au/news/ascs32/Burton.pdf.

142. Burton, "Hades: Cornucopiae, Fertility and Death," 7.

Sweet violet is a shade-loving, low-lying perennial with fragrant purple, dark blue, or white flowers. Violet typically blooms from February to May, although some species may experience a second bloom in August. The petals and leaves are edible. The distinctive light, powdery scent of the flowers is widely used in cosmetics, candies, teas, and syrups. Notes of violet flowers and leaves are popular inclusions in perfumes. Violets make many appearances in Greco-Roman mythology as well; they are specifically noted in the *Homeric Hymn to Demeter* as one of the flowers Persephone gathers for her bouquet before being swept away by Hades.[143]

A little-known Roman festival called the *Violaria* took place around the vernal equinox each year to celebrate the advent of spring and the gathering of violets for food and perfumes. The festival was dedicated to honoring the dead—both the vegetation that would be harvested during the coming months and the human deceased. Festivities of the ancient Violaria included decorating graves and tombs with garlands of violet.[144] Similar to rosemary, violet has the ability to connect us to fond memories, while reminding us to honor and care for our beloved dead. Symbolic of heartfelt love and devotion, violet's gentle spiritus viridis can also help you better understand what kharis means to you and provide valuable insight into how you can best cultivate reciprocity with gods and ancestors in your magical praxis and life.

Thyme

Species: *Thymus vulgaris*

Other Common Names: Common thyme, garden thyme, wild thyme

Toxicity: No reported toxicity. Ingesting thyme is contraindicated for pregnant people and those with a hyperthyroid condition.

Keywords: Bravery, courage, purification, strength, wealth

Indigenous to the Mediterranean region, thyme is an aromatic perennial herb that has been used for purification, to flavor food and beverages, and as a token of courage and strength for thousands of years. The ancient Egyptians used thyme in their embalming practices, while the Greeks and Romans burned it in their homes and temples or added it to their baths for purification. In the

---

143. Evelyn-White, trans., *The Homeric Hymns*, 289–91.

144. Occvlta, "Violet," *Materia Venefica* 20 (April 2023): 21, https://www.occvlta.org/.

Middle Ages, women tucked sprigs of thyme into the armor of knights and warriors and often included it in bouquets of flowers or incense prepared for funerals—thyme was thought to bolster bravery and fortitude in battle and also to ease the transition from living to dead.

Partner with thyme as a magical ally for transitions, such as when starting a new magical praxis or personal endeavor, or conversely, when a commitment, activity, or relationship comes to a close. Bay laurel and rosemary are the herbs most commonly used for khernips, but you may want to experiment with a sprig of thyme used in this manner, too, due to its long association with purification. Adding a few sprigs of thyme to your bathwater on the night of the new moon is a simple but effective rite of purification to begin the next monthly cycle.

Khthonic Bestiary: The Cockerel

A famous *pinax* (votive board) of Hades and Persephone from the eighth century BCE is part of the Magna Graecia collection housed in the Museo Archeologico Nazionale di Reggio Calabria (Italy). This marble bas-relief sculpture portrays the couple enthroned side-by-side: Persephone holds a hen and a sheaf of wheat, while Hades holds a *phiale* (libation bowl) and a stalk of rue or asphodel. A cockerel, or young rooster, promenades next to their thrones.[145]

Roosters have both solar and Underworld associations in ancient Greek mythology, depending on the context in which they appear. When depicted with Persephone and Hades as a couple, roosters are usually symbolic of marriage and fertility. When depicted with Persephone or Hades alone, however, the cockerel may represent souls of the deceased—as noted in chapter 4, Greco-Roman art has many examples of birds, butterflies, and sometimes even bats metaphorically representing the soul departed from the physical body. When I think of a rooster strutting around the barnyard, the phrase that comes to mind is "Walk your talk." If you are going to crow about your relationship with Hades, walk your talk through regular veneration, offerings, and acts of devotion.

---

145. Unknown artist, *Pinax (Votive Relief)*, 700 BCE, Marble bas-relief, Museo Archeologico Nazionale di Reggio Calabria, Reggio Calabria, Italy.

Finding Hades in the Landscape:
Ploutonion Temple at Hierapolis

Hierapolis was a city in Classical Phrygia, in southwestern Anatolia. Natural thermal springs flow here, and the spa city of Hierapolis was established at the end of the second century BCE by the dynasty of the Attalids, kings of Pergamon.[146] The ruins of the baths, temples, and other Greek monuments have been a UNESCO world heritage site since 1988. Ancient Hierapolis can be found adjacent to the modern city of Pamukkale in southwestern Turkey.

On this site, the structure known as Pluto's Gate (*Ploutonion* in Greek, or *Plutonium* in Latin) was built over the entrance to a cave emitting highly toxic gas. The toxic fumes were called "Hades' lethal breath" and killed anything that came near. There is archaeological evidence of ritual and animal sacrifices having been made at Pluto's Gate—pilgrims could watch bulls being sacrificed from the nearby steps, but only priests of the Ploutonion were allowed to stand directly in front of the portal. The noxious fumes were too dangerous to risk exposure, although they purportedly induced necromantic visions for the priests of the temple. Rampaging Christians destroyed most of the Ploutonion during the sixth century CE, and subsequent earthquakes demolished anything that was left.

According to the Greek Reporter, an excavation in 2013 uncovered high carbon dioxide levels being emitted from the ground where the gate was located, explaining the deaths of birds and animals who flew or wandered too close.[147] The excavation was led by Francesco D'Andria, professor of Classical archaeology at the University of Salento, Italy. D'Andria and his team also found a temple, a pool, and steps above the cave that all corresponded to descriptions of the gateway from ancient texts.[148] Columns with inscriptions to Hades and Persephone were among the ruins. After excavation, the stones of Pluto's Gate were restored to their positions and statues erected on the terrace. The site

146. UNESCO World Heritage Centre, "Hierapolis-Pamukkale," accessed January 30, 2023, https://whc.unesco.org/en/list/485/.

147. Tasos Kokkinidis, "Turkey Opens 'Gate to Hell' in Ancient Greek City of Hierapolis," Greek Reporter, June 23, 2022, https://greekreporter.com/2022/06/23/ancient-gate-hell-hierapolis/.

148. Michael Walsh, "Gateway to Hades Said to Be Uncovered by Italian Archaeologists in Southwestern Turkey: Is It Hell on Earth?," *New York Daily News*, April 4, 2013, https://www.nydailynews.com/news/world/gateway-hades-uncovered-turkey-archaeologists-article-1.1307747.

was recently reopened to the public in 2022. A new walkway constructed at a safe distance from the cave allows curious visitors to peek into the ancient Ploutonion.

Invitations to Practice

Hades as Plouton historically represented agricultural bounty; the material wealth of rich soil, precious metals, and minerals; and also the wealth of shades dwelling in his Underworld realm. In a modern context, we can expand our understanding of Hades' wealth to encompass gifts received through kharis: friendship, mentorship, assistance, grace, confidence, and acceptance are just a few of the possibilities. Symbols and correspondences that resonate with the energy of Hades in his aspect as the Wealthy One are the cornucopia, sweet violet, thyme, and the cockerel.

Hymn to Plouton

The following hymn can be spoken or sung to connect with Plouton. Recite this hymn to venerate Hades as the Wealthy One, to invite wealth and generosity (physical or otherwise) into your life, or simply in gratitude for any gifts you receive.

> *Khaire Hades! Khaire Plouton!*
> *Wealthy One, who provides for the collective,*
> *On this day I sing of your generosity,*
> *On this day I lift up your name.*
> *Khaire Hades! Khaire Plouton!*
> *Wealthy One, who nourishes the collective,*
> *On this day I invite your blessing,*
> *On this day I welcome your grace.*

The Sweetness of Devotion

The best way to get to know Hades, and the other denizens of the Underworld, is simply by spending time with them. Or, perhaps said more accurately, by *devoting* time to them. There are myriad ways to show affection and devotion toward the gods. Devotional acts both large and small can be performed with the reciprocity of kharis ("I give, so that you may give") in mind, or simply because you feel called to signify feelings of adoration or gratitude with meaningful actions.

Devoting time to Hades will help you learn to recognize his unique energy, personality, and qualities and cultivate those qualities in yourself, if that is your desire. You might also uncover new or forgotten talents, gifts, skills, and preferences in the process—even a preference *not* to work with Hades, after all—and that's okay too. Try out a few different kinds of devotional activities to see what resonates for you. You can even speak to Hades about this topic, either at your altar or during a trance journey. He may have some wonderful personalized suggestions for you.

Simple Gestures

Simple, everyday gestures can facilitate relationship-building with the gods. Author Patrick Dunn describes saying "Khaire Herme!" when finding a coin on the ground.[149] You might say a silent or quiet "Khaire Hades!" whenever you want to recognize the presence of Hades in your daily life. For example, you might say this phrase when you spot a black animal while out and about, when you encounter one of his sacred plants on a walk, when you find an unexpected treasure at the thrift store, or when your paycheck hits your bank account. Ancient Greeks would sometimes kiss the fingertips of the right hand upon their first sight of the sun or the moon each day or to salute an image or sculpture of the gods. Indeed, I often do this myself, each time I pass my Hades altar. The kiss constitutes a small offering of breath, of the soul.[150]

Volunteer Work and Donations

It's easy to turn community service and volunteer work into an act of devotion by choosing activities that align with Hades' purview: cemetery clean-up, nursing home visitations, archival work, and hospice volunteering are all great choices for Hades devotees. If your lifestyle or physical abilities preclude volunteering your time, you can research causes and groups that are in alignment with Hades' energy and support them through monetary donations. Furthermore, if you have a specialized skill, such as reading tarot cards or offering

149. Patrick Dunn, *The Practical Art of Divine Magic: Contemporary & Ancient Techniques of Theurgy* (Woodbury, MN: Llewellyn Publications, 2015), 122.

150. Dunn, *The Practical Art of Divine Magic*, 123.

energetic healing, you can volunteer to donate your services in the name of Hades or the Underworld.

Hospitality as Devotion

As Polydegmon, the Host of Many, Hades holds hospitality in very sacred regard. Take some time to consider how you welcome your immediate community, such as your friends and family, into your own home. For example, do you feed them nourishing food and drinks? Do they have a clean, comfortable place to rest? Are there special touches that make them feel cared for and important? You need not be overt about the fact that you are dedicating your hosting efforts to Hades; it's the intention behind your efforts that matters.

Ancestry Research

If ancestry research and genealogical charts interest you, this is another area of your life that you can devote to Hades. Chronicling family history, vital records, and other important stories and documents are sacred rites of remembrance. This can be particularly impactful for Black, Indigenous, and other people of color in our communities who have lost much of their history to colonization and enslavement. If you need help getting started, there are many affordable genealogy courses available online, as well as books on the topic to loan from your local library. If you identify as a white person, once you've built some skills as a researcher, consider offering free ancestry research assistance to BIPOC families in the spirit of reparations.

Become a Resource for End-of-Life Planning

Many people resist planning for the end of their lives, oftentimes leaving family members and loved ones scrambling to make difficult decisions during an extremely emotional time. Although it may be uncomfortable in the beginning, Hades' devotees can learn to hold space for important conversations about estate planning, wills, and end-of-life directives in their circles of friends, family, and community. Simply making yourself open and available for these conversations is a great first step. Also consider educating yourself on the essentials, and make sure you have your own affairs in order. Here are three online resources, and a fun card game, to get conversations rolling:

- The Order of the Good Death (www.orderofthegooddeath.com): This website hosts a variety of well-researched, thorough articles about end-of-life planning, funerals, how to choose what to do with your body, and more.
- 5 Wishes Living Will (www.fivewishes.org): This website offers advice on how to talk to family members about your last will and testament, as well as other things, such as health care directives and power of attorney.
- Writing Your Own Will (www.freewill.com): This free online resource walks you through a step-by-step process to complete your last will and testament, and it also has helpful blog posts on related subjects, such as charitable donations, forming a living trust, and more.
- Morbid Curiosity Game (www.morbidcuriositygame.com): This deck contains 162 cards on the topic of death. Some cards are trivia questions about death-related science, history, and pop culture, while others are open-ended conversation-starters. Through humor and storytelling, game participants get to know each other better while also getting more comfortable talking (and laughing) about death.

Memorial Ground Maintenance and Care

The places where we memorialize and inter our dead take many forms, changing across time and cultures. In the past, our ancestors utilized earthen mounds and caves, among other methods, to inter their beloved dead. In modern times, cemeteries, graveyards, potter's fields, and columbariums are four very common types of memorial grounds. Chances are good that you live near one or more of these sites, even if you don't realize it yet:

Cemetery: Designated land where the remains of dead people are buried or otherwise interred. The term cemetery originally applied to ancient Roman catacombs.

Graveyard: Very similar to cemeteries, graveyards are also places where the remains of dead people are buried or otherwise interred. The main difference being that graveyards are attached or in close proximity to a church (i.e., in the churchyard).

Potter's Field: These fields were public burial places for unknown, unclaimed, criminal, or impoverished individuals of the recent past (going back at least one millennium, to as recently as the early-to-mid-1900s) who could not afford cemetery plots.

Columbarium: A building or sometimes a large wall that houses several niches holding funerary urns and cremated remains.

One way we can show care and devotion for these cities of the dead is to participate in their maintenance and repair. Public burial grounds, such as cemeteries and columbariums, often face funding issues. These sites sell single plots or niches but take care of the property as a whole forever. As designated burial grounds become full, no more plots can be sold. Over time, cash flow drops significantly and maintenance funds no longer generate enough income to cover all of the expenses necessary for upkeep. You've likely seen evidence of this decline when driving or walking by cemeteries with fallen markers, sunken soil, illegible headstones, or overgrown grass.

But before embarking on this path, it is critical to remember that the dead still have agency. Sometimes we have to ask ourselves, is this place somewhere I am welcome? Do I have consent to be here? For example, I live in the southern United States. Due to the history of racism and enslavement in this region, there are cemeteries that are divided along racial lines. When I consider working in a Black cemetery, it's important for me to research its history and reflect on whether or not my presence will do more harm (despite all good intentions). Sometimes there are living caretakers or community members that I can consult; other times I have to lean on my guides, gods, divination tools, and common sense to make the best decision I can with current information. The same considerations apply if you identify as a person of European descent and are thinking about participating in care and upkeep of an Indigenous burial site.

The easiest way to begin caring for memorial grounds is simple: litter pickup. Check out the hours that the site you plan to visit is open, and clean up any stray trash you find. Many communities have city and county cemetery preservation organizations—search online to see if one exists near you, or consider forming one on your own. These groups can be great historical and practical resources, and they often teach specialized skills, such as headstone maintenance and repair. However, before you volunteer for any repair or groundskeeping tasks (such as weeding, mowing, tree trimming, planting flowers, etc.), make sure that you have permission from the organization that oversees the memorial grounds to carry out these activities.

In the spirit of respect and reciprocity, there is a certain etiquette to follow when entering and exiting memorial grounds. These protocols can be quite elaborate depending on the type of working you are performing, but for our purposes of simply assisting with upkeep as an act of devotion, here are the basics.

This is the basic protocol for entering grave sites or burial grounds:

- Announce yourself to the dwellers within (residents and spirits of place) by hailing or calling out with your voice, ringing a bell, chanting etc.
- Open the gates (ethereal and perhaps physical).
- Step forward over the threshold with the right foot.
- Leave coins near the threshold as payment (reciprocity) for the guardian spirits of this place.
- Avoid walking directly on graves if possible.

This is the basic protocol for leaving grave sites or burial grounds:

- Take a moment to offer gratitude to the residents and spirits of the place.
- Step backward over the threshold with the left foot.
- Close any gates you have opened (physical and ethereal).
- Cleanse yourself with rue-infused water or fresh running water.
- Eat something to ground yourself (salty food is great).

If you find yourself visiting cemeteries on a regular basis, consider compiling an on-the-go kit to keep in your car or backpack. Here are a few suggestions for your memorial ground go-bag:

- Variety of small monetary coins
- Personal protection talismans that support you in this work
- Drinking water and portable snacks for yourself (such as dried meat, nuts, granola, etc.)
- Salt for quick protective circle-casting, if needed (use mindfully and sparingly so as not to damage the environment by altering the soil content)
- Rue-infused water or spring water for cleansing yourself afterward
- Disposable gloves, waste container, hand sanitizer

Rites of Remembrance

As magical practitioners, it is possible to work toward healing ancestral and collective lineages through time, offering our support and assistance to those who have already crossed the threshold of life and death. Now that I've covered a few basics about working in memorial grounds, I will share one of my favorite devotional rituals: taking a remembrance walk through a cemetery to propitiate the dead.

After I have determined that I have consent to walk within the cemetery I have chosen, I pick a time to visit with offerings in hand—usually black grapes, olive oil, and a blend of nontoxic loose herbal incense (I sprinkle this incense on the ground, rather than lighting it). The path I walk among the graves is random; I follow the whim of my intuition, pausing at several headstones along the way to read the names of the deceased aloud, reassuring them that they are not forgotten. Sometimes I also chant and sing songs to the dead. I leave offerings behind in the name of Hades Agesilaos or Hades Polydegmon. You can ask Hades' daughter Melinoe to accompany and guide you in this work; however, remember that she often travels with restless spirits in attendance. Take care that no unwanted spirits accidentally follow you home.

If you are called to this type of devotional activity, I advise you to be careful that any offerings you plan to leave outside will not cause harm to the flora or fauna of a place and are completely biodegradable. I take along my go-bag with safety gloves, a waste container, and hand sanitizer for all my walks in case I find any refuse that needs to be removed from the cemetery.

Creative Projects

In the ancient world, very few public works of art featured Hades. If Hades was represented, he usually appeared with Persephone, or perhaps with his brothers Zeus and Poseidon, his face half-hidden from the viewer. Greek mythology remains a big part of our cultural narrative; these days, we might recognize Hades' face in movies, art, or cartoons, but it's still rare to see him accurately portrayed. Creative projects, especially those for public display or distribution, are incredibly important acts of devotion—and ones that can have far-reaching impact.

Brithney Morales is an architect, CGI artist, intuitive designer, and Hades devotee. Her Instagram account, the Architect of Hades (@thearchitectof-hades), features a wealth of information on the history of architecture and design and chronicles her Visions of the Underworld (VotU) project, in which she goes into deep meditation to connect with Hades and then creates visual graphics of the locales she is shown. Through her Instagram, Brithney has connected with people all over the world. She shares that not only are people fascinated by her renderings, but they are also inspired to get to know Hades better: "Khthonic architecture focuses on the inner world. Hades offers us depth and inner resources. We come from a womb, from Gaia, the depths of the earth. Working with Hades is something like returning to that origin, to the womb of the Underworld, and it's a natural pull to return to our source."[151] In the coming years, Brithney is excited to continue promoting a more accurate picture of Hades and the Underworld than is often encountered in pop culture.

Brithney's dedicated Instagram account is a great example of how creative projects shift public perception of Hades. Celebrating Hades and the Underworld through works of art, independent zines, social media, educational presentations, videos, podcasts, and similar media are all ways to express your devotion to a larger audience. Need inspiration? Check out this list and see if one of these suggestions appeals to you:

- Compile a slide show about Hades to share on YouTube or at your local public library.
- Compose and record a series of your own devotional hymns.
- Plant an Underworld garden in your yard or community gardening space.
- Construct a replica of Hades' bident, laurel crown, or clothing—or design, thrift, sew, or otherwise craft a completely new, modern take on what Hades might choose to wear now.
- Write an article about Hades or the Underworld for an online magazine.
- Create a blog that serves as a digital altar or devotional photo essay.
- Research and experiment with food and beverage recipes that correspond with Hades. You can publish your favorites in a cookbook (hand-

---

151. Brithney Morales, interview with the author, December 14, 2022.

made or digitally designed) dedicated to ritual feasting. Or celebrate your findings by hosting an Underworld-themed dinner party.

Spiritual Pilgrimage

Myths arise from their landscapes. Making spiritual pilgrimage to the places mentioned in mythological and historical accounts infuses the stories we love with "aliveness" and embodied understanding. If we open ourselves to receive its wisdom, walking the landscape of mythology will teach us many things that intellectual study and theory cannot—and if we are very lucky, we may even encounter the gods themselves in our travels. Hades devotees can discover many places of pilgrimage across the Mediterranean regions of Greece, Italy, and Sicily, spanning all the way to the ancient crossroads of Turkey. Each chapter of this book includes information on specific places to find Hades and his mythology in the landscape. Visiting these sites and supporting them through monetary donations are tangible ways you can express gratitude and reciprocity to the people who have preserved their legacies over millennia.

Traveling abroad to visit these sites in person is wonderful, but it can be equally gratifying to use the digital resources available to us to make virtual pilgrimages to distant lands. Google Maps offers street views of many historical sites and the landscapes surrounding them. You can pin locations on a virtual map or keep track of them utilizing a website or mobile app like Pinterest. Museums around the world offer virtual tours of their collections online. You can look for travel documentaries, television episodes, and YouTube videos that cover the places you are interested in visiting—make some snacks, invite some friends, and go on pilgrimage together from your living room. If the friends who would enjoy sharing this experience with you are long distance, arrange for an online viewing party. Make your virtual pilgrimage an act of devotion by accompanying it with hymns and local offerings for Hades.

CHAPTER 10

OATHS AND VENGEANCE

═══

Hades speaks:

From a secluded spot along the riverbank, I watch the waters of the Styx as they lap against the weathered sides of Kharon's boat. The sound of the river is a rushing susurration of oaths. Styx is called "hated," but why? Perhaps mortals hate the idea of crossing her waters, because it means they are dead. Confined to the Underworld. Or perhaps Styx is hated because she represents objective restraint, unequivocal and unrelenting. There is nothing subjective about swearing an oath on her waters—either you fulfill it or face the consequences. Even the deathless ones cannot escape.

Further downstream, rapids form where her swift waters crash against boulders tossed into the river by perjury. I see Kerberos approach the shore and lean one of his mighty heads down to drink from the river. After quenching his thirst, he shakes his muzzle, sending water droplets flying. My hound is equally unequivocal in his guardian duties; otherwise, these waters would poison him. Tisiphone, one of the triad of Furies, joins him at the riverside. She greets the monstrous beast, patting him on the heads. She carefully folds her massive black wings behind her back before squatting at the river's edge. Tisiphone dips her hands in the water up to her wrists, swirling them to notify Styx that retribution against trespass has been served. It is an ancient language, one they have spoken since long before mortals walked the earth.

As I turn to walk away, I hear one of the boulders crack. The massive rock splits open and disintegrates as it is carried away by the river current. The jagged edges of broken promises are tumbled into smooth pebbles at the bottom of the Styx.

Orkos: Hades of Oaths, or the
Avenger of the Perjured

The epithet *Orkos* refers to two areas of Hades' purview. First, many oaths of the ancient world were sworn on the waters of the Styx, the river encircling his Underworld domain. Second, recall that the Erinyes report directly to Hades and the Dread Queen Persephone. The Erinyes, also known as the Furies, are fearsome dark-winged creatures with serpents twining through their hair, wielding whips and flaming torches of yew. They guard the abyss of Tartaros, but they are also sent to torment oath-breakers, murderers, and perpetrators of other heinous crimes, providing the victims of these trespasses with a sense of justice served.

Oaths in ancient Greece were extremely compelling, often binding two or more people together, and sometimes binding one or more individuals to the gods. These commitments, meant to be kept at all costs, were not considered or undertaken lightly. In antiquity, the word commonly used to signify an oath, *orkos*, was closely related to other ancient Greek words meaning "fence," "enclosure," or "that which confines or constrains." Immortals, just like humans, were also bound to fulfill their sworn oaths. According to Hesiod, gods who committed perjury—in other words, gods who broke or were unable to fulfill their oaths—risked the consequences of falling into a deep sleep and being deprived of their divinity for the duration.[152]

Such a serious commitment required a public ritual. The entire community attended oath-taking rituals. Men, women, and children of the community were present to witness the oath, but these witnesses were also emotionally invested in its successful fulfillment, as a broken oath could possibly influence the luck of the community for the worse. Oath-taking rituals were ancient accountability at its finest. Surveying several primary sources, Classical scholar Irene Berti has identified three recurring elements that featured in ancient Greek oath-taking rituals:

Self-Curse: The self-curse was an acknowledgment by the individual taking the oath that if they should perjure themselves, there would be definite consequences for them, and potentially also for their family and commu-

---

152. Evelyn-White, trans., *Theogony*, in *Hesiod, the Homeric Hymns, and Homerica*, 135–37.

nity members. Sometimes these consequences were named out loud, and other times simply inferred.

Dramatization: The dramatization element of the ritual usually involved a sacrifice or symbolically sacrificial gesture: animals could be slaughtered; blood, wine, or other substances poured on the ground; wax melted; and so on. This sacrificial gesture served as an embodied performance of the self-curse and depended strongly upon the identity of the oath-taker and the nature of the oath itself. For example, a bride may pour out a flask of olive oil or wine to represent the consequence of ill fortune for her household, while a soldier may pour blood on his sword to represent being gravely wounded in battle.

Touching: The element of touching sealed the oath-taking ritual, serving as a kind of sacred transmission of power to bind the oath-taker and witnesses together in the fulfillment of the oath. Again, the performance of this element depended on the oath-taker and the nature of the oath. Participants may all touch an altar, for example, or perhaps the earth, a sword, flowing water, or even each other (as in kissing or shaking hands). The *tomia*, or blood of any animals sacrificed in the ritual, was also sometimes touched by the oath-taker in order to bind themselves to the lifeblood and power of the sacrifice.[153]

At first glance, some of these elements may seem archaic or unrelatable. But think for a moment about modern marriage rituals: an oath of fidelity is spoken between individuals, witnessed by their families and community members (or at the very least, the official or celebrant performing the ceremony), in a ritual that includes physical symbols exchanged in a dramatization of the oath (rings), and is sealed with a final element of touching (the kiss). Depending on the beliefs of the individuals getting married, a god or gods may even be called upon to bear witness to their oath, thus participating with the oath-takers in its fulfillment.

---

153. Irene Berti, "'Now Let Earth Be My Witness and the Broad Heaven Above, and the Down Flowing Water of the Styx...' (Homer, *Mas* XV, 36–37): Greek Oath-Rituals," in *Ritual and Communication in the Graeco-Roman World*, ed. Eftychia Stavrianopoulou (Liège: Presses universitaires de Liège, 2006), 181–209.

Dedication and the Oath-Bound Heart

I took a formal oath of dedication to Hades at the vernal equinox in 2018. I made a set of very specific promises and requested some sureties from Hades in exchange, in a Styx-sworn oath binding us together for nine years. My oath-taking ritual took place in a crepe myrtle grove hidden deep within a historic cemetery, witnessed by four beloved friends. At the time of writing this book, I am still in the midst of fulfilling that oath.

Understanding the gravity of oaths is important when our heart feels called into deeper relationships with the gods. Many gods are extremely ancient beings and have honed their understanding of oath-taking over millennia of interactions with humans. Binding yourself to a god through an oath of dedication gives them a vested interest in your life: it opens up the possibility of them acting on your behalf behind the scenes, influencing your choices, and challenging you in unexpected ways.

The words *devotion* and *dedication* are often used interchangeably. However, I believe there are important differences between these two concepts. Dedicating yourself to a god is one way of formalizing your devotion; Pagan author and artist Morpheus Ravenna uses the phrase *theurgic binding magic* to describe the specific magical technology behind this relationship.[154] *Theurgy* means "divine-working" and refers to rituals or works of magic in which a god or gods participate. Any vow or promise you make to a god is a magical contract. But when you go a step further and bind yourself to them through an oath of dedication, you are inviting them to cocreate your life. Dedicating yourself to a god gives them agency to act on your behalf. It's a very serious undertaking, requiring very serious contemplation.

When Devotion Becomes Dedication

If it's not obvious already, I'll state it clearly for the record: I believe magic is real. It is present all around us, a force operating freely, reflexively, and cooperatively in our day-to-day world. I believe the gods are real, too, and equally present in everyday reality. I don't believe that magic or the gods are inherently dangerous, but neither are they completely safe. Magic always involves risk, and

---

154. Morpheus Ravenna, "Theurgic Binding: Or, 'S#!t Just Got Real,'" *Banshee Arts* (blog), accessed January 6, 2023, https://www.bansheearts.com/blog/theurgic-binding-or-st-just-got-real.

magic involving deities potentially more so. The gods are entities vastly different from humans, and the complete scope of their abilities and reach remains mysterious to us.

Let's imagine that you have spent significant time venerating a particular god at your altar, performing acts of devotion, and studying their mythos. You've evoked them in ritual (solo or in a group). You've spoken with them in trance journey so many times that you've lost count. And perhaps you've even found a few of their other devotees and asked them to share their thoughts and experiences. You've arrived at a place of clear discernment, beyond the initial thrill of infatuation: you understand who this god is, what motivates them, how they operate in the world, and the types of things they expect from their devotees. You may find yourself wondering, what's the next step? Should I take an oath of dedication?

Pause here for a moment. It's important to understand that dedicating yourself to a god or gods is *not* a prerequisite of being Pagan, polytheist, or an adept magical worker. It does not make you cooler, more badass, or part of some elite club. You can have a plethora of deep, life-changing, ecstatically amazing experiences throughout your entire lifetime without ever venturing down the path of dedication. Look at taking an oath of dedication as a horizontal move rather than a vertical one. Before making this decision, slow down and investigate your motives with honest self-reflection:

- Are you feeling pressured to take this step? You should not feel forced or peer-pressured by gods, humans, or any other beings to take an oath. Planned Parenthood has a helpful acronym for remembering the components of consent: FRIES—consent is freely given, revocable, informed, enthusiastic, and specific.[155]
- Is this a passing phase or interest? Taking an oath of dedication is not a reversible scenario like when you get tired of the awesome cereal you've been eating on repeat for three months, suddenly deciding that you never want to taste it again. Oaths of dedication are magically binding contracts.

---

155. "Sexual Consent," Planned Parenthood, accessed October 2, 2023, https://www.plannedparenthood .org/learn/relationships/sexual-consent.

- Is an oath of dedication a filler for something else you feel is missing in your life or existing relationships?
- Do you have codependent tendencies? Could this be influencing your decision?
- The ways of the gods are not necessarily our ways. Perform a risk assessment: Do you have the mental, emotional, psychic, and spiritual preparation necessary to navigate oaths and contracts with gods? Do you need to build more skills before taking this step?
- Do you have a spiritual or magical support network in place?
- Are you ready for your life to change, possibly in unexpected or uncomfortable ways?

After you've considered all these points, here are some ways to help determine if, *yes*, it is the right time for you to take an oath of dedication:

- You can clearly express why you feel called to take this oath, including how you specifically are prepared and suited to fulfill it and how it might benefit you and/or others.
- You've received affirmative synchronicities and signs concerning your decision, either spontaneously or by asking for them.
- You've confirmed your intuition with divination, such as tarot, runes, or augury.

Crafting Your Oath

Similar to engaging in a working relationship with a god, it is advisable to include time constraints and deliverables for both sides when crafting an oath of dedication. What exactly are you offering to the god? For how long are you offering it, and under what conditions? What do you expect to receive in return?

Since you've (assumedly) been devoted to the recipient of your oath for some time now, you may already have a handle on what they desire from you. Trance journey can also be a helpful tool for working out the details of your oath. Just be sure that any beings you are speaking with understand that you are having an informal conversation or brainstorming session, which will not be binding in any way until spoken aloud before witnesses in ritual.

I recommend having a trusted friend or two review the rough draft of your oath, so that they can ask you questions, get clarification, or challenge you on certain points. Their outside perspective can help you avoid potential pitfalls. Three example oaths of dedication are included in the invitations to practice at the end of this chapter.

Planning an Oath-Taking Ritual

Once you've crafted your oath of dedication, the next step is to plan a ritual to formalize and activate it. A customizable oath-taking ritual is outlined at the end of this chapter. As you begin planning your ritual, you'll want to consider such things as magical timing, witnesses, physical place, altar items and material supplies, offerings and libations, symbolic objects, and gifts of gratitude.

Magical Timing

Is there a specific season, moon phase, numeric calendar date, day of the week, and/or time of day that corresponds to the deity you are dedicating yourself to? Choosing the appropriate magical timing will layer more correspondence into your ritual. For example, I chose to have my oath-taking ritual on the vernal equinox, a liminal portal between seasons, and also a time when my witnesses (some of whom traveled a great distance) were able to gather. Refer back to the invitations to practice on page 45 for a list of magical times that correspond to Hades.

Witnesses

Who will you ask to stand as witness to your oath? How many witnesses do you or your god require? Anyone who attends this ritual is considered a witness; their good luck and fortune may be tied to your fulfillment of the oath from that point forward. Witnesses need to be informed of the expectations and solemnity of their role, in addition to being shown a copy of the oath of dedication and the oath-taking ritual in advance, so that they can freely consent to participate.

Don't invite friends or family to an oath-taking ritual without fully informing them about the implications of participation. If you want to share this occasion with others outside of your circle of witnesses, invite them to celebrate with you afterward. Give celebration guests a designated time and place to arrive so that they do not accidentally interrupt the ritual proceedings.

Physical Place

What are the privacy and accessibility needs for you and your witnesses? Will your ritual be conducted inside or outside? If outside, do you have a plan for inclement weather? Do you need to check with anyone to reserve or gain permission to use the space you have chosen?

Altar Items and Material Supplies

Creating a beautiful central altar enhances the sensual experience of your ritual and serves as a hub for material supplies and corresponding items. Fresh flowers and herbs make a lovely centerpiece—choose plants that correspond with the aspects of Hades you want to invite to your ritual. Include representations of his symbols, animals, and the elements of earth and fire. Select an altar cloth that is black, gray, deep purple, or dark blue in color. Add a statue of Hades or a framed art piece if you have one. If you are planning to evoke, or summon, Hades into the ritual circle (which I recommend for oaths of dedication), you may wish to prepare a fluid condenser to house his presence during the ritual. Refer back to the invitations to practice on page 83 for condenser instructions and recommended ingredients.

Offerings and Libations

What offerings are appropriate to show respect to your god? Will you perhaps sing a song, recite a hymn, or perform an act of service (for example, picking up litter in the area)? Will there be offerings of food on the altar? If so, how will you feed the offering to your god? Refer back to the invitations to practice on page 46 for advice on making food offerings to khthonic gods.

Will you be making ritual libations? Do you need special vessels (cups, bowls, pitchers, etc.) to conduct the libations? Do your witnesses have allergies or prohibitions against any type of food or drink? Where will the libation be poured (the ground, a bothros, bowl, etc.)? You can refer to the next section of this chapter, exploring the lore, for more information about ritual libations in ancient Greece.

Symbolic Objects

You may want to select a symbolic object to swear your oath upon, to serve as a physical touchstone and reminder. Common choices for symbolic objects are rings, pendants, braided cords, crystals, staffs, knives, and swords. For my oath of dedication, I selected a ring with a central onyx stone surrounded by silver laurel leaves. If you choose to incorporate a symbolic object in your oath-taking, remember to purify and consecrate it to this purpose before the ritual.

Gifts of Gratitude

Consider gifting each witness with a small token after the ritual, such as chocolate bars, candles, handmade cards, incense blends, braided bracelets, magnets—it's up to your imagination and budget. Honoring your witnesses with a gift supports the spirit of kharis and serves as a memento of this special occasion. Is there a gift of gratitude you want to offer to the guardian spirits of the land on which the ritual takes place (for example, a sprinkling of birdseed outside)? Is there anyone else you need to recognize, such as a partner or spiritual mentor?

Forfeits and Accountability

What if something drastic happens and you cannot fulfill an oath? This is a very valid question. First, if this question is lingering on your mind and heart during the entire process of crafting your oath, you may want to evaluate if the path of dedication is what you need right now. Consider that the gods probably already know whether you will fulfill your oath or not, even before you make it. If you're not getting a strong yes in the early planning stages, maybe it's not the time for a deeper commitment, and that's okay.

Research and study are critically important when considering an oath of dedication. In studying your god's mythology and lore, you might realize that there are consequences for breaking an oath—we've already discussed the ancient Greek notion of broken oaths negatively affecting not only the oath-taker but also any witnesses present for the oath. Breaking your oath could lead to feelings of low self-esteem, guilt, or unworthiness—and may land your name on the "do not hire" list among the gods. You can ask to be released early from your contract, but there is no guarantee the deity will comply.

Many people find it useful to include an alternative forfeit in their oaths in case they are unable to fulfill them. The modern practice of including an alternative forfeit hearkens back to the ancient Greek inclusion of a self-curse in the oath-taking ritual. In some of the oath-takings I've witnessed, common forfeits include donations of time or money as penance for a broken oath. The price of the forfeit—be it money, time, or sweat equity—is usually high, however, and does not represent an easy way out. In other words, the forfeit has to sting a bit. If you have to forfeit or break an oath, I also recommend giving it a good death so it does not continue to haunt you. Release it with proper respect and ritual, and unlike Orpheus, resist torturing yourself by looking back.

On the other side of the coin, what happens if a deity does not fulfill their promises to you? You do have some agency in this situation. You can gather up your witnesses for a group ritual to call them to account. Alternatively, you can petition their retinue (other gods who inhabit the same realm, their consorts, those who are related to them in some way, etc.) to call them to account. Use your divination tools to gain insight into the situation. And last but not least, do not sign up to work with them again in the future.

Finally, just know that there are many ways to look at devotion, oaths, and dedication. These are my thoughts and experiences. Your mileage may vary. Please take away what makes sense to you, with my blessing, and feel free to leave behind what doesn't resonate.

Exploring the Lore

In chapter 5 I discuss how to place a ward of protection in each of the four cardinal directions (north, east, south, and west) and in the fifth direction of center. When casting a circle, many Pagan and magical practitioners also call out to the elements, the spirits of the directions, or to other corresponding unseen beings in each of the five directions—this practice is commonly referred to as *calling the quarters*. Calling the quarters is similar to warding, but in addition to asking for protection, it also calls upon the beings named to lend their energies to enhance or help power a ritual or magical working. You can add another layer of correspondence to ritual or magic involving the Greek gods by calling upon the Anemoi and the Omphalos.

In Greek mythology, the Anemoi are the gods of the winds. The winds associated with the four cardinal directions are Boreas the North Wind, Eurus (or in later texts, Apeliotes) the East Wind, Notus the South Wind, and Zephyrus the West Wind. Each of these winds was personified and associated with a specific season. Boreas was the cold breath of winter. Eurus was the wind associated with autumn harvest, his breezes scented with ripe fruit and golden grain. Notus was the wind of summer heat and stormy rains. Zephyrus was the wind associated with springtime, the gentlest wind, scattering flower petals with his breezes. There are lesser winds, too, but Boreas, Eurus, Notus, and Zephyrus are the gods most relevant to calling the quarters for magical purposes.

The ancient Greeks viewed Delphi as the center, or navel, of the world. The Temple of Apollo at Delphi contained a sacred *Omphalos*—a powerful, egg-shaped stone that allowed the Pythia direct communication with the gods. Hollow channels inside the egg funneled deep earth vapors into the inner sanctuary of the temple, perhaps inducing a trance-like state, or even hallucinations. The Omphalos at Delphi also represented the stone that Rhea fed to Kronos in place of the infant Zeus. The sculpted marble stone has been excavated from the temple ruins and is now housed in the Delphi Archaeological Museum.[156] For the direction of center, call upon the energy and power of the Omphalos in your ritual or magical praxis.

Symbols of Hades: The Phiale

The simple act of pouring libations for the gods was one of the most common expressions of ancient Greek religious practice. Libations could be offered in the morning or evening, at the beginning of meals, to propitiate the dead, or to mark special occasions. Olive oil, milk mixed with honey, or wine mixed with water were common choices for this activity. Once prepared, the libation would be poured from a handled jug into a phiale.

The *phiale* (Greek) or *patera* (Latin) was a shallow ceramic or metal bowl used specifically for the purpose of offering libations. A typical phiale had neither handles nor feet—an indentation centered on the underside, similar to a belly button, facilitated holding the bowl level whilst hymns and prayers were spoken. After the libation was poured from the phiale onto the ground, the remainder of the contents were usually drunk by the celebrant; however, this was unlikely the case if the libation was poured for Hades or the Underworld—in those cases, the entire contents of the phiale were poured on the ground.

The British Museum (London) houses a *kylix*, or wine cup, from around 430 BCE that features a painted scene of the Olympian gods enjoying a feast on the outside of the cup, with Hades and Persephone banqueting in a more

---

156. Unknown artist, *Omphalos*, marble sculpture, 332–323 BCE, Archaeological Museum of Delphi, Delphi, Greece.

intimate setting on the interior.[157] The scene on the interior of the cup would only have been visible once the wine was drunk. In it, Hades and Persephone are seated together on a long couch with embroidered cushions. They are both regally dressed. Hades is easily recognizable by his dark hair and beard, laurel wreath and *tainia* (hair ribbon), and the cornucopia he holds in his left hand. The couple stare directly into each other's eyes. Hades' right arm is outstretched, presenting a phiale toward Persephone, perhaps offering a libation to his beloved.

In His Dark Garden: Myrtle and Poppy

Myrtle and poppy both produce beautiful, ephemeral flowers. At first, their energies may seem fleeting and transient. Delve deeper into relationship with them, however, and you will discover magical gravitas like no other—these plant allies have the ability to bless, enhance, and expand sacred partnerships, as well as connect us with our deepest spiritual longings.

MYRTLE TREE
Species: *Myrtus communis*
Other Common Names: Common myrtle, true myrtle
Toxicity: Somewhat toxic—use caution. Consult a professional herbalist before ingesting, and always keep myrtle out of reach of children and pets. Ingesting myrtle is contraindicated for pregnant people.
Keywords: Celebration, commitment, joy, love, mirth, sacred partnerships

Myrtle is an aromatic evergreen shrub with pointed, glossy leaves. Myrtle trees bloom with sweet-scented flowers, usually white with a hint of pink, whose long stamens give the flowers a soft, fluffy appearance. The blossoms are followed by small, edible purple-black berries. In Sardinia and Corsica, ripe myrtle berries are macerated and fermented in alcohol to produce an aromatic liquor called *liquore di mirto*. Other traditional recipes from the Mediterranean region utilize dried ground myrtle berries to flavor roasted meats and sausages or to serve in place of black pepper.

---

157. Codrus Painter, *Kylix (Wine Cup)*, circa 430 BCE, pottery, red-figure, the British Museum, London, UK, https://www.britishmuseum.org/collection/object/G_1847-0909-6.

Myrtle was sacred to many Greek goddesses, among them Aphrodite and Demeter. Crowns, garlands, and belts woven from flowering myrtle branches were worn for weddings and other festivities in ancient Greece and Rome—indeed, the popularity of myrtle blossoms in wedding bouquets persists to this day. According to folklore, myrtle can be planted on each side of a home to encourage peace and love between all who dwell there.[158] Myrtle is an excellent choice to celebrate sacred partnerships, such as those between gods and oath-bound dedicants. Call upon the spiritus viridis of myrtle to bless your relationships, to seal vows and oaths, or any time you want to recall the connection, emotion, and sense of purpose that nourishes your commitments.

POPPY

Species: *Papaver somniferum*

Other Common Names: Breadseed poppy, opium poppy

Toxicity: Toxic to humans and animals when ingested, with the exception of the seeds, which are used to flavor food. Poppies produce latex sap; people who are allergic to the latex sap of the rubber tree (*Hevea brasiliensis*) should be aware of the potential for cross-allergic reactions.

Keywords: Dreams, expansion, pleasure, sleep, spirit evocation and manifestation

Poppy is an annual plant with hairy, blue-green foliage from which bright, extravagant blooms emerge in late spring and early summer. Poppy flowers can be single or double, in a range of colors that include red, purple, pink, mauve, and white. The individual flowers are delicate and short-lived, each producing a large seed pod. Opium poppy is cultivated for its edible seeds, used to flavor bread, cakes, and other foods, and for its latex sap, called *opion* by the ancient Greeks. The latex sap contains morphine, codeine, thebaine, noscapine, and papaverine, among other naturally occurring alkaloids known as opiates.[159] Opiates have powerful sedative, narcotic, and pain-reducing properties that humans have used recreationally and medicinally for millennia. Opium poppy is considered toxic, however, as misuse or overdose of this plant can lead to addiction, coma, or death.

---

158. Dietz, *The Complete Language of Flowers*, 145.

159. Occvlta, "Opium Poppy," *Materia Venefica* 5 (January 2022), 7, https://www.occvlta.org/.

To experience poppy's energy in a safer manner, consider imbibing a flower essence prepared by a skilled practitioner. Magical herbalist and flower essence expert Nicholas Pearson observes, "Taking the essence [of poppy] invites communion with the infinite and helps align your thoughts and actions with your spiritual principles."[160] Responsibly and respectfully approached, poppy can open a gateway to connect with the gods. Other safer ways to explore the spiritus viridis of this potentially dangerous ally include simply sitting in its presence in a natural environment and drawing or meditating on its image.

Poppy is associated with the River Lethe (Forgetting); Hypnos, the daimon of sleep; and Morpheus, the god of dreams. To gain an answer to a perplexing question, write the query on a piece of paper, then fold or roll the paper and slip it into a poppy seedpod. Place the seedpod under your pillow when you go to sleep to receive an answer in your dreams.[161] Include poppy seeds in offering cakes for the dead, as well as for the denizens of the Underworld. Dried poppy flower petals and seeds can be burnt in a well-ventilated area to assist spirit evocation and manifestation.

Khthonic Bestiary: The Cicada

Cicadas are flying insects with two pairs of membranous wings, prominent compound eyes, and an easily recognizable song. Most modern cicada species are medium to large in size, ranging from 1 to 2 inches (2 to 5 cm) long. More than three thousand species of cicadas have been identified worldwide, with many more species assumed to be unidentified. Male cicadas are responsible for the rhythmic droning song heard on warm spring and summer evenings. Males produce loud buzzing noises to attract and court females by vibrating membranes called tymbals near the base of their abdomen; the hollow abdomen acts like a sound box, amplifying their song. Once mated, female cicadas lay their fertilized eggs in tree shoots or young branches. Newly hatched nymphs drop to the ground, burrowing deep under the soil to suck on the roots of perennial plants. In ancient Greece, as in the United States and other parts of the modern world where these insects are found, cicadas spend their

---

160. Pearson, *Flower Essences from the Witch's Garden*, 396.

161. Dietz, *The Complete Language of Flowers*, 158.

entire nymph stage underground. Depending on the species, this stage can last anywhere from 2 to 17 years.

The cicada's life cycle is largely hidden. Although buried in the ground for long periods of time, the cicada does not die. This natural mystery sparked the imagination of ancient Greek poets, who connected these insects with cycles of death and rebirth, as well as with the power of love and attraction. Poets like Homer and Virgil thought their song to be beautiful. In the *Iliad,* Homer compares the soft conversation of old men to cicada song: "Now through old age these [men] fought no longer, yet were they excellent speakers still, and clear, as cicadas who through the forest settle on trees, to issue their delicate voice of singing."[162]

Cicadas are ancient beings—fossil records of prehistoric cicada-like insects stretch all the way back to the Late Triassic period, approximately 200 to 240 million years ago. They have been serenading each other on the evening breeze since before humans walked the earth. Cicada nymphs molt their exoskeleton five or more times before reaching adulthood, another trait that supports the cicada's khthonic association with transmigration of the soul, and with knowledge that may only be gleaned from katabasis—time spent deep in the Underworld, under the ground. Cicada teaches us that with each season of growth, the song of our soul becomes bigger, truer, louder, and more profound.

Finding Hades in the Landscape: Styx Waterfall

Mt. Chelmos, also known as Helmos or Aroania, is part of a mountain range near the city of Kalavryta in the Peloponnese. The area is known for many attractions: the oldest monastery in Greece, Mega Spileo Monastery; the magnificent Cave of the Lakes; and the Chelmos Observatory perched atop the summit, housing the Aristarchos Telescope. The source of the Krathis River also flows from the summit—this 984 feet (300 m) waterfall is known locally as *Ydata Stygos,* or Styx Waterfall. Local lore holds that these waters travel all the way from their mountaintop origin to the depths of the Underworld, connecting the realm of Hades with the world above.[163]

---

162. Homer, *Iliad,* 3.150–53.

163. RogueChemist, "Styx Waterfall," Atlas Obscura, February 25, 2021, https://www.atlasobscura.com /places/styx-waterfall.

From Kalavryta, you can drive up the road leading to the top of Mt. Chelmos, passing near the observatory. There is a hiking trail from the village of Peristera that provides access to the Styx Waterfall. The trail begins from the side of the road; the trailhead is not immediately obvious, but once found, the path to the waterfall is marked with blazes along the way. The trail is challenging and descends steeply over rough, rocky ground—it is not advised for beginner hikers. To avoid getting lost, hire a local guide from the adventure tour company located in the town center of Kalavryta.

The out-and-back trail is approximately 10.1 miles (16.25 km) in total.[164] The amount of waterfall flow changes with the seasons; in the summer, the water may slow to a trickle. There is a small cave next to the waterfall, where you can pause to catch your breath, enjoy the natural beauty, and touch your fingers to the immortal waters of the Styx.

Invitations to Practice

Invoke Hades Orkos to preside over rituals of dedication and oath-taking, for good luck in court proceedings, to inspire and assist efforts toward social justice, and to bless rites of reparation. Symbols and correspondences that resonate with the energy of Hades in this aspect are the phiale, myrtle tree, poppy, and the ancient cicada.

Hymn to the River Styx

The following hymn is dedicated to Styx, daimon of the revered Underworld river, on whose waters binding oaths are sworn. Recite this hymn when you want to invoke Styx's witness for an oath—but be advised, she will hold you accountable for its fulfillment. Refer back to these words anytime you wish to be reminded of the power of your promise.

> *Oh Styx, Renowned Mother of Truth Tellers!*
> *You, on whose swift and deep waters are sworn*
> *Unbreakable oaths of love, loyalty, desperation, and dedication—*
> *I come this hour, humbly, asking you to bear witness.*
> *Let these words be my adamantine bond.*
> *Hold me to my oath, Beloved and Terrible Styx!*

---

164. AllTrails, "Styx Waterfall," accessed May 1, 2023, https://www.alltrails.com/trail/greece/western-greece--3/styx-waterfall.

Your wild rapids and swirling eddies are the destiny of oath-breakers
Who abandon their promises forsworn, so let me, the oath-taker,
Depend on your steady countenance
For as long as these words be my adamantine bond.

Example Oaths of Dedication

Here are three example oaths of dedication. Remember, it's a best practice to include time constraints and deliverables for both sides when crafting your oath. What exactly are you offering to the god? For how long are you offering it and under what conditions? What do you expect to receive in return? The second example invokes the River Styx for accountability. The third example includes an alternative forfeit, or self-curse.

> **Example One:** I formally dedicate myself to Hades, the Unseen One, who has been my patron for the last three years. I will continue to venerate Hades at my altar and in my routine spiritual practices, and I also offer my divinatory and artistic skills in service to this oath, specifically through providing necromantic tarot readings and opening an online shop to share my Underworld-themed art with the world. In exchange for my formal oath, Hades, I ask for your protection, your continued patronage, and your networking skill to align me with the right clients and buyers. This oath shall last for the next two years, at which time it may be amended, released, and/or renewed.

> **Example Two:** I dedicate myself to Hades Eubuleus, Good Counselor and Consoler, as I embark on a new career as a death doula. In exchange for my oath, Eubuleus, I ask that you teach and support me in providing good counsel and consolation for dying patients and their loved ones. I also ask that you provide relevant opportunities for me to earn a comfortable amount of money while I learn this role. This oath shall last for five years, while I gain skill, knowledge, and experience in this profession. I swear this oath on the River Styx, binding in all the realms.

> **Example Three:** I dedicate myself and my kitchen to Hades Polydegmon, Host of Many, in service to the exploration and observance of his mysteries of hospitality. To fulfill this oath, I vow to host two feasts to honor Hades and the Underworld each year, one at the vernal equinox and one at the autumnal equinox, for the next three years. In exchange for my oath,

Polydegmon, I ask that you connect me with guests who will share my spiritual values and enrich my circle of friends. If I am unable to fulfill this oath, I will donate $600 ($100 per promised feast) to my community food pantry.

Example Oath-Taking Ritual

Here is an example oath-taking ritual that you can customize for your own use. This ritual framework is a fusion of modern magical practice and ancient oath-taking rituals. The magic of this ritual takes place in three central parts: evocation of Hades into the ritual circle, the formal oath-taking, and activation through shared libation or touch.

Feel free to add more ritual elements to this outline if you desire or to alter the wording or form of any part to suit your preferences. For the sake of good magical hygiene and etiquette, however, do not skip the purification, circle casting and warding, welcome, consecration, words of gratitude and farewell, or releasing steps—and if you choose to evoke any gods or spirits, be sure to devoke them as well. Refer back to the invitations to practice on page 82 for instructions on how to perform evocation and devocation.

1. Purification: Purify the ground or floor where your ritual will take place with khernips. Set up your altar and supplies. Next purify your altar, supplies, offerings, yourself, and witnesses with khernips. Check to make sure you have all the materials needed to carry out each step of the ritual.

2. Circle Casting and Warding: Using your preferred method of demarcation, cast a clockwise circle encompassing the entire ritual area, including the altar, yourself, and all witnesses. Beginning in the north and moving clockwise, ward your circle with a sigil of protection in each of the four cardinal directions, finishing with the fifth direction of center. A dedication ritual is a special occasion, so you may also want to call on the Anemoi to bless each direction and the Omphalos of Delphi to hold the center of the circle. Listed clockwise: Eurus (east), Notus (south), Zephyrus (west), Boreas (north), and Omphalos (center).

3. Welcome: Acknowledge and welcome the witnesses who have gathered for this ritual. Feel free to make this short and sweet or more

elaborate if you prefer. A simple welcome statement might sound like, "Welcome, beloved witnesses. I acknowledge the importance of your presence here today. Thank you for agreeing to stand with me as I make this binding oath." After welcoming the witnesses, next acknowledge any other Unseen Ones who may also have gathered with you for this ritual: denizens of the Underworld, ancestors, spirits of place, guides, familiars, elementals, plant spirits, etc.

4. Consecration: Read aloud a statement of intention to consecrate this ritual. This may sound something like, "I consecrate this ritual as a magical container in which to formalize and activate the oath of dedication I swear today."

5. Evocation: Sing or recite a hymn to Hades to evoke his presence into the ritual circle. You can read the Orphic Hymn to Plouton, one of the hymns from this book, or even a hymn that you write yourself— but the hymn you choose should contain the epiklesis, or aspect, of Hades that you wish to evoke. Once the hymn is recited, welcome Hades by pouring a libation on the ground. If you are indoors, pour your libation into a large bowl; carry it outside after the close of the ritual to pour the libation on the ground. As you pour the libation, announce his presence: "Khaire Hades!" Complete this part of the ritual by stomping three times.

6. Formal Oath-Taking: State your oath aloud in the circle of witnesses. You don't have to memorize the oath, unless you want to—reading from a paper is fine. If you have a symbolic object to swear on, hold it up so that all the witnesses can see it as you take your oath. Whether or not you choose to swear your oath on the River Styx is up to you; if you would like to call upon Styx as witness, read aloud the Hymn to the River Styx on page 200. Complete this part of the ritual by stomping three times.

7. Activation by Touching or Shared Drink: This part of the ritual can take many forms. Participants could each approach the oath-taker to place a hand on the shoulder, kiss on the cheek, quickly embrace, or use another consensual touch—you will want to work out the specifics of this before the ritual. Alternatively, participants could share a ritual drink. Pass the vessel containing the drink around the circle

clockwise so that each person can pour a bit into their own cup. Once the vessel makes the rounds, participants are signaled by the oath-taker to lift their cups and drink simultaneously. Since Hades (and perhaps Styx) are also present, be sure to include them in this part of the ritual by touching a representative object on the altar, touching the earth, or by pouring the remainder of the shared drink on the ground (save this portion to pour outside after the ritual if you are indoors). Complete this part of the ritual by stomping three times.

8. Devocation: If you have called upon Styx, offer words of gratitude for her witness and bid her farewell. Next devoke Hades by offering words of gratitude for his presence, blessing, and acceptance of your oath, and bid him farewell.

9. Witness Gratitude and Farewell: Thank the Unseen Ones who gathered for the ritual, offer gratitude for their witness, and bid them farewell. Acknowledge the witnesses that have stood with you with a few final words, such as "Gratitude to all the witnesses who have stood with me today. Thank you for supporting my oath of dedication and holding me accountable to my promises. May the gods bless our community!"

10. Ward and Circle Release: Release your wards by thanking and bidding farewell to them in the opposite direction they were raised: Omphalos (center), Boreas (north), Zephyrus (west), Notus (south), and Eurus (east). Release your circle by sweeping it away counterclockwise with a broom or a sweeping motion of the hands. Once this motion is completed, announce out loud: "It is done."

Your oath of dedication is now magically sworn and activated, so it's time to celebrate! Sharing food and drink is a great way for you, the witnesses, and any friends and loved ones who did not participate in the ritual to celebrate your commitment. You can dance, sing, play music, or tell stories—this is a time to laugh, relax, build community, and have fun. Just make sure everyone is feeling somewhat grounded before traveling home, especially if they are getting behind the wheel of a car.

Once your ritual and celebrations are complete, the real work begins. Pick a time to periodically review the commitments you have made—I like to do this annually on the anniversary of my oath-taking ritual. Evaluate your progress and experiences to date. Has your understanding of the oath changed? Use your trusted tools of divination and trance journey to get clarification if needed. Lean on the strength of group accountability, and give your witnesses regular updates on your progress. Share your successes with enthusiasm and joy!

CONCLUSION

One of my earliest memories of Greek mythology is watching the 1981 cult classic *Clash of the Titans* on a chunky cathode ray tube television that had been wheeled into our elementary school gymnasium on a rainy day. It was humid and stormy outside, and the skin of my thighs was stuck to the tiled floor of the gym. I remember craning my neck at an uncomfortable angle for the entire two-hour duration of the movie, because I was so entranced by Perseus, Pegasus, Medusa, and Bubo the mechanical owl. My legs fell completely asleep as I watched. I went home from school that day with epic visions of heroes, gods, and monsters forever imprinted on my psyche—and I've loved Greek mythology ever since.

You may have noticed that Hades is still very much in the pop-culture zeitgeist. Hades was one of the antagonists in the original *Clash of the Titans* (1981) film, as well as its subsequent remake and sequel (in 2010 and 2012, respectively). Just a decade later, Hades became a fixture character of two popular 1990s television series—*Hercules: The Legendary Journeys* and *Xena: Warrior Princess*. You can also find him in the Walt Disney Studios 1997 full-length animated feature *Hercules*, in which a conniving Hades (voiced by actor James Woods) tries to overthrow the Olympian gods. In the Disney adaptation, Hades' skin is blue and his hair is made of fire.

After the turn of the twenty-first century, Hades continued to make regular appearances in the book and film series Percy Jackson and the Olympians and its various spin-offs, such as the Heroes of Olympus, written by Rick Riordan. First published in 2005, Riordan's books chronicle the adventures of a group of modern-day adolescents in a somewhat Greco-Roman mythological setting. In the world of webcomics, New Zealand artist Rachel Smythe launched *Lore Olympus* in March 2018. *Lore Olympus* is a serial comic retelling the story of

Hades and Persephone. At the time of writing this book, it is the most popular comic on Webtoon, with 1.2 billion views and 6.2 million subscribers.[165] Hardcover and trade paperback versions of *Lore Olympus* have been released in five volumes, and a television adaptation is also in development.

In 2019, the musical *Hadestown* by Anaïs Mitchell burst onto the stage at Broadway's Walter Kerr Theater. *Hadestown* creatively retells the story of Orpheus and Eurydice as an allegory for the modern woes of climate change, industrial exploitation, and systemic poverty. Hades is portrayed, predictably, as the antagonist of this tale. The Broadway production opened to critical acclaim and received numerous awards and nominations. In fact, at the seventy-third annual Tony Awards in 2019, Hadestown received fourteen nominations (the most for the evening) and won eight of them, including Best Musical and Best Original Score.[166]

Hades has also appeared as a character in many video games over the years, including one extremely popular game that carries his name. In *Hades* the video game from Supergiant Games, the player takes the role of Zagreus, a prince of the Underworld who is trying to escape his father's realm. At the tenth annual New York Game Awards, *Hades* won in the Game of the Year, Best Music, Best Writing, and Best Acting categories. It was also the first video game to be awarded a Hugo Award as part of a special video games category introduced for the 2021 Hugo Awards, as well as a Nebula Award for its writing.[167]

These are just a few of Hades' recent appearances in pop culture, among the numerous places he shows up or gets mentioned. This list can get pretty long, especially if you travel down the rabbit hole of romantic fiction and fantasy. Romance writers love the subject of Hades and Persephone! As entertaining and fascinating as these recent portrayals of Hades may be, it's still important to remember that they are modern, fanfiction adaptations of mythology. Many of them are not necessarily true to the lore—or the enigmatic nature—of this complex and ancient god.

---

165. Rachel Smythe, "Lore Olympus," Webtoon, 2018–present, accessed January 31, 2023, https://www
    .webtoons.com/en/romance/lore-olympus/list?title_no=1320.

166. Hadestown, "Hadestown | Official Site," Hadestown, accessed January 31, 2023, https://hadestown
    .com/.

167. Supergiant Games, "Hades," Supergiant Games, accessed January 31, 2023, https://www
    .supergiantgames.com/games/hades/.

So why do we still love, or love to hate, Hades after all this time? I think it is because Hades is uniquely charismatic. His stories are compelling. His mythos includes elements of drama, romance, family dynamics, and power struggles— the kinds of stories that hold our hearts and imaginations captive, like the pull of gravity holding us to Earth. In our modern era of scientific discovery and instantaneous connection, Hades represents something that is still unknowable and unavoidable. He is emblematic of one of the biggest questions we can ask in life: What lies on the other side of death?

Throughout this book, I've shared some of the many ways that Hades challenges us to embrace paradox. Is Hades notorious, or is he a good counselor? He is both. Is Hades sacred, or is he profane? He is both. And yet... he is more. In working with Hades, I've come to see death and desire as two sides of the same coin. And as his mysteries continue to unfold in my life and the lives of those around me, I find that cultivating a relationship with the Ruler of the Dead is unexpectedly life-affirming. Hades' wisdom and presence continues to provide unforeseen gifts of grace, mindfulness, and above all, deep appreciation for the diverse and glorious spectrum of embodied experience we can have in this mortal lifetime. Khaire Hades.

ACKNOWLEDGMENTS

My gratitude goes out to author and paranormal investigator Richard Estep for generously sharing his know-how and experiences with writing and publishing. Richard, I followed your advice and it worked like a charm. I also want to thank Heather Greene, Lauryn Heineman, and the team at Llewellyn Publications for their expertise and excellent caretaking of this book.

To my River Styx Book Club beta readers: thank you for caring so much about me and this project and for your willingness to read my (really) rough drafts. The process of writing this book involved spending a great deal of time in the company of Hades, death, and the Underworld. You kept pace with me every step of the way—some of you with edits, questions, and suggestions and others with your presence and encouragement. All of you made invaluable contributions to my creative process. You are a truly beautiful and intrepid group of humans.

To my teaching collaborator, Murphy, and all the Weavers: thank you for being your authentic, generous, magical selves. I continue to learn so much from all of you, and your passion and commitment to making a difference in the world inspire me to keep researching, writing, and teaching. Magic is real, present all around us, and a profound tool for justice and transformation.

Delicious food, occasional walks, snuggles, and massive amounts of support were provided by the House Hades crew: Jason, RoRo, Bug, and Baci. Our household is its own little Elysium, and you four are my most precious treasures. I also want to acknowledge my maternal grandparents, my mother, and my magical companion Monster, *in memoriam*: I feel you cheering me on from the other side. I love you and think of you every day.

And of course, the utmost respect, awe, and gratitude for Hades himself: Khaire Hades.

Concilio et labore, crescit eundo.

APPENDIX A
TABLE OF CORRESPONDENCES

Symbols	Bident, cornucopia, golden chariot and black horses, Helm of Invisibility, key to the realm, lekythos, meandros, phiale, single tear, soul fire
Plants	Aconite, bay laurel, datura, dittany of Crete, fig, hellebore, Mediterranean cypress, mint, mistletoe, myrtle, narcissus, pomegranate, poppy, quince, rosemary, rue, thyme, violet, white poplar
Animals	Bat, black ram, cicada, cockerel, Kerberos, scorpion, screech owl, snakes and the ouroboros, Underworld black cattle
Colors	Black, gray, dark blue, deep purple
Crystals	Amethyst, black or brown tourmaline, diamond, jet, obsidian, onyx, pyrite, smoky quartz
Oils/Scents	Clove, oakmoss, patchouli, spearmint, vetiver
Elements	Earth, fire
Astrological Sign	Scorpio (ruled by Pluto)
Moon Cycle	Waning dark moon
Time of Day	Sunset twilight

HADES EPITHETS

Epithets as Ruler of the Underworld

Hades Adamastos: Hades the Resolute or Hades the Unyielding

Hades Agesilaos: Hades, Leader of the People

Hades Aidoneus: Hades Unseen

Hades Isodetes: Hades Who Binds All Equally

Hades Eubuleus: Hades of Good Counsel or Hades the Consoler

Hades Khthonios: Hades of the Underworld

Hades Moiragetes: Hades Guide of the Fates

Hades Orkos: Hades of Oaths or Hades the Avenger of the Perjured

Hades Polydegmon: Hades the Host of Many

Hades Polysemantor: Hades the Ruler of Many

Hades Zeus Khthonios: Hades, Zeus of the Underworld

Epithets Related to Descriptions in Mythology

Hades Agelastus: Hades of Melancholy Countenance

Hades Agesander: Hades Who Carries All Away (in reference to the Persephone myth)

Hades Euchaites: Hades the Beautiful-Haired One

Hades Klymenos: Hades the Notorious or Hades the Renowned

Hades Stygius: Hades of the River Styx

Epithets Related to Death

Hades Adesius: Hades of the Grave

Hades Nekrodegmon: Hades Receiver of the Dead

Epithets Related to the Earth and Its Resources

Hades Khamaizilos Dios: Hades of the Earth ("where he likes to be" is implied)

Hades Ploutos: Hades of Wealth

Hades Theon Khthonios: Hades the Terrestrial God

Plouton: The Wealthy One

Epithets Bestowed by Classic Poets

Homer: The Grisly God, the Ruthless King

Virgil: Infernal Jove [Zeus], Stygian Jove [Zeus]

Latin Epithets

Altor: Who Nourishes

Dis Pater: Wealthy Father (in the sense of agricultural and mineral wealth)

Niger Deus: The Black God

Opertus: The Concealed

Pluto: The Wealthy One

Quietalis: The Quiet God (as the dead are quiet when at rest)

Rex Infernus: King of the Underworld

Rusor: To Whom All Things Return

Salutaris Divus: Restorer of the Dead

Saturnius: Son of Saturn [Kronos]

Tellumo: Who Provides the Creative (in reference to the creative power of the earth's resources)

Urgus: He Who Impels

Other Language Epithets

Amenthes: He Who Gives and Receives (Egyptian)

Hades Larthy Tytiral: Hades Sovereign of Tartaros (Etruscan)

APPENDIX C
HADES FAMILY TREE

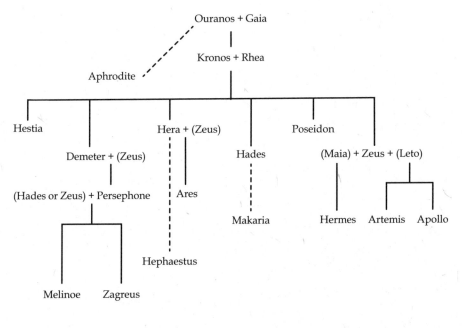

Ouranos + Gaia

Kronos + Rhea

Aphrodite

Hestia

Hera + (Zeus)

Poseidon

Demeter + (Zeus)

Hades

(Maia) + Zeus + (Leto)

(Hades or Zeus) + Persephone

Ares

Hermes   Artemis   Apollo

Makaria

Hephaestus

Melinoe   Zagreus

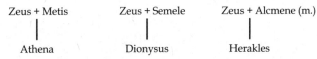

Zeus + Metis

Zeus + Semele

Zeus + Alcmene (m.)

Athena

Dionysus

Herakles

Key

(m.) Indicates a mortal parent

Dashed lines indicate descent from a single parent only

GLOSSARY

AIAKOS (Aeacus): One of the three judges of the dead in the Underworld. In his mortal life, Aiakos was king of the island of Aegina.

AKHERON (Acheron): The Akheron is the River of Woe or the River of Misery, and in some source texts it is the principal river of the Underworld, instead of the River Styx. In those tales, the ferryman Kharon transports the shades of the dead across the Akheron from the upper to the lower world.

ANEMOI: The Anemoi are the gods of the winds. The winds associated with the four cardinal directions are Boreas the North Wind, Eurus (or in later texts, Apeliotes) the East Wind, Notus the South Wind, and Zephyrus the West Wind. Each of these winds was personified and associated with a specific season.

ASKALAPHOS (Ascalaphus): An orchardist who is transformed into a screech owl for reporting that Persephone had eaten pomegranate seeds while in the Underworld.

ASPHODEL FIELDS: Most shades of the dead are assigned to drift through the Asphodel Fields. This is the Underworld home for mortals who were neither particularly good nor particularly bad.

BIDENT: A two-pronged metal implement similar to a pitchfork. Similar to Zeus' single-point lightning bolt and Poseidon's three-pronged trident, Hades' bident serves as a symbol of his authority over the third realm, the Underworld.

BOTHROS (plural, *bothroi*): A ceremonial pit dug in the earth that served as an altar to receive sacrifices made to Hades and the Underworld.

COCKEREL: A young rooster.

DAIMON: A term from Greek mythology describing a category of lesser deities or spirits who were oftentimes humanoid personifications of abstract concepts.

ELYSIAN FIELDS: The Elysian Fields, or Elysium, are the Underworld home for shades of mortals who lived virtuous lives or perhaps were initiated into various mystery cults. These fields are sunny and pleasant, abundant with food, drink, and conversation.

EPIKLESIS: The epithet used to evoke the desired aspect of a deity during religious ceremonies.

EPITHET: An adjective or short description that expresses the character of a person or thing—essentially, an illustrative nickname or surname. Ancient Greeks commonly used epithets to honor the gods in poetry, literature, art, and statuary.

EREBOS (Erebus): The primordial god of darkness. Erebos is elemental, being the substance of darkness, rather than an anthropomorphized god. Erebos encircles the Underworld, and his darkness fills all the hollow places of Earth.

ERINYES: The Erinyes, also known as the Furies, are fearsome dark-winged creatures with serpents twining through their hair, wielding whips and flaming torches of yew. They guard the abyss of Tartaros, but they are also sent by Hades and Persephone to torment oath-breakers, murderers, and perpetrators of other heinous crimes.

HALLS OF HADES: The Halls of Hades are the home of the god himself and his wife Persephone, when she is at residence in the Underworld. It is in these halls that we find their audience room and the dual thrones symbolic of their sovereignty.

HEKATE (Hecate): Hekate is the Titan goddess of magic, witchcraft, ghosts, the moon, and the night. Although she traverses many realms, Hekate spends a good portion of her time in the Underworld. She has the responsibility of guiding the Dread Queen Persephone to and from the Underworld each year.

HELM OF INVISIBILITY: A mythical helmet that renders the wearer invisible. Hades is the owner of this helmet and lends it to others on occasion.

HERMES KHTHONIOS: The god Hermes in his khthonic aspect, guiding the shades of dead mortals to the border of the Underworld.

HYPNOS (Hypnus): The daimon of sleep. He travels from his home in the Underworld each night with his mother, Nyx, granting rest to mortals. He is the brother of Thanatos.

KATABASIS: A trip to the Underworld. This term is usually associated with Greco-Roman mythology but is also sometimes used in other mythological and spiritual traditions as a general term to describe any journey to the realm of the dead.

KATADESMOI (singular, *katadesmos*): Curse tablets, referred to as *defixiones* in Latin, made from thin sheets of lead that were inscribed, rolled up, and then pierced with nails or needles. The purpose of katadesmoi was to petition the gods, the dead, or the spirits of a place to compel someone to do something or to enact some form of retribution.

KERBEROS (Cerberus): The fearsome canine or beast who guards the gateway to the Underworld. Kerberos has three heads, a serpentine or dragon-like tail, and various smaller snakes writhing from different parts of his body.

KHAIRE: Classical Greek expression of salutations and honor. It means "rejoice!"

KHARIS: An offering made in the spirit of reciprocity—"I give, so that you may give." Kharis can also refer to the spirit of reciprocity present in a devotional relationship with a god(s); it is the sense of grace, good fortune, or providence that is felt on behalf of the giver and the receiver.

KHARON (Charon): The daimon who ferries the shades of the dead across the river Styx (or Akheron) to the Underworld. The fee for his services is a single obol—a coin placed beneath the tongue of the dead.

KHERNIPS: An ancient Greek purification technique (literally, "hand washing"). Khernips is created by lighting a sprig or leaf on fire and, once it is smoldering, plunging it directly into a bowl of water. The water is then considered purified and can be used for hand washing or sprinkled on objects, offerings, and spaces.

KHOAI: Ritual libations, offered to gods or the deceased, consisting of either olive oil, a mixture of milk and honey, or a mixture of wine and water.

KOKYTOS (Cocytos): The ice-cold River of Wailing or River of Lamentation. Its waters are filled with the desperate cries of those who have no obol for Kharon.

KORE: Another name for Persephone. *Kore* is translated as "maiden" or "daughter."

KRONOS (Cronus): Kronos was the king of the Titan generation of gods and the god of time, particularly time viewed as a destructive, all-consuming force. After it was prophesied that he would be overthrown by one of his own children, Kronos swallowed each of his offspring as they were born.

LEKYTHOS (plural, *lekythoi*): A narrow vessel used by the ancient Greeks to store oil and, in particular, the precious olive or perfumed oil set aside for purposes of ritual anointment.

LETHE: Lethe is the River of Oblivion or the River of Forgetfulness. Upon entering the Underworld, shades of the dead drink the waters of Lethe to forget their earthly existence. Eventually their souls will be born again, but they will remember nothing of their previous life.

LEUKE (Leuce): A nymph whom Hades loved. Leuke lived with Hades in the Underworld, and when the span of her life was over, Hades transformed her body into a white poplar tree in the Elysian Fields.

MAKARIA (Macaria): Daughter of Hades and goddess of the blessed dead. In the Underworld, Makaria rules over the Elysian Fields.

MANTEIS: Diviners who were not officially licensed by the city-state.

MELINOE: Daughter of Hades and goddess of ghosts, night terrors, and propitiating the spirits of the dead. As the daughter of Hades and Persephone, representing both darkness and light, one half of her body is deepest black while the other half is stark white.

MENOITES (Menoetes): The Underworld daimon who keeps watch over Hades' herd of immortal, sable-black cattle. He suffered a broken bone while wrestling Herakles.

MINOS: One of the three judges of the dead in the Underworld. In his mortal life, Minos was king of Crete. He was given his position in the Underworld as a reward for the establishment of law among mortals.

MINTHE: An Underworld nymph who had an affair with Hades. After hearing Minthe boast that Hades would put aside his consort and return to her bed, Persephone (or sometimes Demeter, depending on the source text) trampled the nymph under her feet, turning her into the mint plant.

MNEMOSYNE: The goddess of memory who keeps an Underworld pool located near the Halls of Hades. Scholars speculate that the ability to drink from the Pool of Mnemosyne and remember past lives may have been a boon granted to initiates of mystery cults—such as the cult of Demeter and Persephone at Eleusis.

MOIRAI (Moirae): The goddesses of fate. The Moirai consist of three sisters: Clotho, Lachesis, and Atropos. Clotho, with a distaff in her hand, presides over the moment we are born. Lachesis, working the spindle, turns out the hours and days of our lives. And Atropos, the eldest sister of the trio, ends the thread of our human life with a sharp pair of scissors.

NEKROMANTEION: A temple or other sacred precinct where the living could speak to the dead. Hades was the patron god of necromantic oracles in ancient Greece.

NYX: The primordial goddess of night. Her home is the Underworld, which she leaves each evening to trail her dark cloak across the sky. She is accompanied by her son, Hypnos, the daimon of sleep.

OMPHALOS: The ancient Greeks viewed Delphi as the center of the world. The Temple at Delphi contained a sacred omphalos—a powerful, egg-shaped stone that allowed the Pythia direct communication with the gods.

PERSEPHONE: Fertility goddess, consort of Hades, and the Dread Queen of the Underworld. She spends half of her time in the land of the living, heralding spring and the growing season. She spends the other half in the Underworld, sharing the responsibility of rulership with her husband.

PHIALE: The *phiale* (Greek) or *patera* (Latin) was a shallow ceramic or metal bowl used specifically for the purpose of offering libations. A typical phiale had neither handles nor feet; an indentation centered on the underside, similar to a belly button, facilitated holding the bowl level.

PHLEGETHON: Phlegethon is the River of Fire. It is called so because it travels directly to the depths of the Underworld, passing through lands filled with the flames of funeral pyres, eventually leading to the abyss of Tartaros.

PSUCHAGÔGOI: "Soul-drawers," specialists who evoke uneasy ghosts in order to coax them into being at rest.

PSYCHOPOMPÓS: A figure that serves as a guide of souls. The role of the psychopomp is not to harvest or judge the deceased but simply to guide them on the way to their next home.

PYXIS: A decorative cylindrical box with a lid, commonly used to house cosmetics, trinkets, or jewelry.

RHADAMANTHYS: One of the three judges of the dead in the Underworld. In his mortal life, he was a famously just lawmaker.

RHEA: The Titaness mother of the Olympian gods, Rhea is the Queen of Heaven and consort of Kronos. She is emblematic of motherhood, birth waters, menstrual blood, flow, and ease.

SHADE: The ephemeral or ghostly semblance of a mortal's last physical form. Mortal souls appear as shades in the Underworld.

SPIRITUS VIRIDIS: The green spirit of plants.

STYX: The Styx is the principal river of the Underworld. It is a branch of the Oceanus river and encircles the border of the Underworld seven times, separating the realm of the dead from the land of the living. Mortals and gods guarantee their most solemn oaths by swearing them on the waters of the Styx.

TARTAROS (Tartarus): An impenetrable Underworld dungeon imprisoning the fallen Titans and the worst of mortal offenders. Archaic poets and playwrights describe Tartaros, Nyx, and Erebos existing even before Ouranos—the primordial sky god and father of the Titan Kronos.

TEMENOS: A grove, cave, grotto, or parcel of land set aside and dedicated to a god; a sacred precinct.

THANATOS (Thanatus): The winged daimon of death, Thanatos is the supernatural being who brings a peaceful end to mortal life. He reports to Hades.

TITANOMACHY: The overthrow of the Titan generation of gods by the Olympians and their sympathizers.

VOTUM (plural, *vota*): in ancient Roman religion, a votum was a vow or promise made to a deity and also a reference to that which fulfilled the vow: the actions, offerings, statues, or temples that were promised. Vota represented contractual agreements between mortals and gods.

ZAGREUS: Called "the first-born Dionysos," Zagreus is a god of the Orphic Mysteries. According to Orphic tradition, he is the son of Zeus and Persephone. The Dread Queen Persephone was seduced by the Olympian god in the guise of her husband, Hades, or possibly as a serpent.

BIBLIOGRAPHY

Achilles Painter. *Terracotta Lekythos (Oil Flask)*. 440 BCE. Terracotta; white-ground. The Metropolitan Museum of Art. New York, NY. https://www.metmuseum.org/art/collection/search/255949.

Agrippa, Henry Cornelius. *The Philosophy of Natural Magic*. Translated by L. W. de Laurence. Chicago: de Laurence, Scott & Co., 1913. Electronic reproduction by John Bruno Hare, Internet Sacred Texts Archive, 2008. https://sacred-texts.com/eso/pnm/pnm34.htm.

Albinus, Lars. *The House of Hades: Studies in Ancient Greek Eschatology*. Aarhus, Denmark: Aarhus University Press, 2000.

AllTrails. "Styx Waterfall." Accessed May 1, 2023. https://www.alltrails.com/trail/greece/western-greece--3/styx-waterfall.

Alm, Johan August. *Tartaros: On the Orphic and Pythagorean Underworld and the Pythagorean Pentagram*. San Pablo, CA: Three Hands Press, 2013.

Apollodorus. *The Library, Volume 1: Books 1–3.9*. Translated by James George Frazer. Loeb Classical Library 121. Cambridge, MA: Harvard University Press, 1921.

Apuleius, Lucius. *The Golden Asse*. Translated by William Adlington. London: Thomas Harper, 1639. Project Gutenberg, 2022. https://www.gutenberg.org/ebooks/1666.

Atsma, Aaron J. "Flora 1: Plants of Greek Myth." Theoi Project. Accessed January 22, 2023. https://www.theoi.com/Flora1.html.

———. "Flora 2: Plants of Greek Myth." Theoi Project. Accessed January 22, 2023. https://www.theoi.com/Flora2.html.

———. "Hades Cult." Theoi Project. Accessed January 22, 2023. https://www.theoi.com/Cult/HaidesCult.html.

Bacon, Francis. "Of Delays." In *Essays*, 83–84. New York: John B. Alden, 1885. https://books.google.com/books?id=LhgCAAAAYAAJ&source=gbs _navlinks_s.

Bardon, Franz. *Initiation into Hermetics: The Path of the True Adept*. Salt Lake City, UT: Merkur Publishing, 2014. Kindle.

Bat Conservation International. "Bats 101." Accessed April 24, 2023. https:// www.batcon.org/about-bats/bats-101/.

Berti, Irene. "'Now Let Earth Be My Witness and the Broad Heaven Above, and the down Flowing Water of the Styx …' (Homer, Mas XV, 36–37): Greek Oath-Rituals." In *Ritual and Communication in the Graeco-Roman World*, edited by Eftychia Stavrianopoulou, 181–209. Liège: Presses universitaires de Liège, 2006.

Black, Annetta. "Cave of the Sibyl—Antro della Sibilla." Atlas Obscura. December 31, 2009. https://www.atlasobscura.com/places /cave-of-the-sibyl-antro-della-sibilla.

———. "Necromanteion of Ephyra." Atlas Obscura. March 27, 2010. https:// www.atlasobscura.com/places/necromanteion-of-ephyra.

Blackie, Sharon. "The Mythic Imagination." Online Course. 2016. https:// sharonblackie.net/.

Boyer, Corinne. *Plants of the Devil*. San Pablo, CA: Three Hands Press, 2017.

———. *Under the Bramble Arch: A Folk Grimoire of Wayside Plant Lore and Practicum*. London: Troy Books, 2019. Reprint, Woodbury, MN: Llewellyn Publications, 2020.

———. *Under the Witching Tree: A Folk Grimoire of Tree Lore and Practicum*. London: Troy Books, 2017. Reprint, Woodbury, MN: Llewellyn Publications, 2020.

Burton, Diana. "Hades: Cornucopiae, Fertility and Death." 32nd Australasian Society for Classical Studies Conference, 2011. https://www.ascs.org.au /news/ascs32/Burton.pdf.

———. "Worshipping Hades: Myth and Cult in Elis and Triphylia." *Archiv für Religionsgeschichte* 20, no. 1 (2018): 211–27. https://doi.org/10.1515 /arege-2018-0013.

Burton, Neel. *The Meaning of Myth: With 12 Greek Myths Retold and Interpreted by a Psychiatrist*. Acheron Press, 2021. Kindle.

Campbell, Joseph. *The Hero with a Thousand Faces*. Novato, CA: New World Library, 2008.

Causey, Faya. *Ancient Carved Ambers in the J. Paul Getty Museum*. Los Angeles: The J. Paul Getty Museum, 2012. https://www.getty.edu/publications/ambers/objects/groups/8/.

Clark. "Hades Daughter: Everything You Must Know about Her Story." Ancient Literature. September 20, 2022. https://ancient-literature.com/hades-daughter/.

Claudian. *Claudian, Volume II: On Stilicho's Consulship 2–3. Panegyric on the Sixth Consulship of Honorius. The Gothic War. Shorter Poems. Rape of Proserpina*. Translated by M. Platnauer. Loeb Classical Library 136. Cambridge, MA: Harvard University Press, 1922.

Codrus Painter. *Kylix*. Circa 430 BCE. Pottery; red-figure. The British Museum. London, UK. https://www.britishmuseum.org/collection/object/G_1847-0909-6.

Corbin, Henry. "Mundis Originalis, or the Imaginary and the Imaginal." Translated by Ruth Horine. *Colloquium on Symbolism* 6 (1946): 3–26. http://www.bahaistudies.net/asma/mundus_imaginalis.pdf.

Danforth, Loring M. *The Death Rituals of Rural Greece*. Princeton, NJ: Princeton University Press, 1982.

Dash, Mike. "The Unsolved Mystery of the Tunnels at Baiae." *Smithsonian Magazine*, October 1, 2012. https://www.smithsonianmag.com/history/the-unsolved-mystery-of-the-tunnels-at-baiae-56267963/.

Department of Greek and Roman Art. "Death, Burial, and the Afterlife in Ancient Greece." Metropolitan Museum of Art. October 2003. https://www.metmuseum.org/toah/hd/dbag/hd_dbag.htm.

Dietz, S. Theresa. *The Complete Language of Flowers: A Definitive and Illustrated History*. New York: Wellfleet Press, 2020.

Diggle, James, B. L. Fraser, P. James, O. B. Simkin, A. A. Thompson, and S. J. Westripp, eds. *The Cambridge Greek Lexicon*. 2 vols. Cambridge: Cambridge University Press, 2021.

Doughty, Caitlin. "What Death Positive Is NOT." The Order of the Good Death. January 25, 2018. https://www.orderofthegooddeath.com/article/what-death-positive-is-not/.

Dunn, Patrick. *The Orphic Hymns: A New Translation for the Occult Practitioner*. Woodbury, MN: Llewellyn Publications, 2018.

———. *The Practical Art of Divine Magic: Contemporary & Ancient Techniques of Theurgy*. Woodbury, MN: Llewellyn Publications, 2015.

Empedocles. "Empedokles of Akragas." In *Early Greek Philosophy*, trans. John Burnet, 227–289. London: Adam and Charles Black, 1908. Project Gutenberg, 2022. https://www.gutenberg.org/files/67097/67097-h/67097-h.htm.

Encyclopaedia Britannica Online. S.v. "asphodel." Accessed August 12, 2021. https://www.britannica.com/plant/asphodel-plant.

———. S.v. "diamond." Accessed April 7, 2023. https://www.britannica.com/topic/diamond-gemstone.

———. S.v. "hell." By Carol Zaleski. Last modified May 18, 2023. https://www.britannica.com/topic/hell.

———. S.v. "lekythos." Accessed March 23, 2016. https://www.britannica.com/art/lekythos.

———. S.v. "Styx." Accessed March 3, 2023. https://www.britannica.com/topic/Styx-Greek-religion.

Evelyn-White, Hugh G. trans. *Hesiod, the Homeric Hymns, and Homerica*. London: William Heinemann, 1914. https://books.google.com/books?id=942RUUhzE98C.

Fourcade, Patricia. "Mythology." In *Snakes: A Natural History*, edited by Roland Bauchot, 184–93. New York: Sterling Publishing, 1994.

Freuler, Kate. *Of Blood and Bones: Working with Shadow Magick & the Dark Moon*. Woodbury, MN: Llewellyn Publications, 2020.

Garland, Robert. *The Greek Way of Death*. Ithaca, NY: Cornell University Press, 1988.

Gill, Nikita. *Great Goddesses: Life Lessons from Myths and Monsters*. New York: G. P. Putnam's Sons, 2019. Kindle.

Goepel, Masha. "All You Ever Wanted to Know about the Magical Hellebore Plant." Garden and Happy. Accessed November 10, 2022. https://gardenandhappy.com/hellebore/.

Gruben, Michelle. "Rare Occult Herbs: Dittany of Crete." Grove and Grotto. April 12, 2017. https://www.groveandgrotto.com/blogs/articles/rare-occult-herbs-dittany-of-crete.

Hadestown. "Hadestown | Official Site." Accessed January 31, 2023. https://
hadestown.com/.

Harasta, Jesse. *Hades: The History, Origins and Evolution of the Greek God.*
Self-published, CreateSpace, 2013. Kindle.

Hard, Robin. *The Routledge Handbook of Greek Mythology.* 8th ed. London: Routledge, 2022.

HellenicGods.org. "Persephone: The Epithets." Accessed May 2, 2023. https://
www.hellenicgods.org/persephone-the-epithets.

———. "Ploutōn: The Epithets." Accessed January 22, 2023. https://www
.hellenicgods.org/plouton---the-epithets.

Hillman, James. *The Dream and the Underworld.* New York: HarperCollins, 1979.

Homer. *The Iliad of Homer.* Translated by Richmond Lattimore. 1951. Reprint,
Chicago: University of Chicago Press, 1961.

———. *The Odyssey.* Translated by Emily R. Wilson. New York: W. W. Norton
& Company, 2018.

Hornblower, Simon, Antony Spawforth, and Esther Eidinow. *The Oxford Companion to Classical Civilization.* 2nd ed. New York: Oxford University Press,
2014.

Johnson, Robert A. *Owning Your Own Shadow: Understanding the Dark Side of the
Psyche.* New York: HarperCollins Publishers, 1991.

Johnston, Sarah Iles. *Restless Dead: Encounters between the Living and the Dead in
Ancient Greece.* Berkeley, CA: University of California Press, 2013.

J. Paul Getty Museum. "Underworld: Imagining the Afterlife." Accessed
November 10, 2022. https://www.getty.edu/art/exhibitions/ancient
_underworld/inner.html.

Jung, Carl Gustav. *The Collected Works of C.G. Jung.* Vol. 12, *Psychology and
Alchemy.* Edited by William McGuire, Herbert Read, Michael Fordham, and
Gerhard Adler. Translated by R. F. C. Hull. Princeton, NJ: Princeton Univer-
sity Press, 1980.

Just a Fat Boi. "Cerberus's Honey Cakes: 2000 Year Old Recipe, Myth and History." *Just a Fat Boi* (blog), March 15, 2021. https://justafatboi.com
/cerberuss-honey-cakes/.

Kapach, Avi. "Hades." Mythopedia. Last modified December 7, 2022. https://mythopedia.com/topics/hades.

Kerenyi, Karl. *Hermes: Guide of Souls.* Thompson, CT: Spring Publications, 2015. Kindle.

Kershaw, Kerry. "Scorpio Full Moon Penumbral Eclipse." *Magic of I.* (blog), May 5, 2023. https://magicofi.com/blogs/moons/scorpio-full-moon-penumbral-eclipse.

Kokkinidis, Tasos. "Turkey Opens 'Gate to Hell' in Ancient Greek City of Hierapolis." Greek Reporter, June 23, 2022. https://greekreporter.com/2022/06/23/ancient-gate-hell-hierapolis/.

Kouris, Athanasios. "Trail Minthi Mountain." Athanasios Kouris Productions. March 27, 2019. https://athankproductions.com/en/trail-mountain-minthi/.

Macfarlane, Robert. *Underland: A Deep Time Journey.* W. W. Norton & Company, 2019. Kindle.

Mastros, Sara L. *Orphic Hymns Grimoire.* Braddock, PA: Mastros & Zealot, 2019. PDF.

Matthews, Caitlin. *The Psychic Protection Handbook: Powerful Protection for Uncertain Times.* London: Piatkus Books, 2005.

Matyszak, Philip. *Ancient Magic: A Practitioner's Guide to the Supernatural in Greece and Rome.* New York: Thames & Hudson, 2019.

Merriam-Webster. "Is It 'Invoke' or 'Evoke'?" Accessed January 14, 2023. https://www.merriam-webster.com/words-at-play/is-it-invoke-or-evoke.

Nicholas, Chani. *You Were Born for This: Astrology for Radical Self-Acceptance.* New York: HarperOne, 2020.

Occvlta. "Hellebore." *Materia Venefica* 18 (February 2023). https://www.occvlta.org/.

———. "Opium Poppy." *Materia Venefica* 5 (January 2022). https://www.occvlta.org/.

———. "Thornapple." *Materia Venefica* 7 (March 2022). https://www.occvlta.org/.

———. "Violet." *Materia Venefica* 20 (April 2023). https://www.occvlta.org/.

Ogden, Daniel. *Magic, Witchcraft, and Ghosts in the Greek and Roman Worlds: A Sourcebook*. 2nd ed. Oxford: Oxford University Press, 2009.

Online Etymology Dictionary. S.v. "rape." By Douglas Harper. Last modified July 27, 2022. https://www.etymonline.com/word/rape.

Order of the Good Death. "Death Positive Movement." Accessed January 28, 2023. https://www.orderofthegooddeath.com/death-positive-movement/.

———. "Our Story." Accessed January 28, 2023. https://www.orderofthegood death.com/our-story/.

Overly Sarcastic Productions. "Miscellaneous Myths: Hades and Persephone." February 12, 2021. YouTube video, 20:28. https://www.youtube.com /watch?v=Ac5ksZTvZN8.

Ovid. *The Metamorphoses of Ovid*. Vol. 1. Translated by Henry T. Riley. London: George Bell & Sons, 1893. Project Gutenberg, 2007. https://www .gutenberg.org/ebooks/21765.

———. *The Metamorphoses of Ovid*. Vol. 2. Translated by Henry T. Riley. London: George Bell & Sons, 1893. Project Gutenberg, 2008. https://www .gutenberg.org/ebooks/26073.

Pausanias. *Complete Works of Pausanias*. Translated by W. H. S. Jones. Hastings, East Sussex, UK: Delphi Classics, 2014.

Pearson, Nicholas. *Flower Essences from the Witch's Garden: Plant Spirits in Magickal Herbalism*. Rochester, VT: Destiny Books, 2022.

Plato. "Cratylus." In *Plato in Twelve Volumes*. Vol. 12. Translated by Harold N. Fowler. Cambridge, MA: Harvard University Press, 1921.

———. *Phaedo*. In *The Dialogues of Plato*. Vol. 1. Translated by Benjamin Jowett. New York: Scribner, Armstrong, and Co., 1874. https://books.google.com /books?id=m1cMAAAAIAAJ.

———. *The Republic of Plato*. Translated by Benjamin Jowett. Oxford, UK: Clarendon Press, 1888. Project Gutenberg, 2017. https://www.gutenberg.org /ebooks/55201.

Pliny the Elder. *The Natural History*. Edited and translated by John Bostock and H. T. Riley. London: Taylor and Francis, 1855. https://www.perseus.tufts .edu/hopper/text?doc=Plin.+Nat.+toc.

Popham, Sajah. *Evolutionary Herbalism: Science, Medicine, and Spirituality from the Heart of Nature*. Berkeley, CA: North Atlantic Books, 2019.

Pursell, JJ. *The Herbal Apothecary: 100 Medicinal Herbs and How to Use Them*. Portland, OR: Timber Press, 2015.

Ranieri, Luke. "How to Pronounce χαῖρε in Greek: Classical Greek, Attic Greek, Koine Greek, Modern Greek." polýMATHY. August 19, 2019. YouTube video, 7:46. https://www.youtube.com/watch?v=yCv5dK1DOgw.

Ravenna, Morpheus. "Theurgic Binding: Or, 'S#!t Just Got Real.'" *Banshee Arts* (blog). Accessed January 6, 2023. https://www.bansheearts.com/blog/theurgic-binding-or-st-just-got-real.

Richter, Darmon. "Cape Matapan Caves." Atlas Obscura. July 2, 2013. https://www.atlasobscura.com/places/cape-matapan-caves.

Roach, Mary. *Spook: Science Tackles the Afterlife*. New York: W. W. Norton & Company, 2006. Kindle.

Roberts, Ellie Mackin. *Heroines of Olympus: The Women of Greek Mythology*. Nottingham, UK: Welbeck Publishing Group, 2020.

———. *Underworld Gods in Ancient Greek Religion: Death and Reciprocity*. Abingdon, UK: Routledge, 2020. Kindle.

Robinson, Murphy. "Trance: A Working Guide," October 2019, 1–4. https://drive.google.com/file/d/1uY8xyzUky9VpV9BdXRugHjWDP_0k6aaV/view?usp=drive_link.

RogueChemist. "Styx Waterfall." Atlas Obscura. February 25, 2021. https://www.atlasobscura.com/places/styx-waterfall.

Sabouroff Painter. *Terracotta Lekythos (Oil Flask)*. Circa 450 BCE. Terracotta; white-ground. The Metropolitan Museum of Art. New York, NY. https://www.metmuseum.org/art/collection/search/251043.

Sekita, Karolina. "Hades and Herakles at Pylos: Dione's Tale Dismantled." *The Classical Quarterly* 68, no. 1 (May 1, 2018): 1–9. https://doi.org/10.1017/S0009838818000216.

Shakespeare, William. *Hamlet*. Edited by Charles John Kean. London: Bradbury and Evans, 1859. Project Gutenberg, 2009. https://www.gutenberg.org/ebooks/27761.

Smythe, Rachel. *Lore Olympus*. Webtoon. 2018–present. https://www.web toons.com/en/romance/lore-olympus/list?title_no=1320.

Strabo. *The Geography of Strabo*. Translated by H. C. Hamilton and W. Falconer. London: George Bell & Sons, 1903. http://www.perseus.tufts.edu /hopper/text?doc=Perseus%3Atext%3A1999.01.0239%3Abook%3Dnotice.

Strand, Sophie. "What Is the Underworld?" *Wimblu* 6, no. 3 (November 2022): n.p.

Suda, and Katina Ball, trans. "mu,51." Suda On Line: Byzantine Lexicography. Edited by David Whitehead and Catharine Roth. Last modified April 28, 2013. http://www.cs.uky.edu/~raphael/sol/sol-entries/mu/51.

Supergiant Games. "Hades." Accessed January 31, 2023. https://www.super giantgames.com/games/hades/.

Taunton, Gwendolyn. *The Path of Shadows: Chthonic Gods, Oneiromancy & Necromancy in Ancient Greece*. Colac, Victoria, Australia: Manticore Press, 2018.

Taylor, Sonya Renee. *The Body Is Not an Apology, Second Edition: The Power of Radical Self-Love*. Oakland, CA: Berrett-Koehler Publishers, 2021. Kindle.

Temple, Robert K. G. *Oracles of the Dead: Ancient Techniques for Predicting the Future*. Rochester, VT: Destiny Books, 2005.

Tommasi Moreschini, Chiara O. "Bats in Greco-Roman Antiquity." *Bats* 29, no. 2 (July 20, 2011): 6–8.

Tserkezis, Eleftherios. "What Are the Names of Hades' Stallions in Greek Mythology?" Quora. May 9, 2017. https://qr.ae/py76RB.

UNESCO World Heritage Centre. "Archaeological Site of Elis." Accessed January 31, 2023. https://visitworldheritage.com/en/eu/archaeological -site-of-elis/5f1f5051-f0d2-494a-8eed-c46269f483f1.

———. "Hierapolis-Pamukkale." Accessed January 30, 2023. https://whc .unesco.org/en/list/485/.

Unknown artist. *Omphalos*. 332–23 BCE. Marble sculpture. Archaeological Museum of Delphi. Delphi, Greece.

———. *Pinax (Votive Relief)*. 700 BCE. Marble bas-relief. Museo Archeologico Nazionale Di Reggio Calabria. Reggio Calabria, Italy.

———. *Marble Statue Group of Isis-Persephone and Serapis-Hades*. 180 CE. Marble. Heraklion Archeological Museum. Crete, Greece. https://www.heraklionmuseum.gr/en/exhibit/isis-persephone-and-sarapis-hades/.

———. *Terracotta Funerary Plaque*. Circa 520–510 BCE. Terracotta; black-figure. New York, NY. The Metropolitan Museum of Art. https://www.metmuseum.org/art/collection/search/254801.

Vasilopoulos, Christos. "4 Gates of Hades Locations Not to Miss in Greece." Mindful Experiences Greece. April 13, 2023. https://mindfulexperiences greece.com/gates-hades-underworld-greece/.

Vaudoise, Mallorie. *Honoring Your Ancestors: A Guide to Ancestral Veneration*. Woodbury, MN: Llewellyn Publications, 2019.

Virgil. *The Aeneid of Virgil*. Translated by J. W. Mackail. London: Macmillan and Co., 1885. Project Gutenberg, 2007. https://www.gutenberg.org/cache/epub/22456/pg22456-images.html.

Walsh, Michael. "Gateway to Hades Said to Be Uncovered by Italian Archaeologists in Southwestern Turkey: Is It Hell on Earth?" *New York Daily News*, April 4, 2013. https://www.nydailynews.com/news/world/gateway-hades-uncovered-turkey-archaeologists-article-1.1307747.

Ward, Terence P., ed. *Host of Many: Hades and His Retinue*. Orlando, FL: Bibliotheca Alexandria, 2020.

Warrior, Valerie M. *Greek Religion: A Sourcebook*. Newburyport, MA: Focus Publishing, 2009.

Watson, Lindsay C. *Magic in Ancient Greece and Rome*. London: Bloomsbury Academic, 2019.

Winter, Sarah Kate Istra. *Kharis: Hellenic Polytheism Explored*. 2nd ed. Self-published, CreateSpace, 2019.

Woodfield, Stephanie. *Dark Goddess Craft: A Journey through the Heart of Transformation*. Woodbury, MN: Llewellyn Publications, 2017. Kindle.

———. *Dedicant, Devotee, Priest: A Pagan Guide to Divine Relationships*. Woodbury, MN: Llewellyn Publications, 2021. Kindle.

Zarrelli, Natalie. "'O, Shrill-Voiced Insect': The Cicada Poems of Ancient Greece." Atlas Obscura. June 23, 2016. https://www.atlasobscura.com/articles/o-shrillvoiced-insect-the-cicada-poems-of-ancient-greece.

To Write to the Author

If you wish to contact the author or would like more information about this book, please write to the author in care of Llewellyn Worldwide Ltd. and we will forward your request. Both the author and the publisher appreciate hearing from you and learning of your enjoyment of this book and how it has helped you. Llewellyn Worldwide Ltd. cannot guarantee that every letter written to the author can be answered, but all will be forwarded. Please write to:

Jamie Waggoner
℅ Llewellyn Worldwide
2143 Wooddale Drive
Woodbury, MN 55125-2989
Please enclose a self-addressed stamped envelope for reply,
or $1.00 to cover costs. If outside the U.S.A., enclose
an international postal reply coupon.

Many of Llewellyn's authors have websites with additional information and resources. For more information, please visit our website at http://www.llewellyn.com.